A WALK ACROSS MONGOLIA

LESSONS IN PROGRESS
FROM SACRED MOTHER MOUNTAIN
TO MOTHER LAKE

by William C. Engels, Obl.S.B.

Antiquæ Libri

Published by:
David L. Whelchel
Antiquæ Libri
Pullman, Washington USA

Publisher provided Cataloging-in-Publication Data

Engels, William C.
  A Walk Across Mongolia: Lessons in Progress from Sacred Mother
    Mountain to Mother Lake/ William C. Engels – 1st ed.
        p. 271 23 cm.

    Includes bibliographical references and index
    ISBN- 979-8-9862728-2-5 (cloth)
    ISBN- 979-8-9862728-0-1 (paper)
    ISBN- 979-8-9862728-1-8 (ebook)

    1. Mongolia—Description and travel – 2. Mongolia—Social life and
    customs – 3. Mongolia—History – 4. Mongolia—Archeology –
    5. Mongolia—Ecology – 6. Mongolia—Flora and fauna – 7. Mongolia—
    Democratic revolution – 8. Central Asia—Description and travel

To read this book is to enter into the tranquility of rural Mongolia. You will feel the space, color of the rocks, and connections to the herders and the human past. The people, locales, archaeology, and natural world are described with a curiosity yet humanity and respect that is not so common in travel books trying to attract attention. I enjoyed traveling in the book as the author guided me through a trajectory I have never traveled before. We bypass many important sites when we travel by car, but the hiker-author didn't miss those details. Anyone interested in traveling in Mongolia should read Mr. Engels' book *A Walk Across Mongolia: Lessons in Progress from Sacred Mother Mountain to Mother Lake.*

Oyungerel Tsedevdamba, former Minister of Culture, Sports, and Tourism of Mongolia and author of *The Green-Eyed Lama*

To my mother

BILLIE RAE ENGELS
(1927-2001)

True lover of wisdom

"'Well, see all you can. That's what it comes to. Worry about nothing.'" Henry James, *The Wings of the Dove*

"Margaashiin makhnaas önöödriin uushig." ("Today's lung is better than tomorrow's meat.") Mongolian proverb

Acknowledgements

My heartfelt thanks to the beautiful Mongolian people who showed kindness to me—whether accepted or not—during the hike, those who extended hospitality, offered rides, provided directions, spoke words of encouragement and friendship, offered food, agreed to interviews. An expression of my deepest appreciation and gratitude to my guide, Boldsaikhan, is long overdue. He was a patient, honest, and hardworking assistant during the crucial first two weeks in the Gobi Desert. My sincere thanks also to those Mongolian scholars who aided me in my research, D. Erdenebaatar, Dovdoin Bayar, Damdinsürengiin Tseveendorj, G. Menes, and Ts. Ochirkhuyag, archeologists; Kh. Terbish, zoologist; D. Ganbold, botanist; Tseveljid, director of the Museum of Famous Persons in Uliastai; Sereenendorj, director of acquisitions at the Khövsgöl Aimag Museum in Mörön; and others.

I am deeply grateful to my friends Theresa Horgan, who sent my GPS compass to me from the U.S., the biologist Lkhagvasüren, who taught me how to program the compass, Ts. Boldchimeg, who secured my guide, and Baigalmaa, who bailed me out in two emergencies on the hike. I would also like to thank those friends and relatives, including D. Bolortuya and A. Ariunjargal, who translated texts or interviews. Many thanks as well to my friends Jungmi Park, Donald Bellomy, Anne Whelchel, and Pat Caraher and to my late relative Jane Noble (Janey B. Hendrix), who read from and provided feedback on the manuscript. An additional "thank you" goes to Pat Caraher for his excellent work in proofreading the final version before printing. To my friend David Whelchel for assistance with locating research texts online, using the bibliographical formatting tools on Microsoft Word, and preparing the manuscript for publication with Antiquæ Libri, my warmest thanks.

Of course, there is one person whose role in this project entitles her to a major share of these Acknowledgments. Without the assurance of her love to lighten my steps, I might not have completed the journey. Without the benefit of her linguistic skills, which she was always ready to share, incorporating much of the research material in Mongolian and Russian and many local place names in the book would have been much more difficult, if not impossible. To you, my dear wife, Enkhjargal, I give my boundless, undying thanks.

Finally, thank you very much to many more who helped make the hike and book possible yet are not mentioned here.

Prefatory Note

In writing this book about my adventures, encounters with the land and people, and psychological journey during a trek across Mongolia from China to Russia in the summer of 2002, one of my priorities was providing an accurate account. I relied heavily on the detailed and up to date journal I kept on the hike. I wrote the initial, much longer draft while in Mongolia for most of one year following the hike, so the memories were still fresh. Nonetheless, some incorrect details have probably crept in. Also, despite my good intentions and efforts, the information I include from my research on Mongolian culture, history, and natural history is probably inaccurate in places. This is more likely the case where the original was in Mongolian and Russian, making translation necessary. The spellings of place names from my 1:500,000-meter scale maps, which I didn't replace after they were lost in shipment from Asia to the U.S. in 2006, and responses reported from tape recorded interviews, for example, probably contain errors. The bibliographical information of some of my print sources was lost, apparently in the same shipment. I was not always able to recover the dates of interviews and may have gotten a few of the dates wrong. Minor liberties were taken with the wording in passages of dialogue, usually very short, that aren't part of the taped interviews. These avowals hopefully won't detract from the reader's sense of getting a faithful record of my experiences and portrait of Mongolia in this book. In a few cases, to help preserve a person's anonymity, I omitted the name. Otherwise, the name of the person is given.

For sources printed in English, I generally used the sources' spelling of Mongolian names in my bibliographical references and Index. In converting Mongolian tögrögs (MNT) to U.S. dollars (USD), I used the rate at that time. The rate on July 10, 2002, about midway through the hike, was 1,000 MNT = .91 USD. The front and back cover photos and most of the photos of people and places in the ten chapters covering the hike were taken en route by me or, where I am in the picture, by someone else present. With the exception of photo #44, the rest were taken by me on later visits to the area.

Table of Contents

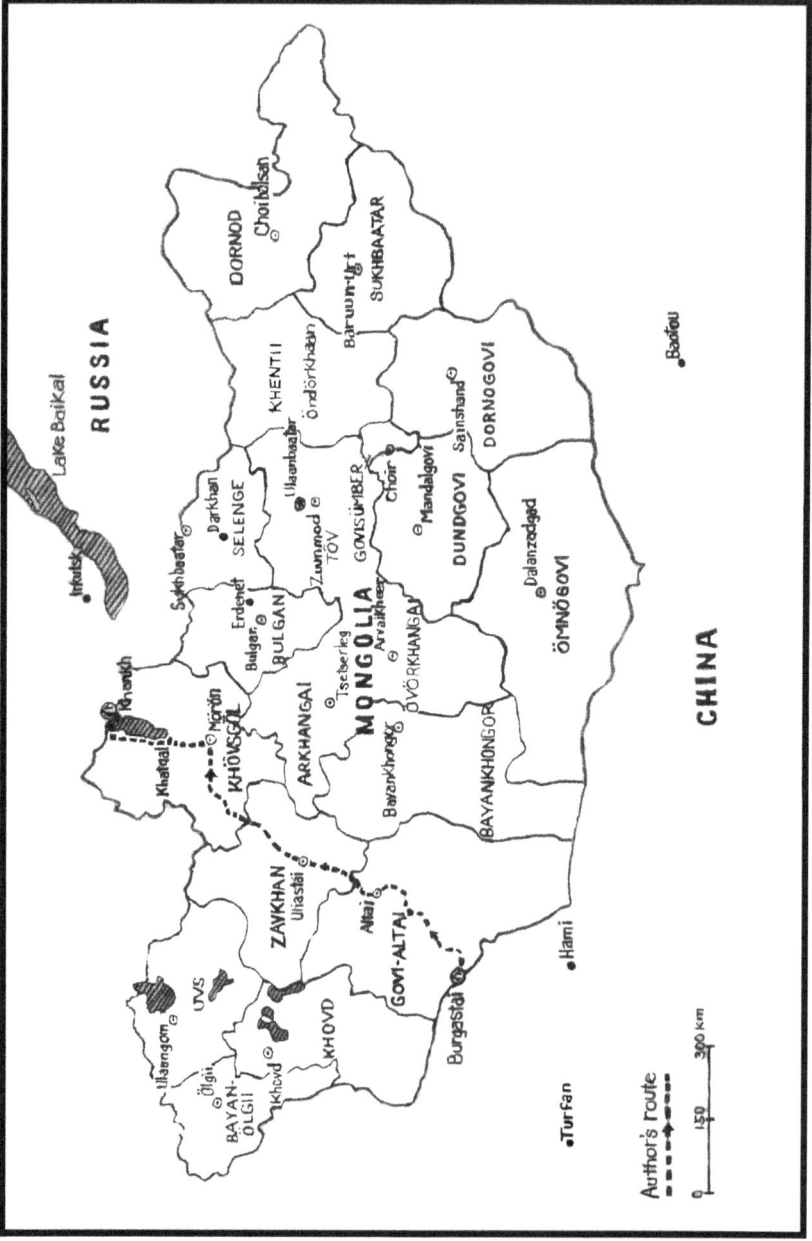

Map of Mongolia

Prologue.
Awakening

"Arise, my love, my fair one,
and come away;
for now the winter is past,
the rain is over and gone.
The flowers appear on the earth;
The time of singing has come,
and the voice of the turtledove
is heard in our land.
The fig tree puts forth its figs,
and the vines are in blossom;
they give forth fragrance.
Arise, my love, my fair one,
and come away." (Song of Solomon 2.10-13)[1]

I stood at the table spread with memorabilia from my mother's life, the photos, academic certificate or two, household articles that had somehow survived a long succession of homes. I had picked up and was flipping through a box of homemade vocabulary flashcards from her German studies in graduate school in the 1980s. It was July 24, 2001, the day before her funeral, and the family had gathered for the wake in the parlor with the opened coffin. I had come to the U.S. that summer from Mongolia, my home for the past three years, chiefly to see her, bedridden for more than two and a half years with a strange complex of diseases, one of which was diagnosed as Parkinson's. Having kept her promise at the time of my previous summer visit to remain alive at least until my next one, she had died within a week after my arrival.

Selecting an index card from the box at random, I read on the English side, in utter amazement, the words "I accuse you of motion." With her still corpse lying nearby, this statement, which didn't resemble the sort of common idioms language students memorize, struck me as a sardonic thrust at the world of fortunate animate beings from the deceased. Prankish expressions of envy were wholly alien to my mother's character, though. Another interpretation of the statement soon began to suggest itself. She had never learned to drive and the comparative restriction of physical movement and activities this imposed probably encouraged her pursuit of reading and, in her later years, scholarship as well. At one time

I had followed a personal creed that the physical freedom and rapid movement experienced in driving an automobile were detrimental to the clear thinking and mental vigor required for literary scholarship and writing. However, about ten years before I had succumbed to societal pressure and bought a car. During this summer visit I even considered buying my sister's extra used Toyota Camry after my brother remarked that I looked good in it. The expression on the index card now resonated as a subtle reproach or challenge from my mother's spirit for becoming content with a lifestyle geared toward "motion."

For the past year or so I'd had my sights on a backpacking trip across Mongolia. Though an avid hiker, apart from my annual two-day walk from Ulaanbaatar (Red Hero) to Gorkhi-Terelj National Park on a scenic route pieced together a few years before, I had done no hiking in three years in Mongolia.

1 - At Khasbaatar's ger enroute to Gorkhi-Terelj National Park

I had heard a great deal about stunning desert, lake, and mountain scenery, the site of the ancient capital Karakorum, dinosaur fossils. Maybe it was time to venture further afield in the vast, exotic land that stretched fenceless from my doorstep.

I also wanted to write a book about the experience. Certain circumstances—like a student's polite question in a journal entry, "Why don't you write a book, Dr. Engels?"—were pointing me in that direction.

Current travel books on Mongolia were still comparatively scarce. The additional exposure in the West provided by my book might attract more visitors, benefiting the tourist industry and, through it, the nation's struggling economy.

The greatest challenge the project seemed to pose was not the physical distance to be covered but the disruption of my comfortable academic routine and support system. For the past three years since earning my doctorate, I had been hired on a semester or yearly basis by the University of Colorado at Denver as the English instructor at their International College of Ulaanbaatar, a job that provided a benefits package and wage well out of proportion to the cost of living here. Would I have the courage to give up the security of this position for a semester, possibly longer, to complete the hike and write the book?

I had taken a few initial steps, consulting a road map for likely routes and enrolling in a short tutorial course in the Mongolian language, before I left for vacation in the States that summer. By the time of the incident at my mother's wake, I still hadn't made definite plans about whether and when to hike. I now saw this long-distance trek as a way of recovering my earlier unhurried disposition and the mental strength that flowed from it. In his essay "Walking," after giving a derivation of the word "saunterer," one who goes "a la Sainte Terre," Thoreau remarks, "For every walk is a sort of crusade, preached by some Peter the Hermit in us, to go forth and reconquer this Holy Land from the hands of the Infidels."[2] The hike would be a crusade for the liberation of my mind. My mother's death itself seemed to sanction the enterprise for it made a visit to the States the following summer unnecessary. I would take the hike at that time—and in honor of her memory. I did not buy the Camry but saved my money for the trip.

As I would soon discover on the hike, though, slowing down involved more than simply traveling by foot instead of car. I could be driven by the same speed mentality whether driving or walking, and learning to appreciate the unfolding journey instead of rushing to get to the goal would prove a major part of my struggle for mental freedom on the hike.

Before returning from the States, I purchased most of the required equipment, including a lightweight one-person tent and sleeping bag, backpacker's stove capable of running on gasoline—white gas being out of the question in rural Mongolia—half-length, self-inflatable mattress, two disposable cameras, microcassette recorder, and pair of top-grade hiking boots handmade in Italy. On the plane ride back to Mongolia in mid-August, I happened to have as fellow passengers two friends from the Ulaanbaatar community of the Missionaries of Charity. When I told them of my plans for next summer, one of the Sisters alerted me about the dangers inexperienced travelers in rural Mongolia face from the frequent unmarked forks in dirt roads. It was "no joke" to be lost in the countryside, where travelers often go long distances before encountering people and water. Thanks to this timely warning, by the following spring I had purchased a lightweight GPS compass through a friend in the U.S. and secured a guide for at least the initial stage of the journey.

Boldsaikhan (Fine Steel) was a tall, rawboned, twenty-four year old with large, swarthy hands, a crew cut, and a broad, engaging smile. Only three years in Ulaanbaatar, where he worked as a construction laborer, he still had the wide-eyed innocence and bashfulness, as well as tanned complexion, of the young herdsman recently come from the steppe. We agreed that I would employ him for the first two weeks, after which we might renegotiate for another stage or more.

What will be my starting point? My guide was from the area northeast of Altai, capital of Govi-Altai Aimag, or province, in southwestern Mongolia. His knowledge of this general region might be tapped into if I were to start at the border in Govi-Altai. There was also, according to my map, a road north from a post on this border by which I would be able to bypass vast stretches of the Gobi Desert in the lower reaches of the aimag. Seasonal weather conditions seemed to suit a northward, better than a southward, course on a hike taken from early June to August or September, my anticipated schedule. The worst of the spring winds in the Gobi would be over by June and the heat might be insufferable there in August. I would start, then, at the Burgastai (With Willows) Post, which my map placed on the border of Govi-Altai Aimag and China.

In early spring my guide and I met several times with Enkhmaa, anglicized to Emma, the English-speaking marketing manager at Juulchin Tourism Corporation, to gather information on practicalities like weather conditions, availability of food and water, and appropriate gifts in return for hospitality. I also asked her about the location of historical sites on or near my intended route in Govi-Altai, Zavkhan, and Khövsgöl Aimags. After additional consultations with two archeologists and a historian at the Institute of History, as well as some book research, I compiled a two-page facts sheet on historical and scenic points of interest. I then marked the detailed 1:500,000-meter scale topographical maps I had purchased from the Department of Geodesy and Cartography in Ulaanbaatar with numbers keyed to this list.

I drew up a list of questions, handwritten in Mongolian in Cyrillic script, about rural life and culture that I would use with the microcassette recorder in interviewing locals. Some questions covered the extent to which things had changed since the soviet era and locals' response to the changes. It had been only a dozen years since Mongolia declared itself independent of Russia and began to embrace democracy.

One change would get a little help from me. From my parish church, Sts. Peter and Paul, I got a one to two-page synopsis of the Catholic faith written in Mongolian and made several photocopies for distribution along my way. I wanted to live out Jesus' words about going forth and spreading the Good News, and a country where religious expression had been outlawed for decades might especially benefit from hearing it. Then, too, I could claim some remote kinship with William of Rubruck, the 13th-century Franciscan missionary who visited the imperial court of the Mongols. There was also, I regret to say, the mercenary motive of purchasing some insurance for divine protection.

I obtained documents from two government offices in Ulaanbaatar: a permit to approach the borders with China and Russia from the Headquarters of Border Troops and a statement verifying the starting and ending points on my hike from the Bureau of Immigration and Naturalization. To avoid having to carry large sums of money, I deposited $2,000 at a bank with branches in the aimags where, I was assured, I would be able to make withdrawals.

On the weekend of June 1st and 2nd, after outfitting Boldsaikhan with hiking gear purchased or taken from my surplus stock, we took a practice hike to Gorkhi-Terelj National Park, following my accustomed private route. I discovered that the ancient metal-frame pack from my attempt of the entire Appalachian Trail in 1973 bit into my back, so after the hike I purchased a capacious internal-frame "Northface" that turned up at Naran Tuul (Sun River), the largest outdoor market in town. Chimgee (Ts. Boldchimeg), a friend who had introduced me to Boldsaikhan, secured the ride by minivan to Burgastai. The date of our departure would be on or around June 10th, the day the border port opened. In this way we would be more likely to encounter traffic on the desert road should any emergencies arise.

Do I really know what I'm getting into? During this last stage of intense preparation, the thought that I was embarking on a far more difficult enterprise than I realized and had not made adequate inquiries about the distance, terrain, availability of water, etc. frequently occurred to me. I would be surprised by my rashness and presumption and shamefacedly return to Ulaanbaatar early. One day Amar, the Administrative Assistant at my school, voiced my worst fears.

"Why are you doing this—walking across Mongolia? It's dangerous. You don't know when you might meet up with bad people. What if your electronic compass breaks?"

I mentioned precautions I'd taken—the guide, bank deposit—then added, "I don't doubt that I'm running risks, but sometimes you have to just take the chance and venture forth in spite of the threat of mishaps." If I sounded confident, it was due to practice; I'd had this dialogue more than once with myself.

Shortly before my departure date, though, a danger of another sort began to loom, one which might prove more detrimental to the trip than a roadside bandit or broken GPS. Somebody had said something to me some time back. It was a trivial incident in itself, but one my suspicious, obsessive-prone brain was capable of making momentous, especially under the ideal conditions of solitude and physical duress. Moreover, there was a confirmed pattern of increased vulnerability to obsessing right before and during a trip. I began to worry. I thought of preparing a short script and springing it on the person, a fellow parishioner at Sts. Peter and Paul, if she appeared at next Sunday Mass; I was scheduled to leave early the Sunday after. This little extra-liturgical ritual might spare me months of anxiety or even a breakdown on the journey, I told myself. On the other hand, I knew from experience that such magic-wand waving too often only transformed one worry into another, even more groundless one. Obsessing—confronting—obsessing: This had largely been the story of my life for the past twenty years, at least. Try turning the other cheek and letting it go, I reasoned. I decided to try. The walk was to be an adventure on both the physical and spiritual plane, with the second terra incognita possibly the more perilous of the two. If I could complete the journey, however, I might from that time forward be less prey to compulsive behavior and enjoy more inner freedom. In this way also, then, my hike would be a crusade a la Sainte Terre.

ʔ ʔ ʔ

Map of Govi-Altai Aimag

Chapter 1
Passing by Sacred Mother Mountain:
Govi-Altai Aimag from Burgastai to Tseel

Your sparkling eyes and your smiling character,
Your rejoicing face and your calm behaviour
Relieved my depression and refreshed my mind,
And cheered my spirit gladdening my heart. (9-12)[1]

"Whumph!" The sagging sack of my full eight-liter collapsible water container hit the ground after unraveling the string like a spinning top's from the tree limb. Neither the pun on the word "collapsible" nor the sudden unplanned improvement in the container's design for a shower fixture, the use I was trying to put it to just now, occurs to me. I am staring with horror at the two or three prongs of spray, thinking what the timing of this accident might mean. My very first action on the first morning and I have ruined a vital piece of equipment! Is God or Fate set against this trip? The night before last in Altai at Boldsaikhan's cousin's place, where we lodged on the minivan trip down, there was the incident of the GPS slipping off my belt and falling into the outhouse pit. I'd had to retrieve it with a long pole and clean the cloth holster with repeated applications of detergent and water. I was able to laugh at that, later at least, but a damaged water container in the Gobi? So, it is with a sinking feeling of despair and cynicism, rather than the excitement and enthusiasm I expected, that, a short while later, I am walking with Boldsaikhan down the sandy knoll from last night's campsite to begin my hike across Mongolia.

How different this feeling from my exultant mood when we got off the minivan last night. We had presented my papers from Border Troops at the yellow, turreted, post building at Burgastai and then, following instructions, ridden two kilometers back to the unmanned gate. As fellow passengers and the driver looked on, I gathered a pinch of soil and placed it in a plastic zip bag. "This dirt," I announced, "will be deposited in Lake Khövsgöl at the end of my walk across Mongolia!" Minutes later, the hubbub of hilarity and bantering, words of encouragement and farewell that we had stood in the midst of were an echo in the steady pounding of our feet on the lonely dirt road. We walked a short way, then made a quick camp, sleeping out in the open. Now, in the clear, matter-of-fact morning light, my soaring spirits had come crashing down with that water container. I would discover later that it was still usable if filled half full and kept upside down in my pack and that, in any case, my guide's container sufficed for both of us. In the meantime, though, I have to fall back on what reserves of faith I can muster to get going this morning.

I have rested fairly well, in spite of the windy, cool night. The ground of gray gravel, stretching away on either side of the east by southeast road, has low saxaul shrubs scattered plentifully about, though there are broad barren spots. An isolated stand or two of the same swamp cottonwood we slept under last night can also be seen growing on low sand ridges. Also called poplar, this species, scientifically named diversifolia, puts out leaves of different shapes and sizes.

We pass two boys on horseback herding a flock of molting camels and later, at 11:00 am, a young couple leading two more camels loaded with their dismantled ger—the round, low-domed felt tent called the "yurt" in Russia—a small herd of camels in tow. The day before, as we were traveling in or near the Shargiin-Mankhan Natural Reserve in the vast waterless plain of the Shargiin Gobi (Yellowish Desert), we saw, running on our right, a herd of wild camels.[2] The young woman is wearing a squat, conical hat, called "tsomoo" in Chinese, the kind worn by laborers in the rice paddies of southeast Asia.

During this morning's walk I have occasionally looked behind us and to the right in the direction of Turfan in northwest China, recalling Mildred Cable's captivating description of it from the 1920s and 30s in *The Gobi Desert*. I had inadvertently chosen as my starting point one of the border posts nearest this historic oasis. It is situated in a depression that approaches a depth of over three-hundred meters below sea level at its lowest point, reputedly the lowest on the earth's dry land surface. Cable reports that, partly owing to its extremely low elevation, Turfan is among the hottest places on the globe during the summer months, reaching a temperature of about fifty-four degrees Celsius.[3]

Guided by the parallel line of telephone poles, we follow a road that we have been told leads to the village of Altai, namesake of the town we stayed overnight in. Lizards scurry off to the right and left and golio, a type of cicada resembling a large plump cricket and having a striped black-and-pink back, just manage to scuttle out of the way of our boots. The gray gravel eventually gives way to porous black pebbles of common vesicular basalt—a heavier version of volcanic lava. In the distance to our left lie the snow-dotted peaks of the Aj Bogdiin Nuruu range, home to the snow leopard; argali, or wild mountain sheep; wild goat; and Altai snowcock.[4] The range is a sub-chain of the Mongol Altain Nuruu, which has elevations of more than four-thousand meters, the highest in Mongolia.

We pass low sand dunes. Later we come to a fenced-off patch of tall Gobi feathergrass, or "broom grass," which is being raised as fodder in one of the aimag's excursions into agriculture. The grass continues well beyond the enclosure and in one spot we come upon a family preparing to depart for a new house site after dismantling their ger and loading it onto a truck. There is a well-defined circular clearing in the grass. The large blue truck with a high wooden frame in back is the Zil 130, once widely imported from Russia and still ubiquitous in Mongolia.

At three o'clock we reach Altai, circumventing enclosed vegetable gardens and crossing several springs. Altai is a "sum," the center of an administrative district, also called a "sum," roughly equivalent to a county in the U.S. The city named Altai that we visited as overnight guests of Boldsaikhan's cousin's two days before and are walking back to is the capital of Govi-Altai, one of twenty-one larger administrative districts in Mongolia called "aimags."

Inquiring about a guanz, that is, a canteen or roadside café, we are directed to a building on one side of the square. A sign, still projecting above the edge of the roof, identifies it as a former government warehouse for the purchase and storage of animal hides, wool, and cashmere. We enter a room with peeling, white-washed walls and wooden floor and sit down at a table with a bench like a church pew but partitioned with arm rests into individual seats. During the soviet era the bench probably accommodated workers attending the mandatory weekly organizational meetings of the local animal husbandry industry. A doorway in the back wall leads to a family's living quarters. Two middle-aged women, who introduce themselves as Alimaa (Apple) and Altanchimeg (Golden Ornament), begin making buuz, steamed beef dumplings traditionally served in great numbers at Tsagaan Sar (White Month), the Mongolian lunar New Year. I watch as one of the women kneads dough at a long wooden desk while the other chops the meat. They make dough balls, roller pin them, and fill them with meat. A fire is made in the stove using dried plants, probably eurotia or pea shrubs. After steaming for twenty minutes, the buuz are ready.

During the food preparation, Boldsaikhan converses with the cooks about the next water source. They confirm the report about a stream twelve kilometers away that we got from a group of drivers who were among our fellow passengers on yesterday's trip to Burgastai. Amazed by our walk from the border post about twenty kilometers away, they must be rather alarmed when he tells them about our intended hike to Russia.

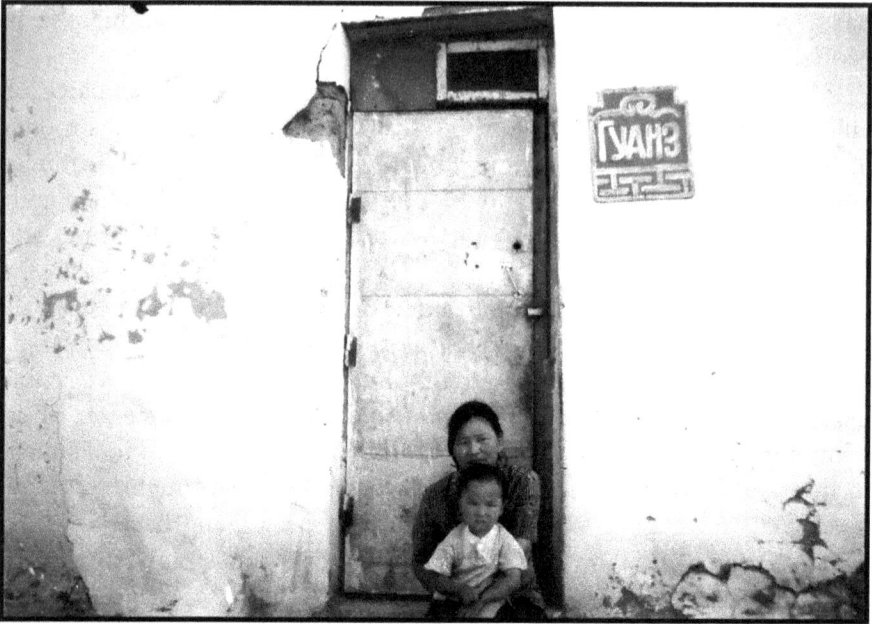

2 - *Alimaa and child*

As the conversation continues during the meal, I understand them to say they are friends and began operating the establishment in 1990, the year of the democratic revolution in Mongolia. Dating from the country's first turning from state-owned operations to entrepreneurship, this private guanz in a former government warehouse is a living chronicle of Mongolia's recent political history. Alimaa says she plans to take a typing course—she simulates operating a keyboard—in Ulaanbaatar in September.

Word has apparently gotten around town about the two strange men at the guanz, for young women begin arriving as we are preparing to leave. Bidding our hostesses goodbye, we follow the road out of town, passing a concrete monument atop a hill on our right. This construction—a horizontal ring with a tall pillar attached to the inside edge—is called Bayan Ovoo (Rich Heap of Stones), which is also an earlier name of local origin for this settlement. We pass tall, rounded hillocks resembling giant coal piles composed of black basalt pebbles. Rounding one of these hills, the road climbs slightly. Reaching a well, we stop by the ger of Enkh-Amgalan (Peace Tranquility), one of the drivers we consulted about the route on yesterday's minivan ride. He tells us our spring is in a large grove of aspen and willow trees that can be seen far ahead.

When we are nearing this grove, we ask further directions of a boy who approaches riding a donkey with large silver-toned stirrups. He accompanies us for a while out of curiosity. I had seen a saddled donkey inside one of the fenced-off vegetable gardens we passed on our way into Altai Sum. Soon we can hear the shouts and laughter of many voices coming from the grove, a sound wildly incongruent with the peaceful desert setting. As we enter the fenced-in grove through a gate, a woman calls out from a ger beside the enclosure, ordering us to stop. Thirsty, exhausted, and furious, I sit down inside the fence while Boldsaikhan talks to her at the ger.

But all is well. He returns with directions to a spot where the spring meanders briefly outside the fence and we drink and collect the cool, delicious water there. A cuckoo's loud note in the trees mingles with the uncouth din of the party. This is Khadnii Us (Rock Springs). We cross the sand out of earshot of the noise and find a campsite affording a beautiful view of the Aj Bogdiin Nuruu, which has grown more distinct since this morning. It is 8:30 pm. Soon after our dinner we are lying comfortably in our sleeping bags under the darkening sky.

༄

Govi-Altai is the Texas of Mongolia. Just as the state is the second largest in the U.S., the aimag ranks second in size among the country's twenty-one provinces.[5] Like Texas, it is located in the southwestern region of the country and the aimag's lower margin forms part of the country's southwestern border. The two have similar shapes, with projections at the top, bottom, and left, though Govi-Altai does not have the distinctive panhandle. Raising livestock is the principal means of livelihood in the aimag, Mongolians being a nomadic people, but the aimag stands out in this area, as the land of the longhorn does among the fifty states. The year before my hike, Govi-Altai ranked fourth among the twenty-one in the number of livestock and fifth in herding households.[6] It was this Mongolian Texas that I was to spend the next two and a half weeks getting to know intimately, walking a jagged southwest to northeast diagonal across its very heart.

Breaking camp the following morning, June 12th, we filled our one-liter bottles at the spring and headed east across the peneplain in the direction of our road. The sky was clear except for a long slender wisp of cloud above the northeast horizon. When we had gone about two-hundred meters, I stopped, noticing an unusually shaped shard of black stone at my feet. Examining it, I confirmed that it was indeed a flake left from tool manufacture. We made a brief reconnaissance. Boldsaikhan

found a second flake and I a third. I was ecstatic—a newly discovered
Stone Age site in Mongolia! I wrote down the position coordinates from
my GPS and dropped one or more of the flakes into my plastic bag of
flower samples.

Periodically during our walk that day, I would imagine the primitive
camp or settlement at Khadnii Us and think of how the perennial water
source had brought these early people here as it had brought us. Perhaps
the ancestral trees of this same grove had alerted them to the site of the
spring and—who knows?—a forebear of the cuckoo that we heard
singing in the grove last night was heard by them.

> The voice I hear this passing night was heard
> In ancient days. . . . (63-64)[7]

3 - Khadnii Us

Much later I was informed by Damdinsürengiin Tseveendorj,
Director of the Mongolian Academy of Sciences Institute of Archeology
in Ulaanbaatar, that ten joint Mongolian-Russian expeditions conducted
in recent years had discovered the site of numerous Stone Age
settlements in the area of the Mongol Altain Nuruu. There were three
Paleolithic sites near the village of Tögrög on our minivan route to
Burgastai two days before. According to archeologist Tseveendorj, the
ecology of the region was much different at that time, water and

vegetation being much more abundant. The isolated grove at Khadnii Us, then, was apparently the relic of an extensive woodland.[8]

The following summer I returned to this spring and found a half-dozen stone tools, fragments, and flakes. Consulting two other archeologists in Ulaanbaatar, I was told that one of the stones seems to have been an abandoned attempt at a side-scraper. The edge had apparently been retouched using an antler bone or a similar tool. The size of the tools and the technology used in their manufacture pointed to a date within the Mesolithic period in Mongolia,[9] possibly around 10,000 B.C., they said. One of the flakes was made of clouded chalcedony, while all or most of the others were of a black-colored agate, a fine-grained chalcedony with a hardness rating of six-and-a-half to seven on a one to ten scale of hardness. Diamonds rate ten and a Swiss army knife five.[10]

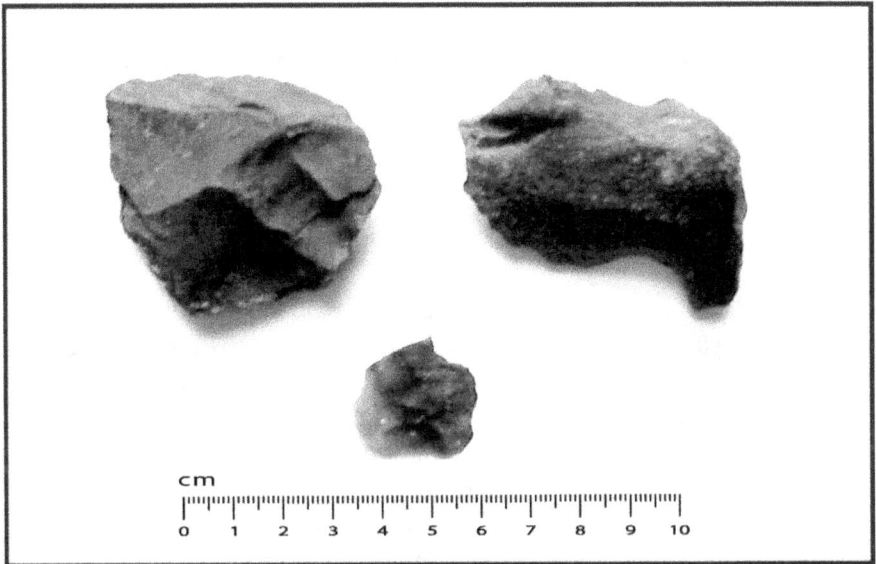

4 - Stones found at Khadnii Us

Reaching the line of electricity poles, we began following it since it would eventually converge with our road. The ground surface, rather evenly sprinkled with low saxaul shrubs, had more small stones than gravel, making walking rather difficult. A strong cool wind was at our backs and whenever we made a halt, choosing from among numerous dry gullies created by mountain run-off during the spring thaw, we leaned back in our packs against the windward bank to enjoy the coolness on our chest and face.

That afternoon we passed the first major turning on our route as we veered northeast, leaving behind the southeastward road I had originally planned to take because of its natural features and historic sites. Little-known traces of an old caravan stop on the initial, southernmost stretch were part of the road's appeal. An archeologist in Ulaanbaatar had told me about constructions of parallel shelving that were used to support the camels' load while they rested, thus sparing the trouble of unloading and reloading them.[11] But there is danger attached to the siren attractions on this road—a ninety-kilometer waterless stretch—so, like Odysseus tied to the mast, I bypass them.

At 3:00 pm we finally met up with our road again and were soon improving the time in an English tutorial on the first six cardinal numbers. At 4:15, near the end of the plain, we came to an abandoned, dry well with the pump pulled out and the cattle trough, a metal pipe slit lengthwise, pulled off to one side. Nearby stood a solitary ger with a saddled dark-brown donkey tied to a post, and we stopped to inquire about the next water source. A short middle-aged man emerged with a boy who wore a T shirt with "Servicemax" or "Servicemag" printed on the front. They were the first people we'd seen all day.

I understand the man to say the nearest water source is thirty kilometers away! I am beginning to despair of my life until I find there is a spring here; he apparently meant the water source nearest this one. It was to be the first of several confusions due to incomplete or inconsistent communication at "Babbling Springs," as I've christened this spot—after the Tower of Babel, rather than the sound of the water, which is as stagnant and scummy as a cow pond. Now, it seems, the man is reporting another water stop just fifteen to twenty kilometers away. We decide to fill our bottles only, adding iodine tablets. Then I see a man whom I take to be a neighbor of his coming to gather water a little downstream from us. I send my guide to inquire of him, with the result that we now have a new report to work with—no water until twenty-five kilometers. I was not to learn until going over the incident with Boldsaikhan and an interpreter in Ulaanbaatar months later that the "men" were one and the same person and that what we were getting were the vacillating opinions of an uninformed advisor.

My guide suspects that the twenty-five kilometer figure is wrong and is for proceeding with enough water for fifteen kilometers, as originally planned. I point out that if the fifteen-kilometer figure is wrong we will be "nas barsan" ("died")—my clumsy rendering of "dead ducks" in Mongolian. We must therefore also fill the good eight-liter-capacity container here. To my surprise, he refuses to cooperate, so I have to insist, warning him that if there is a second incident we'll have to part company. The draconian administrative approach is a regrettable about-face after our friendly interactions earlier today; it imparts a tone of constraint to our relations for the rest of our journey together, which lasted only until the town of Altai. Viewing the incident from a knowledge of what we later found to be the actual distance to the next water stop, it seems that Boldsaikhan was more certain of finding water in fifteen kilometers than he could communicate to me in Mongolian.

We finally left the peneplain and began ascending the southeast slope of the Aj Bogdiin Nuruu not far from Khüren Toson Uul, the aimag's second-highest mountain.

5 - Entering Aj Bogdiin Nuruu

After the road crested, we walked amid mountains painted green, light red, and other tones. Soon there were only reddish-brown slopes on our left and a plain on our right. A small plant, probably sagebrush, was among the sparse vegetation.

We passed another played-out well. The cool wind continued to blow lustily through the late afternoon. Around 6:45 we left the road and followed the line of telephone poles left into a narrow gulch with a dry stream bed. While resting in the shade, we were visited by a male and female wagtail. The sight of these slender birds bobbing their long tails up and down would become very familiar to me in the weeks ahead.

At about 8:30 we emerged onto the road again. Thinking that Boldsaikhan had expected to find the fifteen-kilometer water source in the stream gully, I called a halt for the day. We made a campsite on a fairly level and soft stretch of a dry stream bed hidden behind a hillock. The next morning would bring the discovery that we had stopped within two or three kilometers of water.

June 14th, the third full day, we set out at 8:20 am, our earliest yet. The night was chilly and I didn't sleep well. From now on I would always erect the tent when camping outdoors. Today there was less wind and the sky was mostly clear. It was on this morning that I first prayed at least one Mystery of the rosary, counting off the beads with one hand as I walked, an activity that soon became a routine. Before long we entered another gully where the telephone poles diverged from the road. After coming to a well-constructed but now ruined stone corral, we met a handsome boy descending the gully. He wore a brown deel, the national costume, a gown with a high collar and long sleeves—features apparently derived from Manchu dress—and an overlapping front fastened on the right side with metal buttons. We asked him about the location of water and he pointed to the well a short distance up the gully. We found a ger there, with part of another in the process of being dismantled by two men and two women. A jeep was parked between the tents. We refilled our one good eight-liter container and, perching it on the ledge of a small cliff near the well, bathed the upper half of our bodies, shaved, brushed our teeth, and cleaned the utensils used in last night's dinner. Then we went to the ger, accepting an invitation to tea.

Following guest-behavior protocol, we entered carefully so as not to step on the threshold, then walked to the left, or west, since the door always faces south,[12] and sat down. Our host, whose name is Ravdan, is lying on the floor in the back area, called the khoimor, which contains a Buddhist shrine and family treasures and photos.[13] This particular shrine features, among other objects, a photo of the Dalai Lama and a painted clay statuette of a standing bear dressed like a human. Ravdan's wife, Baigalmaa (Nature), sits on the bed across from us on the right side of the room. She is in her late twenties, rather pretty, and above average in height. Their young daughter and two of Ravdan's younger brothers and a young sister were also present during most of our visit. Another brother was the boy we'd passed and who, we were told, had been going to get two horses that we'd seen grazing near our road.

As the conversation about our trip got underway, we were given süütei tsai, traditional salted milk tea; boortsog, squares of dough kneaded with baking soda, oil, water, sugar, and salt and cooked in oil; and a bowl of what appeared to be soft cheese. Serving tea and tsagaan idee (white food), that is, dairy products, is the custom in the hospitable Mongolian home. Later, Baigalmaa would go a step beyond this by offering us cream to protect our lips and skin from the sun's intense rays. The broad band of sunlight streaming through the circular opening at the top of the ger was made palpable by the smoke from Ravdan's cigarette. The room had a more rustic aspect than I was used to seeing in gers. Along the wall between me and the door was one dismantled ger—a large stack of felt folded up, the orange wooden roof poles, and the folded khana, or wooden lattice work that is spread out to make the wall sections. In front of this stack was a saddle made of animal hide, the fur still stuck to it, stretched over a wood frame. This left side of the ger is the male domain and equipment-storage area. The right side, the female domain, contains domestic articles, such as the water barrel and kitchen utensils.[14] We learned that the family had been here one month and was getting ready to move to higher ground, where the grass was better. They told us that they have all five traditional kinds of domestic livestock: horses, camels, cattle—that is, cows or yaks—sheep, and goats.

When we had shouldered our packs in front of the ger and bid our friendly hosts farewell, we climbed the gully, occasionally inhaling the fragrant scent of an herb, probably wild thyme, which was growing in abundance. Besides what appeared to be buttercups and yellow iris, there were several wildflowers I didn't recognize. It was hot until the road reached a higher elevation. Cirrus clouds had begun forming in the depths of the sky. The top of the pass was very arid, a combination of brown sand with little vegetation and brown-gray stones with a rough, granular surface splotched with reddish-brown lichen. A Siberian marmot whistled a warning to the neighborhood while we sat resting.

Later that afternoon we came to a small, deep valley with a lone ger in it. Ravdan had told us to look for water there; not finding any, we signaled to a herder boy who had sighted us from a hilltop. He informed us there was water in five kilometers on a road that was not on our route. We ascended a hogback slope under the glaring sun, the boy on horseback escorting us at a distance. I had tied the detachable, lower section of my pant legs to my short shirtsleeves to protect my forearms and hands, now sunburnt and swollen. We descended steeply to a small stream with a chain of gers along its bank. The water is apparently runoff from melting snow. A herdsman informed us that we would find water in the stream bed again five kilometers from here but none after that until the village of Bum on the other side of the Aj Bogdiin Nuruu. Following this stream would also bring us to our road again.

6 – Herding sheep, Aj Bogdiin Nuruu

The grassy bank where we rested and slaked our thirst was swarming with the same tiny grasshoppers with striped legs that we had been unavoidably stepping on during most of the day's hike. A man in a jeep stopped. It was Ravdan!

> "Sain baina uu?" ("Hello." Literally, "Are you fine?")
> "Sain." ("Fine.")
> "Say, I thought you said there was water in the valley five kilometers back. We couldn't find any."
> "I said in this valley, not that one!"
> "Oh."

Such was my interpretation of the brief conversation between him and my guide, judging from Ravdan's angry expression and abrupt departure at the end of it. Boldsaikhan has since confirmed the accuracy of this rendering. Mongolian men in the countryside, I was finding, often preferred making confident assertions in answer to questions about directions and distances—even when not so sure of the facts—to simply saying "I don't know."

After about five kilometers, noticing a pool of water in a stream bed intersecting our road and a flat, grassy stretch on the bank, I decided to camp. It was very windy. We erected our tents for the first time, and, at Boldsaikhan's suggestion, I lay down, exhausted and cold, while he prepared dinner wearing our one rain jacket-windbreaker. The other one was with the box of food and gear we had decided to leave at his cousin Tsetsegsüren's ger until our arrival back in Altai. Using the light, handleless rolling pin he had brought, he rolled the dough into patties for gambir, a sweet unleavened bread fried in oil, on a large plastic zip bag spread on his tent floor. When he had cooked the gambir, along with six eggs and instant mashed potatoes, in a niche of the rocky hillock near our camp, I joined him for dinner in his larger, two-person tent. We each drank two cups of hot chocolate for dessert. Then we rushed to clean the utensils and put everything away before dark.

In the early morning I was awakened by my tent's flysheet flapping violently in the wind, which had increased since nightfall. Entering Boldsaikhan's tent to get the earplugs in my pack and to tell him he might have to share his sleeping quarters tonight, I noticed that his tent was about as noisy and returned to mine. I tried turning around, lying with my head in the narrow, foot area, where it was a little quieter. Feeling a slight surge of panic from claustrophobia, I placed my closed pocketknife beside me to reassure myself that, in the event of a serious panic attack, I could slice open the tent wall in an instant. I slept.

🐏

We left our still-windy campsite about ten o'clock and, passing through a small valley with several gers in it, came to a rude stone pillar which my guide called a manuukhai chuluu, which is translated "scarecrow stone," though the purpose seems to be to scare off wolves. There is a cloth version, the manuukhai, which is sometimes set up near cultivated fields or on the roof of gers where cheese is drying to keep birds away.

Our road, which we have recovered, proceeded over hilly terrain in an extremely desolate landscape—sand or eroded sand-colored rock. Later, purple-colored mountains entered the not-too-distant background. A thin layer of cloud was spread into streaks in the sky. When we were within about thirteen kilometers of Bum, the road seemed to descend; we had all but conquered our first mountain range. The way down had gotten steeper when the rock walls of the pass, light gray and splotched with brown lichen, became pocked and gouged, creating various contorted shapes on their surfaces. Sagebrush was sometimes scattered over the walls' face, making the effect even more striking. When this rock eventually gave way to the purple mountains, their color now appeared to be light brown with an oily, dark-gray sheen on one side of many of the stones.

7 - Landscape, Aj Bogdiin Nuruu

Around 5:00 pm we emerge from the Aj Bogdiin Nuruu onto a small plain surrounded by mountains and hills and are soon at the unfortunately named Bum, a brigad, or village, within the administrative district of Altai Sum. Bum, pronounced "boom," is a collection of twenty gers and a few buildings constructed of gray brick and plaster, which is falling off in places. The population count, I was soon to learn, is between fifty and sixty. A green patch on the west side of the plain is the site of Büngiin Gol spring.

Walking toward a ger to inquire about the next water stop and a lodging place, we are approached by several young men, one of them on a bicycle, and a young woman. They inform us that it is thirty-five kilometers to the next water source, which is within a day's walk on the flat terrain ahead, and that we can stay overnight with them. As we are following one of the men and the woman to a ger, I tell Boldsaikhan that we are doing this, instead of camping, in honor of his daughter's second birthday, which is today. If, in consulting my map this morning, I balked at the thought of stopping at a place with such an inauspicious name, after walking all day I am quite reconciled to the idea.

8 - Ovoo, or sacred cairn, Aj Bogdiin Nuruu

We pass a stone shed with a lot of dried saxaul, looking like beached driftwood, stacked as fuel against one wall and a wooden churn painted yellow. With the increase in coal and other fuel prices in recent years, the use of saxaul for firewood had become more popular in the Gobi. This was a cause of the significant decrease in the growth rate and size of saxaul "forests," high density areas of tree growth, over the last twenty-five years.[15] The churn was apparently used for making airag, fermented mare's milk, though this standard Mongolian beverage was traditionally made by placing milk in a sheep's stomach sack and pounding it with a stick for an hour before letting the milk ferment for three to four hours.[16] Several paces from the firewood and churn in physical space but eons from them in time is a satellite dish.

On entering the ger we are greeted by a comely young woman whose small daughter is sleeping on the floor; her stroller is parked in the ger. The group of us converse with the rasping, dolorous moan of camels in the background. Ariunaa, the woman who met us entering Bum, is also quite attractive and speaks some English, having studied the language for four years at a private institute in Ulaanbaatar. She now teaches English at an elementary school in the aimag capital, Altai, her home. Her parents live in the area of Bum, while her husband, apparently the man who accompanied her to the ger, is from Ulaanbaatar. Her friend, our hostess, is also a grade school teacher.

One part of the ger wall is covered by a carpet representing the celebrated silver tree fountain at the ancient palace in Karakorum, capital of the Mongol Empire. At the base of the tree, four silver lions spewed airag and, near the top, four pipes entwined with gilt serpents dispensed wine, refined mare's milk, boal—apparently mead—and rice wine. The tree was surmounted by an angel, whose trumpet blast signaled when to refill the pipes with liquor.[17] The ger is also furnished with a television set, as the dish outside indicated, and before long it is on, tuned-in to a station in Ulaanbaatar. Our hostess makes boortsog, the fried pastry, giving each cut square of dough a few taps with her butcher knife before tossing the square onto the pile for frying.

Several neighbors stop by, curious about the new arrivals. After a while, I take a wooden stool and my copy of a few short American novels torn from an old paperback anthology to save weight and sit down in the shade of the stone shed to read. Behind the low mountains across the plain, distinct on the horizon's rim, rise the twin horns of Eej Khairkhan (Sacred Mother Mountain), an extinct volcano. Looking up occasionally from Edith Wharton's *False Dawn* to take in the scene, I debate whether to accept an offer made by the young people to taxi us there and back tomorrow. The mountain is one of the points of interest bypassed when we turned off the southeastern road on the second day. Ariunaa has told me she can show me the sights, the rock pools, caves, and rock carvings, which led to the site being declared a Natural and Historical Monument ten years before.[18] It is an inviting proposal and at one point I even resolve to accept, but the expense—about $60—as well as the damage to our morale that I fear will result from disrupting our routine so early, eventually leads me to decline.

> And thus the native hue of resolution
> Is sicklied o'er with the pale cast of thought. . . .
> (3.1.86-87)[19]

Here was the first instance of a contradiction in my journey that would often recur. Traveling on foot across a country would seem to involve a leisurely progress allowing plenty of unplanned side trips. In fact, my hike was to become more like a runners' marathon requiring adherence to the route. The slow, arduous mode of travel meant that to cover such a long distance and reach my goal I had to conserve time and energy by being selective about the sidelights. What did this mean for my crusade to recover from the enervating effects of a motion-based lifestyle, or, to adapt the familiar term, "motion sickness"? How ironic that the means of conquering my propensity to haste had become an occasion for it. I was walking, yes, but with the mentality of a long-distance runner, if not a speed car driver.

Several children who had approached me shyly in the ger found me out behind the shed. A herdsman who had gotten wind of my arrival was also introduced to me there. He was handsome and swarthy, a polite forty-six-year old gentleman who had lived in or around Bum all his life. He told me some Americans on a hunting expedition after the argali, or wild mountain sheep, had visited here three years ago. The animal is hunted for its meat and horns.

When I returned to the ger at nightfall, I was shocked to find it packed with people sitting rapt before the luminous, flickering TV screen. It is Saturday night at the movies in the oasis hamlet. I explain to our hostess that, as my guide and I must get up early to resume our trip, it is time we turned in. Most of the audience soon disperses and when the stragglers have savored a few more precious moments before the tube, the power generator outside is switched off and we retire.

2

We rose early as planned and, having thanked our hostess—in words and cash—and bidden farewell to our young friends, entered the dusty plain in the direction of the spring. We stopped to collect water and, in my case, wash clothes. The midge flies, whose reputation among the locals had preceded them, were terrible, leaving an itching sensation all over. We had just gotten underway again when I found three small black stone flakes, traces of tool making. Another Stone Age settlement or camp in Mongolia come to light after thousands of years! I recorded the GPS position coordinates and put the lightest chip in the right front pocket of my trousers.

When I returned to the site the next summer to collect a surface sample of stones, I discovered the ground several meters back from the spring, closer to the road, rather abundantly littered with black agate stone tools, fragments, flakes, and cores for making flakes. According to the same archeologists in Ulaanbaatar whom I consulted about the Khadnii Us stones, a four-and-a-half-centimeter fragment from my sample had apparently been intended as a knife or side-scraper. One tool I collected, a five-and-a-quarter-centimeter end-scraper with a nice serrated edge, was never used for some reason.[20] Had it been lost just after being made until I happened upon it about a dozen thousand years later?

9 – Büngiin Gol outside Bum

After traveling through a long corridor of low hills, we entered a plain with a range of low mountains, the Toroin (Piglet's) Nuruu, lying beyond it. Eej Khairkhan could be seen standing off by itself and to the right of the range. We were now in the Zakhui Zarmangiin Gobi, like the Shargiin Gobi crossed en route to Burgastai, one of the ten well-known sub-regions of the Gobi Desert in Govi-Altai.[21] Locals gather at Eej Khairkhan on designated holy days each month to pray to the mountain. They offer mutton, milk products, and vodka with a khadag, or blue silk scarf representing the sky. Childless women ask for the blessing of children.[22]

For the rest of that day and in the afternoon of the following one, "Sacred Mother" would escort us as a guardian spirit on our desert journey, just as, I trusted, the spirit of my own mother, in whose memory I was making this trip, was guiding and protecting me. As we proceeded northeast, I observed the changes in the mountain's silhouette as the alignment of the two horns shifted. At a point more nearly parallel with the mountain, while we were resting against the bank of a dry stream bed, I made a pencil sketch of the mountain's outline. The distinctive configuration has inspired an earthy folk tale.

Once upon a time long ago Sacred Mother was on her way to the mountain Aj Bogdiin Uul, whom she wished to befriend. Seeing her, Burkhan Buudai Uul, with whom she had already formed a friendship, became envious and began running after her. She had stopped to take a crap when Burkhan reached her. Picking up some sand, he angrily hurled it at Eej Khairkhan, who fell back on the ground. That is why the mountain has the form of a woman lying on her back.[23]

10 - Stones found at Büngiin Gol

As I looked at the jagged volcanic-crater shell across the plain, it was also easy to imagine a lush late Cretaceous wetland seventy to seventy-five million years ago, the giant flesh-eating Tarbosaurus stalking its prey and duck-billed Saurolophus grazing, a smoking green volcano in the background. The Mongolian Gobi is one of the world's prime hunting grounds for dinosaur fossils. The American explorer Roy Chapman Andrews' discovery of the first dinosaur eggs in Ömnögovi Aimag in the 1920s is especially well-known.

As we neared the Toroin Nuruu in the afternoon, we crossed the forty-fifth parallel, the line of latitude equidistant between the equator and north pole and lying along the north foot of Eej Khairkhan. During the last several hours of our walk across the plain, sand dunes detached themselves from the front of the range, and when we finally reached them numerous saxaul bushes and swamp cottonwood trees could be seen on them. This was the oasis descriptively named Nariin Toroin (Thin Piglet's) and, alternatively, Buurin Bulag (Male Camel's Spring).

After stopping briefly in the saxaul "forest," the horseflies not allowing us to stay longer, we veered to the right, leaving the road to look for a campsite near water. We passed a lone ger on our left. The sky had become overcast and around this time it rained lightly. It seemed strange, these water drops falling on the desert sand, yet there were tall spears of grass and a surprising variety of colorful wildflowers, among other plants, growing here. After we had climbed two sand dunes to see if we could spot a few gers together, indicating a water source, and Boldsaikhan had searched the oasis for a while on his own, we returned to the area of the one ger. We found a spring beside it flowing in a channel artificially cut in the sand. This was the next water source that our friends in Bum had told us was thirty-five kilometers away.

I went up to the spring head, a pool with roiling water and a sandy bottom, to fill my drinking bottle. We decided to pitch our tents behind the ger, which was unoccupied, and next to the spring, where the horseflies and other insects were less numerous. We ate a cold dinner, finishing our granola and muesli brought from Ulaanbaatar, in Boldsaikhan's tent, then retired to rest. Once, getting up in the dark to relieve myself, I saw headlights slowly tracing a rough line in the distance: travelers, like ourselves, headed toward the village of Tseel.

༃

I was cutting a moleskin patch to cover a nasty blister on the inside of my left heel the next morning when a jeep bounced into camp and several jovial passengers got out. They had come to freshen up and collect water at the spring. We learned from them there was no water stop on the road we were traveling until Tseel, one-hundred kilometers away, but that there might be a little water on an alternative route. Good thing they happened by! It was drizzling when we departed on this second road about 10:00 am.

Since the start of the hike, I had habitually kept to the left rut of the road, my guide the right. Today, taking advantage of a discovery made the previous day for lessening the boot's pressure on my blistered left heel, I treaded the left slope of the median strip between the ruts. Later, when the inside of my right-foot heel blistered from so much left-favored walking, I would also tread the right slope with the right foot. In this way,

I became a staunch middle-of-the-roader over the next few weeks. Only after I had finally begun carrying out my own instructions to my guide for preventing blisters or calluses, namely, wearing a thin pair of socks under the thick woolen pair, did I shift back to the leftist rut I began my career in. Why had I thought my feet were special and didn't require the second pair of socks?

We entered the Toroin Nuruu. The landscape was extremely arid—black gravel on brown sand dotted with saxaul shrubs and, often, outcroppings of rock on the adjacent hills. It was amid scenes like these that I found myself turning to thoughts of the dear woman I had last seen several days before walking up the busy street from the Ulaanbaatar bus depot where we parted.

> If you miss the train I'm on, you will know that I am gone
> You can hear the whistle blow a hundred miles. . . .

Snatches of a song I'd sung on a date with her one evening at a karaoke rose up in that emptiness.

> Lord, I'm one, Lord, I'm two, Lord, I'm three, Lord, I'm four
> Lord, I'm five hundred miles from my home. . . .[24]

I'd come to this faraway place and was she, a porter on the Ulaanbaatar-Beijing railway line, traveling away from me this very moment? Instead of being a hindrance on the hike, as I'd feared when I asked Enkhjargal (Peace Happiness) to think of me merely as a friend while I was away, her image was an invaluable aid, sustaining my spirits and resolve, dispelling loneliness and anxiety—including any that might have arisen from the incident with my fellow parishioner. If a threatening obsessive thought or image did surface at that time, I have no record or recollection of it. The realization that I could be peaceful and energized thinking about Enkhjargal was a major turning point on the hike, maybe even in my life. Through the rest of the two weeks to Altai, I would often resort to imagining our conversations on the phone when I reached there and in person at the end of the summer in Ulaanbaatar. It was the start of a journey away from self and toward the other.

We came to an area where the mountain rock on both sides of the road had an oily black or purple luster. I think it was here that I noticed, lying in the loose gravel on the left side of the road, a rather peculiarly shaped piece of rusted metal—a flat oval tongue with a small spike attached at one end, the whole probably about fifteen centimeters long.

Boldsaikhan, coming over as I stood examining it in my hands, seemed to think it was an ancient artifact.

"No," I decided, letting it drop. "It is from an automobile." It was a little heavy for its size and the slightly tilted attached spike, ringed where it joined the tongue, was rather quaint looking, but both sides of the tongue were perfectly flat and smooth. An ancient hand-made tool would surely bear some traces of hammer strokes, and a weapon would have a ridge down the middle of the blade and sharpened edges. It was too bad we weren't crossing Mongolia in the opposite, north-to-south direction, as I had briefly considered doing. Nine days later at the museum in Altai, I discovered an exhibit of many of these "automobile parts" of various shapes and sizes neatly mounted on a board labeled "Some Types of Mongolian Warrior Spearheads from the Iron Age in the 13th-17th Centuries." Although the Iron Age in Mongolia was much earlier— between the 7th and 3rd centuries B.C.[25] —and, as I was to learn later, "Arrowheads" would have been more accurate, the exhibit served to bring home the fact that I had picked up and tossed down a precious historic artifact. The opinion of archeologist D. Erdenebaatar, that the arrowhead I found was from the 13th century, corroborated the dating suggested by the museum exhibit.[26] The smooth finish of the blade that had led me to think it was machine-made does credit to the skill of blacksmiths in those days.

We were resting amid the rock with the dark-purple sheen when a Zil 130 truck with a motorcycle in back coming from the opposite direction stopped. A thick-set middle-aged man got out. As we stood talking, the gruff, torpid expression on his face was rather forbidding until he began flashing broad, snaggle-toothed smiles expressing guileless, boyish wonderment about our trip. Sükhbaatar, as he called himself, overcome with curiosity, bent down with his face close to the zip bag of flower and stone flake samples at my belt and, later, snatched up Boldsaikhan's backpack resting on the ground.

"Wow!" he exclaimed in the Mongolian equivalent for the interjection, hoisting the pack onto his back with one arm to test its weight. He or the woman in the passenger seat handed us an unlabeled plastic bottle filled with Coca-Cola to take a swig or two from, as well as a thick cookie each. Sükhbaatar told us there was water in twenty kilometers but none for the remaining fifty to Tseel.

This stretch of mountain pass, doubtless subject to bitter winds in the winter, was littered with the carcasses of livestock. I noticed at least one horse's and one camel's. For the past three winters parts of Mongolia had suffered from zuds, or onslaughts of unusually heavy snowfall, covering pasture grass and resulting in the loss of millions of stock. Herdsmen who were relatives or friends of Boldsaikhan's cousin had mentioned to us on the evening of our visit losing many animals the previous January. While some losses during the bitter Mongolian winters have always occurred, since the advent of democracy the lack of government support for the maintenance of livestock and lifting of restrictions on the size of flocks have meant greater losses.

We descended to the plain again and made a long, gradual upward march northeast toward the eastern edge of the Aguitiin (Cave's) Nuruu. While resting we heard the melodious song, a mixed chirrup and gurgling sound, of the boljmor, or lark, of which there are nine species in Mongolia.[27] An oasis, Bayan Tooroi (Rich Poplar), with the tutelary Sacred Mother mountain in the background, became visible on the plain on our right. Reaching the site of Bosgiin Bulag (Threshold's Springs) at the crest of a hill, we found a meadow verdant with humps of tall grass, a large patch of cane, and buttercups on long stems, but no running water. An animal carcass lay near one of the stagnant pools. We decided to push on for another ten kilometers to a spring that I had not noticed on the map until then.

11 - *Plain after Toroin Nuruu, looking west*

After continuing the ascent along the margin of a wide, dry riverbed, we notice, shortly before 8:00 pm, three green patches at a point where the road enters a high wall of mountain up ahead. Flowing from the left-hand one is a runnel of sparkling water. This is apparently Khachigchin Bulag, a spring in the region known as Tayan Nakhis Gazar. Tracing the trickle of water back to a gulch, we find our first good campsite, a delightful spot with tall sheer cliff faces on either hand; rock squares and ledges to serve as furniture; flat, stoneless patches for our tents; and, of course, pools of cool mountain water. I expect to see others camped nearby, but some bits of paper in the spring bed are the only signs of our fellow humans. We are in what is technically called a slot canyon, formed, like its better-known counterpart in Zion National Park in Utah, by the spring's steady channeling of the rock over the ages.[28]

We are in excellent spirits tonight. Our two-week march to Altai, where Boldsaikhan has indicated he plans to stop walking and return to Ulaanbaatar, is now half done.

The next morning, a man traveling with his boy by motorcycle stopped at our camp and told us we could get to Tseel on this road leading through the gulch in a little over thirty kilometers. We hope to reach Tseel today and then catch up on our weekly one-day-of-rest schedule. We breakfasted on one large gambir patty, prepared, as usual, by Boldsaikhan, and a half-liter of orange Metamucil each. I have not slept well due to the aching of my sunburnt arms and the noise of the strong wind, which returned during the night.

It is warm as we proceed through the gully, but there is a breeze. After passing through the Aguitiin Nuruu we begin a long gradual ascent north to Baga (Little) Tayangiin Nuruu. We enter this range to find ourselves among barren hills of a strange light-green color. Also unusual is a monument beside the road consisting of a large squarish block of stone with several colonies of smaller stone blocks ranged around it. Atop the central block is a pile of small rocks, and wrapped around two crossed short stout sticks is a blue silk khadag, the ceremonial scarf. The other blocks also have a pile of small rocks on them. The whole faintly resembles a castle or a Buddhist lamasery. It commemorates, I later learn, the physical strength of Mongolian wrestlers and, in particular, one Byaluudash, who is said to have lifted the central block singlehandedly.[29]

When the road finally begins to level out, we come to an ovoo, a cairn marking a spot, usually at the top or the pass of a sacred mountain, for making offerings and prayers. We circle it thrice in a clockwise direction, and I toss onto it a small stone, one of the traditional offerings. In this way the traveler petitions or gives thanks for a safe journey and good fortune. To be really orthodox I could have added the wish "May you grow tall and may I make lucky finds." Mingled with the stones of a typical ovoo are horses' skulls, empty vodka bottles, food, and pairs of crutches, among other items offered in supplication or gratitude. The whole is often surmounted by a wooden pole draped with one or more khadags. All digging, moving of stones, tree cutting, hunting and fishing, and polluting of lakes, rivers, and streams in the vicinity of the cairns are taboo.[30]

It was about 3:30 pm when we sat resting at the ovoo. Checking the distance to Tseel, I found that we were about thirty kilometers out; the man on the motorbike had miscalculated. Descending the pass, we surprised, in a hidden niche of the gully, a small herd of gray camels, their stone corral nearby. They stopped grazing to stare at us. After another turn, we beheld the vista of an enormous green valley, the electricity poles entering it from the gully we are in and eventually blending to form a brown line: the route to Tseel. It was the first turning in the gray semi-desert ground toward the greenness we would find further north; we are making progress. The name of this valley was Sukhaitiin Khooloi (Sukhat's Throat).

12 - Sukhaitiin Khooloi valley before Tseel

Light rainfall and, later, bands of dark cloud and far-off sounds of thunder as we plodded along on the flat, dusty road helped account for the sudden increase in vegetation. A party in a jeep stopped to offer us a lift and in their conversation with Boldsaikhan reported that it was forty kilometers to Tseel. He was in favor of accepting the ride, but I angrily turned it down, reminding him that by our last reckoning it was only thirty or so. After this incident, his manner assumed a quietly rebellious tone, creating tension between us that spoiled my enjoyment of the lovely green landscape.

At some point on our hike during the past two days, we must have crossed the path that Idu'ud Khan of Turfan, the oasis town in northwest China, took on his way east to meet Temüüjin in present-day Zuunmod near Ulaanbaatar. Idu'ud, who brought gifts of great wealth, was favorably received and honored with the khan's daughter Alaltun in marriage. This was in or around 1206, the year Temüüjin was formally given the title "Genghis Khan" as ruler over a unified Mongolia.[31]

The terrain rose slightly before becoming level again. A rainbow appeared straddling a small hill on our right. Though still covered with low vegetation, the ground was much sandier than before, or at least appeared to be because we had left the road and were walking along the straight line of electricity poles to save time. At about 8:30 pm the distance to Tseel was about fourteen kilometers. When we were within six or so of our destination, we decided to camp since night was falling and the hotel in town that we'd heard about would not be admitting guests now. We also each had a half-liter of water left, enough to get us through the night. Almost the very moment we finished putting up our tents it began to rain—hard. We were lucky to have stopped when we did. Still, I slept little that night on account of going supperless to bed.

ᲠᲠᲠ

Chapter 2
Three Villages and Three Ranges:
Govi-Altai Aimag from Tseel to Dötiin Davaa

Here is a deer!
Running at top speed,
Antlers carried high.

There is an ibex!
Jumping with all its strength,
Horns upheld.

. . . .

In these granite rocks
Washed with rain and snow,
Over which the swallow flits
And the eagle circles,

That ancient artist
The author of these works,
Climbed grazing his knees and elbows,
And scratching his hands and fingers. . . .¹ (1-6, 41-48)

We continued our pursuit of Tseel about 7:00 am after another windy night. The rain had just resumed, to continue during the rest of that day and all night. We passed a long low building of modern construction for housing livestock. On a hill in the town far ahead, a palatial-like plaster-walled building with a long row of windows was a token of civilization, beckoning with the promise of order, prosperity, and repose. Our approach to the town by way of the telephone poles led us by a back route across a stream and through the dumpsite. Finally arriving, we came to a small brickworks, then passed up the sleeping neighborhood and ascended to a collection of colorful, plastered buildings, including a small, yellow-roofed monastery, in search of the hotel. A lone passerby directed us to a building with a sign "Buudal" ("Hotel").

"Baikhgüi" ("Not there"), in other words, "No rooms available." A well-favored, early middle-aged woman answering the door delivered the all-too-frequent reply in Mongolia to inquiries about people, products, and services. She might be able to find us a ger, though. Invited to come in out of the rain, we entered a large room, empty except for a massive billiard table in the middle. Huge tawdry plaster medallions bearing leaf designs were affixed to the pink walls at intervals. The ceiling, a dirty gray stained brown in places, was badly cracked and sagging. Clearly, the place belonged to a more prosperous era: the days of soviet town planning. Was it originally a hotel or had it undergone a transformation, like the former warehouse in Altai village, in private hands?

13 - Tseel

At the far end of the room was a door with a small arc-shaped and glassless window covered by a short white curtain. The rounded, sagging, plywood ledge evidently once served as a ticket counter for the billiard hall patrons. We proceeded through this door into a combination kitchen and bedroom, where we sat down in our wet clothes while the woman ran for breakfast at a nearby guanz. A little girl slept on the bed beneath the one window. Across from the bed stood a large unlit stove cluttered with pans, an upturned pan lid with some raw meat lying in it, and four empty beer bottles.

Tümenbayar (Ten-Thousand Happiness), our hostess, returned with two oval metal plates overflowing with budaatai khuurag, a rice and mutton dish, and a thermos of hot milk tea. After quickly dressing her child, she went off again in search of lodgings for us while we ate. The little girl is a beautiful three-year old. She prattles on and gambols about, coaxing my constant attention. Stitched onto her trousers is the cryptic slogan

Happ
y Babies

The small radio on the windowsill above the bed broadcasts a morning program from Ulaanbaatar. Among other things on the ledge are a large electronics battery bearing Chinese characters and two different-sized sets of playing cards, both designed from the U.S. $100 bill. It seems a bit strange, Ben Franklin's benevolent, bovine face looking up at me from the windowsill of a poolhall backroom in Tseel, Mongolia.

Tümenbayar brings news of a lodging place, and we follow her across the street to a log building with a kitchen and furnished sleeping room. It is rather grimy and run-down but roomy and, except for a slow drip from the ceiling, dry. I secure it for only five-hundred tögrögs, or about fifty cents. Water for washing and firewood will cost another thousand tögrögs.

I am finally in the process of taking off my wet trousers when company arrives: three men, then a woman and girl, probably the one we have just left at the billiard hall. They are curious about us and our trip. I must abide the trousers a while longer. I am astounded at the open-door policy in force here and make no effort to play the host. Others drop in later while I am lying in bed in my one dry article of clothing, a pair of undershorts unearthed in my pack. One fellow swings by the kitchen to rummage through our two food bags on his way out.

On the wall across from my bed are two large 1998-99 Mongolian wrestling posters and a smaller one of a smiling President Bagabandi. More interesting to me is the kitchen's huge laminated photo-poster of a table setting featuring a multi-decked hamburger and French fries, a verdant park showing through the window in the background.

On the back wall between my bed and Boldsaikhan's, a dresser displays family photos. Many more, including one of a young couple, the man in a uniform and Russian fur cap, are pinned up on a second dresser by the window. We are set up, then, in somebody's home. This may explain the glut of visitors; Mongolians like to stop in on their neighbors. Still, they saw we were strangers. No doubt I indulged in some condescending comparison of cultures as I sat up in bed. Clearly the respect for privacy and personal space in the U.S. is not part of traditional Mongolian thinking. The irony, which escaped me, was that I was showing about as much respect for others' privacy as Goldilocks.

In the afternoon, we went to eat at the guanz in a ger next to the pool hall. The three women in their middle to late years working inside had opened the establishment only a month before. Like the one in Altai Sum and many more I would stop at on my hike, this guanz was evidence of the rise of private enterprise with the coming of democracy. In spite of the rain, many people came and went while we were there. One, an electrician, tackled the job of repairing the light switch with his knife. A woman who was a friend of the proprietresses also used a knife for a novel task. After eating the meat left on one of the bones boiled to make our soup, she hit the bone with the sharp edge at the top of the joint end, then stoutly whacked it in a circle all around the middle until the upper half dropped off. Now for the marrow.

This operation reflects Mongolians' belief that animal food products should not be wasted. Parents tell their children the following tale: There was once a wealthy herdsman who owned many livestock animals—horses, camels, sheep, goats, and cattle. Whenever he slaughtered one, he would eat only the meat on the outside of the bone, tossing the picked bone away. Over time he became very poor. He went to a lama to ask him what he must do to recover his wealth. "Eat the marrow of the bones you threw away," the monk advised him, so he found the pile and began doing so. Sure enough, in time, he became a wealthy man again.[2] Mongolians' taboo against wasting animal food products is part of both their spiritual heritage as worshippers of nature and their culture as nomads surviving in a harsh environment.

I have a bowl of lavshaa—soup traditionally prepared with homemade flour-noodles, mutton or beef, and a vegetable, usually onions. The house lavshaa at this guanz also includes sliced carrots. I ask our three hostesses, Chinbaatar, Nüden, and Dagina, if they have ever seen an American in Tseel before and they answer "No." All three were born here. They estimate the population of the sum, the administrative district with Tseel as its capital, at slightly more than two thousand.

Leaving the guanz about 5:00 pm, we intended to buy groceries but found all of the delgüürs, or small grocery stores, closed. "Baikhgüi." Now we must wait until they reopen, probably around 10:00 am, before departing tomorrow. Then, as the proprietor of our lodging brought in the firewood and water we had ordered, three men followed him in and began gawking at our wet clothes on the line strung across the room and asking questions about our trip. Why didn't I lock the door behind us after reentering? I managed to keep from blowing up and suddenly shouting at them to get out. I finally did complain a little, though, when some drunken fellows, the last of our visitors that day, kept my guide engaged in conversation in the kitchen until late. I looked in at them from the kitchen doorway. It worked, though as a solution to frequent downpours, complaining is comparable to setting out drip pans. We eventually had four or five of them out that night. Better to repair the roof—that is to say, oneself.

ॐ

We had heard that it might rain the next day as well, but when I woke in the morning the sky through the window showed some blue. It was time to resume our journey to Altai, still two-hundred kilometers away. Besides, another visitor had already burst in on us, this time an indignant elderly woman who may have inadvertently been our actual host. Apparently, she had not been consulted in the matter. It was becoming uncomfortably clear that the resentful trespassed-upon one had himself been the main trespasser all along.

The first delgüür we found open after our breakfast at the guanz was outfitted in the back of a jeep. I bought the usual chocolate bars, crackers, powdered cream, Chinese-brand instant noodle soup, etc. from the couple who ran this "shop." About a week later, as we were nearing Altai, the same jeep would stop on the road and the driver hail us as the two backpackers who shopped from him in Tseel. At another, conventional delgüür, I bought four half-liter plastic bottles of spring water, filling our two drinking bottles and leaving the empty ones at the store. I justified this environmentally irresponsible action by the lack of good drinking water at the stream following yesterday's heavy rain. Larger bottles would have saved a little plastic, but there were none to be found here or at the other stores we visited.

Touring the delgüürs with our backpacks on, we attracted a lot of attention, especially among the children, who seemed ready to follow us, like the Pied Piper, out of town.

As we finally set out about 11:00 am, we passed a long two-story elementary school, probably the stately building I had set my sights on as we were approaching Tseel. During our stay I had noticed near our lodging place the bust of a man holding a lamb mounted on a tall concrete pedestal. Long afterwards I would learn that it was a monument to one Sereeter Punsal (1915-1963), who had apparently made, in the manner of the Good Shepherd, the ultimate sacrifice for his sheep.

We were following a road beside the muddied stream out of town when two men in a jeep overtook us. One held out for my inspection a sparkling green-tinted rock shaped like a half-egg, a geode covered with silica. I noticed that the gray rock at our feet also sparkled. Judging from the mineral exhibit at the Altai museum I saw a week later, Tseel is especially rich among the sums for crystals and other minerals.

14 - Tseel

On the opposite side of the stream, another party was proceeding on foot roughly parallel to us: a woman, who was carrying a large sack of flour, and three children. Later, I noticed one of the children carrying the sack. The road soon entered a region of low blunt hills. When we were about to make our first rest stop, probably around noon, we came upon an elderly man and two small girls playing pitch-and-toss with a volleyball. We sat down together on the hill's slope, and I gave the girls a few pieces of candy bought from the jeep delgüür. They were named Davaasüren and Myagmarsüren, presumably after the days of the week, Davaa (Monday) and Myagmar (Tuesday), on which they were born. The first, exceptionally pretty, was in grade four, the second, first grade. Their grandfather was wearing a deel of light black with orange-colored designs on it and a ski cap. Both of these articles of clothing were dirty and the inside edge of one of the deel's two front flaps was torn. He pulled out a long pipe with a metal bowl and mouthpiece attached to a stem of shiny red wood or a semi-precious stone such as jade.

"How do you like the Mongolian countryside?" I understood him to ask.

"I like it, especially this green color," I replied, referring to the increased vegetation since the valley before Tseel. His eyes were red and lips caked with dried spittle.

"How long have you lived in this area?" I asked.

"Four years."

His previous home was Ulaanbaatar and before that Baga Nuur (Small Lake), a town due east of it. As we were parting, I gave him two small gifts for the girls, a red pencil and a bookmark from the U.S. I observed the Mongolian custom of holding out the gift in both hands to the oldest member of the family present.

The road, undulating over the low hills, headed for our next mountain range within the Mongol Altain Nuruu. A large stream bed with wet sand in the bottom appeared. I deliberately selected a rest stop affording a view of a large, weirdly colored rock outcropping: brown with two wide bands of purple sandwiched in. Soon after, the greenness in the landscape became more intense and there were even some places of thick, lush growth; grass was replacing the sand and gravel. This alteration in the land was accompanied by an increase in the number of gers, the size of flocks, and the kinds of livestock. We saw at least one herd of

15 - Tsagaan Gol canyon

cows and two of yaks—with some khainags, offspring of cows and yaks, possibly included. "This is the kind of country you'll find in Zavkhan," was my guide's encouraging remark. Zavkhan was the next aimag to the north.

In the early evening we reached the canyon of the Tsagaan Gol (White River), lying roughly perpendicular to our road. This segment of the Altain Nuruu contained Burkhan Buudai Uul, the third mountain in the folktale about Eej Khairkhan given earlier and the focus of the 52,110 hectare Burkhan Buudai Gol Nature Reserve created in 1996.[3]

After entering the valley, we passed a road sign advising caution by the symbol of an exclamation mark, then crossed a dry stream bed on a small concrete bridge. Both sign and bridge were first-time occurrences on our hike. Just before the water in the riverbed played out, we stopped for the night at a spot partially sheltered from the wind, which was blowing lustily. Huddled in a tiny gully near our tents, we ate a hasty international meal of Chinese noodle soup and Russian crackers. When I was about to turn in, I noticed, high above us, a mountain peak rising on the other side of the river steeped in brilliant bronze by the setting sun.

ꝗ

June 21st, the summer solstice, was beautiful—cloudless and windless. As we proceeded down the canyon in the steadily increasing heat, I noticed a homemade toy truck lying beside the road. The chassis was a board, wheels polygonal circles sawed out of a board, and cab cut out of a white plastic canister. The toy suggested the remoteness of this region, yet, as we were resting a short time afterward, a large yellow truck with bulging dark-green tarpaulin over the bed followed by a jeep passed us heading south: Chinese merchants, Boldsaikhan said. I wondered why they were taking what I had been told was a less frequented road to the Burgastai port.

We reached a stranded family changing or repairing a tire on their Russian minivan. It looked a bit dangerous—vehicle trouble on a hot day in the Gobi. The father was serious and scarcely interrupted his labors as he answered the questions I put through my guide about the location of some "Turkic inscriptions" in the area. He and his pretty, petite wife indicated there was a historic monument not far down the road.

As we were resting where a stream, the Dairgantiin Am, flowed into the dry riverbed, a man on horseback herding goats stopped and dismounted. He was wearing a jeans jacket and trousers. A short iron goading stick hung from the saddle. Bayarsaikhan (Gladness Beautiful), who had lived in the area for ten years, gave more precise directions to the "Turkic inscriptions."

Continuing downstream, we passed two or three gers where the occupants were fleecing sheep, a process the animals must have appreciated on such a warm day. "This picture of today," the narrator remarks in the sheep-shearing episode in Thomas Hardy's *Far from the Madding Crowd*, showed little "contrast between ancient and modern. . . . In comparison with cities, Weatherbury was immutable. The citizen's *Then* is the rustic's *Now. . . .* In these Wessex nooks the busy outsider's ancient times are only old; his old times are still new; his present is futurity."[4]

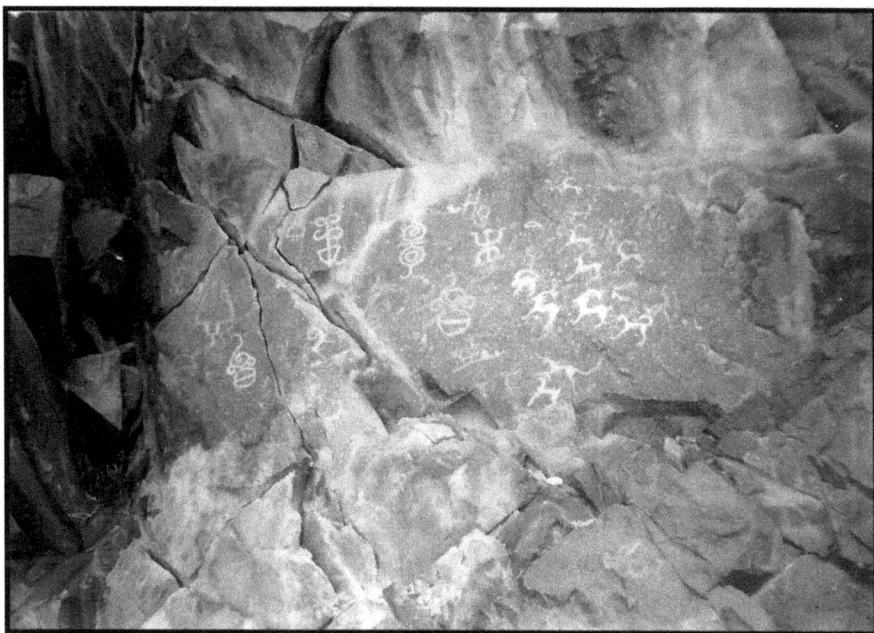

16 - Rock carvings, Tsagaan Gol canyon

What was the age of the rock carvings we encountered just down the road? The 6th to 8th centuries of the Turkic period? That I thought so at the time marks me as a "busy outsider"—one whose inflated notions of time result in placing what is past far too near the present. I may have been incapable of seeing them as products of a culture predating the Turks' by hundreds of years.

Of the three-hundred or so images, including wild and domestic animals, human figures and dwellings, and abstract seals, delicately scratched in the gray canyon wall on the opposite side of the river,[5] two figures standing together, each holding an upright spear, were identified as a product of 1st to 4th-century A.D. Xiongnu culture by at least one source[6] I later consulted.

17 - Anthropomorphic figures, Tsagaan Gol canyon

The Xiongnu, also spelled Hsiung-nu, were a nomadic people who some scholars believe were ancestors of the Huns. Their empire, which endured the longest of those in Central Asia before the Mongols' in the 13th to 14th centuries, flourished in the 3rd to 2nd centuries B.C. and was in decline around 300 A.D.[7] According to Ts. Dorjsüren in his article on the site, these two figures resemble hunters wearing big furry hats, short deels, and soft leather boots with fur lining, while sporting a game bag hanging from their belts.[8] Among other figures is a man on horseback wearing a cap with large horns attached and shooting a bow and arrow. The design of an unhitched cart in one image is similar, researchers claim, to that of carts depicted elsewhere in Central Asia, Kavkaz in Russia, and Scandinavia.[9] The image of a running man carrying a spear impressed me by its vivid suggestion of motion.

18 - Anthropomorphic figure, Tsagaan Gol canyon

In the late afternoon we emerged from the descending canyon road to behold, rising above a green valley, the multicolored face of another subchain of the Mongol Altain: the Khan Taishiriin Nuruu, its red, brown, and light-yellow foothills intensified by the bright sunlight. The plain lying between us and the mountains was the southwest corner of the immense Shargiin Gobi we saw on our way to Burgastai.

It was a long walk northwest up the plain to the village of Khaliun. In the evening we raced the sun, suspended directly above the town on the horizon. If it reached Khaliun first, we would not be able to find lodgings, for everything closes at sundown. It seemed a remarkable stroke of luck that today was the longest day of the year. In spite of our rapid pace, though, the town did not seem to get any larger, as if it retreated a step for every one of ours.

When we finally neared the village, we passed a large enclosed grove, a twenty-five hectare orchard and garden owned by some thirty families and begun around 1970 with the planting of apple trees from Siberia. At the present time, the plot also produced plums, black currants, and sea buckthorn berries.[10]

Just after ten o'clock, with daylight lingering in the sky, we entered the town, having walked thirty-one kilometers that day. We stopped to ask a woman for directions to the hotel. A bare-chested man emerging from a nearby house escorted us across the village past a park of unmown grass, bedraggled shrubs, and full and pollarded trees, many of them dead. On either side of town, splendid mountains glowed in varied hues. Unlike Tseel, Khaliun had more wooden houses surrounded with board palisades than gers and plastered buildings.

19 - Mountains and palisades at Khaliun

Our escort brought us to the town hall, then disappeared, apparently to seek the person in charge of guest accommodations. Displayed above the entrance was a sign in Mongolian, the Cyrillic in gold on a blue background: The Leaders of the People's Congress of Govi-Altai Aimag's Khaliun Sum / The Office of the Governor."

We sat, exhausted, on a few of the old radiators that stood in a line buttressing the dirt terrace next to the concrete walkway. A voice blared fuzzily on a Mongolian National Radio program broadcasted from a building with a satellite dish in front and an antenna like the mainmast of a schooner. I wondered whether this practice—I was told the broadcasting went on every day from 10:00 am to 11:00 pm—was a relic of the age of communist propaganda, when insecure party leaders sought to sway mass audiences. How insistent custom is. In a peaceful, remote village bounded by glorious mountain scenery, a constant flood of unearthly noise is tolerated, probably, just because it is what people are used to.

A woman wearing laborer's clothes and carrying what looked like a diploma or certificate in one hand and the lid of a large cooking pot in the other came out of the building, greeted us, and passed through an opening in the palisade. In a short time she returned with another woman and they showed us a room at the far end of the building—and opposite to the side the noise was on. It was the answer to my many "Hail Marys" since our arrival this evening and, in consequence, the cause of an increase in my religious faith: a large white-walled room with five empty beds, each with a fringed, brightly woven coverlet; carpet with a similar design covering half of the shiny linoleum floor; and chair and small table at one end spread with a white cloth of red poinsettia-and-bow pattern—very Christmassy. Clean bed sheets and water for the dispenser receptacle above the sink in one corner were brought. We ordered and ate a late dinner of mutton and rice prepared at a nearby guanz before turning in.

ਕ

I spent a restless night with a stomachache, probably brought on by the mutton. Though it had not been a week since our rest in Tseel, I declared a rest on the next day since Boldsaikhan would leave at the end of the second week and otherwise miss the second day off with pay. I was also too sick to walk and did little but lie in bed or sit until late afternoon. At one point during the morning the man who had assisted us in finding lodgings entered, without knocking, accompanied by another man. Both sat down on an empty bed. I had instructed Boldsaikhan to avoid encouraging visitors, should any turn up, so as not to repeat the scene at Tseel, and he now continued reading the newspaper in bed after briefly responding to the man's greeting and efforts at conversation. After several minutes of this cold-shoulder treatment, he rose abruptly. Boldsaikhan finally volunteered a sentence or two as a way of softening the insult, while the two made their way to the door. When they were gone, I congratulated him on having routed the enemy. I would regret the incident later. That I returned this man's generous favor to us the night before with rudeness was not a pleasant thought, once the threat of unexpected company had passed.

In the afternoon we went out to buy groceries and gasoline and to collect water. The discovery that only one delgüür—a small establishment on a corner thronged with men and boys around a billiard table—was open and a misunderstanding between my guide and me related to the gasoline purchase drove my spirits down to an all-time low on the trip. Back at the hotel, I tried a home remedy taught me by Enkhjargal for stomachaches—soda mixed with water—and recovered sufficiently to visit a delgüür now open next door.

I found the owner typing in his apartment adjacent to the store. He was a short, spruce, middle-aged man with a face expressing intelligence, mental alertness, and self-discipline. Like Maya Angelou's Uncle Willy behind the counter of his store, he walked with a pronounced limp as he assisted me. I returned with my microcassette recorder and requested an interview.

We sat in his kitchen, probably to avoid disturbing his wife sleeping in the next room. Producing my list of questions written in Mongolian in Cyrillic script, I read the shorter questions, he the longer ones. Zayabaatar (Lucky Hero), fifty-two, had lived in Khaliun for the past thirty years. He originally worked as an animal husbandry specialist, then as Chairman of the Youth Committee in the local sum government. He was currently Chairman of the sum's Mongolian People's Revolutionary Party, which had been the sole, socialist party in the nation prior to democracy. His wife was a physician at the local hospital.

To the question "How is life different since the democratic revolution?" he replied, "In 1990 democracy came to Mongolia and the changes in all aspects of Mongolian society and the nation's economy are still going on." The situation in Govi-Altai was the same as in all parts of Mongolia. "Sometimes life is difficult, sometimes easy—it varies. My lifestyle is simple, as it was in previous years, before democracy. In our sum and aimag this winter we lost many animals due to the snow. That's why the people's life is difficult. However, we are trying to develop agriculture and to increase job opportunities in order to overcome the difficulties." In spite of the problems, when he compared the situation of people before and after democracy his general assessment was that "it was worse before."

Regarding the geography, history, and industry of the region, he said that small forests of Siberian larch could be found growing on the "very beautiful" mountain chains flanking the town. His statement coincided with the predominance of wooden houses that I'd noticed earlier. He mentioned there were also saxaul forests in the desert. Thus, the sum contained a combination of khangai, or mountainous, forested land containing plentiful water and rich pasturage, on the one hand, and desert, on the other. Numerous species of wildlife inhabited the area.

20 - Zayabaatar

"The weather conditions are very harsh. In winter there is heavy snow and extreme cold and in summer it becomes very hot. Storms occur year-round. . . . During the heavy snow last winter and spring, we lost fifty percent of our livestock. We are now enjoying summer weather, and I believe that the surviving animals will be able to grow fat."

The sum, established in 1959, now had more than eight-hundred families, or a population of about three thousand, and, while large business enterprises were few in number, it maintained hospitals, schools and kindergartens, a bank, and a post office. The sum's day-to-day operating expenses were funded by the national income tax.

"During the socialist period, local industry developed and the sum's reputation spread throughout Mongolia." A lot of attention was given to animal husbandry.[11] He spoke of "a tradition of agricultural development" in the sum. "We established a 510-hectare area for growing seeds but at present are using only about one-hundred hectares. Up to ten years ago, we had an irrigation system in Khaliun Sum; it is no longer in use."

On the availability of medical care, he was optimistic: "My health is good, God be praised, but I can get any kind of medical care in my country." One wonders, though, whether being the husband of a physician gave him readier access to this commodity than the average citizen. The report of a resident of Altai town whom I would later interview was basically consistent with Zayabaatar's, while that of a herdsman in Naran, a small village between the two towns, was not.

21 - Khaliun

Asked what he thought of foreigners, especially tourists, he replied that Mongolia had become better known abroad during the last ten years and tourists had begun flocking to his country. "In the same way, you came from America far away and during your work and residence here are hiking with the intention of going from southern to northern Mongolia. . . . We understand that foreigners', especially tourists', interest in Mongolia is good for our country's development. Therefore, I would like to provide hospitality to the tourists who come, and I hope that your hike will be very successful because, in this way, Mongolia will be introduced to more Americans."

"Have any Americans come before to Khaliun?" I asked, venturing off the question sheet a moment.

"Six years ago, an American from Texas visited my home for two days. He owned a stallion ranch and he and his wife were on their honeymoon. We became well-acquainted and I have a photograph which I will show you afterwards. Nice American, nice old man."

Finally, I asked him to share a local legend or anecdote. "Every place has a lot of legends, tales, and other things of interest," he said, "and I could tell you many legends if we had time. I will, however, tell you one to comply with your request." It concerned the origin of a local place name, apparently 2,870-meter Mogoin Tolgoi (Snake Hill) outside of Khaliun. "Forty-three years ago, when the sum was founded, . . . as people say, many large snakes were once seen from a distance wriggling on a slope of this hill. Since our sum was established, the snake has been seen very rarely."

Handed the photograph he referred to earlier, I saw, in a large group shot taken out of doors, a rather portly middle-aged American couple, the man, invested with traditional Mongolian garb, smiling broadly. In my peevish humor, I marveled at his engaging, extroverted personality that could create a completely different Khaliun experience—like a neighborhood barbeque—from mine. Or maybe it was his rancher's sympathy with the Mongols' traditional esteem for the horse. At any rate, I envied him his popularity.

At the end of the interview, Zayabaatar's wife, Lkhamjav, came into the kitchen from the other room and a male friend of his named Pürevdorj entered from the front door. We made a lively group, though once, when Lkhamjav learned that the man crossing Mongolia on foot was forty-nine, she shook her head ruefully, as if she were pitying a convicted juvenile delinquent. It was not the sort of reaction I would have preferred from a doctor. I asked them whether Naadam, the national sports holiday held in July, would be observed in town, and they said it would be, with people gathering from all over the sum. I had visited a little amphitheater with a damaged proscenium on the edge of town when Boldsaikhan and I went to collect water. This was the focal point of the festival; during the wrestling competition, the two tiers of concrete seating would be filled.

During my visit, my host had not forgotten the offices of Mongolian hospitality, of course, offering me milk tea and slices of bread with a yellow spread called öröm, a thick cream skimmed from boiled milk. I took a photograph of my three companions standing in front of the delgüür, where, cheered by the novelty of my visit, they lingered a while after I bid them farewell.

Thunderclouds were gathering when I returned to our lodgings and it rained that evening, washing the air clean of the screeching radio music for a brief time. We seemed to have chosen by chance the two wettest days in June to rest on.

We left our snug room the following morning, a Sunday, after a breakfast of warm rice gruel—I was leery of guanz meat at the moment. Our bill for the two beds for two nights and four shared meals was 13,200 tögrögs, or about $12. Taking an easterly, rather than the same southeasterly, road, we traveled back past the orchard, but with it again on our right, and over the same plain. The sky was clear except for a fringe of cumulous clouds along most of the horizon. The delicious warbling of darting larks hung in the air. As for the ground—and one gets to know the ground very well on a backpacking trip—striped lizards, a species called multi-cellated racerunners,[12] as well as black beetles, appeared for the first time. Many small white morning glories and fewer large pink ones, coaxed out by last night's thundershower, bloomed beside the road. Mingled with the clumps of Gobi feathergrass were pea shrubs and eurotia. Both plants are a local source of fuel, which may explain why we passed a woman in a blue deel and girl gathering sticks.

But no familiarity with the ground would yield a trace of the hoof prints, wheel tracks, horse dung, campfires, or other vestiges of the forces of Temüüjin, the later Genghis Khan, and his ally Ong Khan, who apparently passed somewhere in the area of present-day Khaliun on their way west to attack Buyruq Khan, a leader of the Naiman tribe.[13] The pursuit and defeat of Buyruq's forces was part of Temüüjin's unification of Mongolia, which set the stage for his far-flung conquests abroad. According to *The Secret History of the Mongols*, the 13th-century epic of the khan's life and campaigns, the episode occurred in or around 1202,[14] too long ago to hope for more than a fragment of rusted metal–a platelet or boss fallen off of a cuirass or saddle, a broken buckle or knife blade left in camp—and then only by the most fortuitous chance, like the one that brought the stone flakes and iron arrowhead before my eyes.

Shortly after stopping to shake some sand out of my boot, I reached for my rosary, which I had conveniently put in the upper right pocket of my trousers, and accidentally pulled out with it the stone flake found in Bum. Backtracking and inspecting the ground as soon as I noticed the flake was missing proved fruitless. I engaged in a private battle with the giants Cynicism and Despair as we continued on our way. "Without this tangible proof of your discovery," they mocked, "the archeologists in Ulaanbaatar aren't going to be persuaded that the site exists and is worth investigating."

We passed the point, due south, where we emerged from the Tsagaan Gol canyon two days before and circled thrice the ovoo at the entrance to the Övöljöönii Nuruu. The terrain and, with it, a cool wind, began to rise. We were following a road pointed out by locals that was not on my

1:500,000-meter scale map; it would provide a more direct route to Naran (Sun) Brigad, our last village before Altai. Prickly pea shrubs with small yellow blooms and sagebrush grew in abundance. Later, as we were resting on the slow, steady ascent, a small brownish-gray owl atop one of the poles of the telephone line on our route disrupted the quiet with its strange, high-pitched cry—a combined squawk and wail. Though there are eleven species of owls in Mongolia,[15] not once during the hike would I hear any of the nocturnal hooting associated with owls in the West:

> Tu-whit, tu-whoo—a merry note,
> While greasy Joan doth keel the pot. (5.2.901-902)[16]

After three hours of pulling up the relentless incline under a hot sun—though often in a cool breeze—we each had only about a quarter liter of drinking water left. Just before the ovoo at the beginning of the ascent, two handsome young herdsmen had ridden by and told us there was a well in twenty kilometers. We knew by now the importance of getting a second opinion, but no ger, passing driver, or other equestrian appeared. The absence of gers and, except for one herd of camels, livestock marked this as a dry region.

Finally, the vehicles, always tardy on Sundays, begin appearing. Two men on a motorcycle report there is a spring just up ahead. We pass a man in a deel sleeping beside his beloved motorcycle in the shade off the road. The motorbike seems to be an enormously popular mode of transport in rural Mongolia, rivaling, if not surpassing, the horse as the favorite mode. Of course, it costs less and is more fuel efficient than a car or truck. It is also better at negotiating the stony, roadless steppe. But most important, perhaps, motorcycles look and ride a good deal more like the culturally iconic horse.

Soon we notice, much to our relief, water running in the roadbed. Following it to its source, a little pool next to the road, we sit down to celebrate another day's victory over the harsh land we are crossing on foot. Oh, the heavenly draught, so cool and clean, satiating me in a minute! This area is known locally as Khökh Morit (Dark-Blue Horse).

It was now around 6:30 and we had walked about thirty-six kilometers. After briefly scouting for campsites up the road, I decided on a stone-strewn ledge slightly downstream from the pool to be close to water. A family—father and mother and about five teens and preteens—came down the road in a Zil 130 truck as we were pitching our tents. All but the mother, left standing in the back of the truck, piled out, and soon Boldsaikhan and I were seated and chatting with the father. They had come from the city of Altai, their home. Suddenly, I spied the mother standing behind the truck preparing to serve milk tea or airag. I rose and walked back to my unassembled tent. The man whom we had passed sleeping now appeared, roused by the agreeable sound of a social occasion in the making. I indicated to one of the boys who had come up to help me with the tent that I preferred to do the job myself. Before long, they were all gone, the tea or airag, unserved, with them.

As we were cooking a dinner of borsch from one of our powdered soup mixes, a jeep stopped and three men and a woman got out.

"Sain baitsgaana uu?" ("How are you all?"), one of the men, short and rather thin, wearing a clean office shirt, calls out, walking up with the others. His act of sitting down on a stone is answered by mine of turning to tend the pot. He rises.

"What work do you do?" I ask him, in a belated gesture of friendliness. Not understanding the reply, I turn to my guide. "Not a herder?" I ask.

"No." Another of the men, thick set, in a tight-fitting office shirt, smoked a cigarette. The third man was elderly and seemed to have lost the use of one arm in a stroke. The pleasant-featured woman came around and peeked into the pot on the stove. Then the group left.

I now learned from Boldsaikhan that the man who greeted me was the governor of Khaliun Sum and his companions local government staff. Seeing more clearly on this occasion what I had missed by my discouragement of visitors—an interview with the governor would have made a nice addition to my log—I had a serious self-reckoning that night. I was turning into a misanthrope. Unless I could control my initial impulse to brush people off and be more accepting of them in all of their supposedly undisciplined and overly inquisitive selves, my travel account, not to mention my life and personality, would be impoverished. Toward nightfall the wind died down, a rarity around here, and I could hear a new sound as I prepared for sleep: the delicate notes of birds in the distance.

꒰

At 10:00 am the next day, June 24th, an hour out of last night's campsite, we were resting in a broad green spot where the road through the pass finally crested. Some camels grazed nearby. I was miserable, my stomachache having returned. It was also getting hot; there was no wind today and the only clouds were high and thin cirri in the north. After descending to the valley, we stopped again at a well. The bucket attached to a rope that we used to fill our drinking bottles had been improvised from a section of tire, imparting a musty tang of rubber to the water. Adding a powdered citron mix, we were sitting on the edge of the concrete trough drinking the cool, green beverage when a boy and girl came down the slope from a ger to draw water. She was a few years older and, when I addressed her, the expression on her brown, wind-polished face as she looked back at me was serious and earnest. Evidently, her duties as big sister had fostered in her a precocious toughness and reserve. Of course, she was probably also busy registering a new kind of physiognomy.

I was too sick to make further attempts at conversation and soon went off to sit on the ground and try the soda-and-water remedy. It failed as an emetic this time, maybe because the water was too cool and refreshing, but by afternoon I would be well again. Several camels, probably the same we encountered at the top of the pass, gathered at the trough. Camels have the habit when taking a drink of hoisting their head back and shaking it vigorously with a snort, spraying the droplets around, as if they aren't used to having water, instead of sand and dust, in contact with their nostrils.

We crossed the wide Gyalgariin Khooloi (Shiny Throat) valley, apparently a northwestern prong of the Beger Depression, which was home to Siberian ibex and the rare saiga antelope, argali sheep, and khulan, or Asiatic wild ass. Much earlier, dinosaurs ranged here; fossils have been discovered at or near Naran Brigad, the village we would soon enter across the valley.[17] About all we saw was a plain teeming with golio cicadas and grasshoppers.

Naran was a collection of gers, several small, dilapidated, gray-brick buildings, and a few larger one-story white-plastered ones. The last group included a trim, well-proportioned schoolhouse with a green metal roof. Hoping to arrange an interview, I directed our steps to one of the gers. Two men, one unshaven and shirtless, wearing green short pants, high leather boots, and a black straw hat with a bent-over brim, the other, mustachioed, in a gray-green deel and a ski cap, sat inside. The wife of the first man, a sleepy-eyed, frowsy-haired woman dressed in a green deel, served us milk tea. The ger interior was less tidy than most, if not all, of the homes we had visited.

The second man offered us his khöörög, or snuff bottle, enacting a well-established ritual of hospitality, as we sat down. The bottle, usually embellished with carvings, is typically made of a semi-precious stone, such as jade or chalcedony, though other material, including bone, glass, steel, silver, porcelain, and even mother of pearl, have also been used.[18]

It is received in the right hand with the right elbow in the palm of the left, as in accepting a bowl of tea. The recipient either puts a little snuff between the thumb and forefinger of the left hand using the tiny, long-stemmed spoon attached to the inside of the cap or merely takes a whiff after barely unstopping the bottle. It must be returned, placed in the upturned palm of the right hand, to the owner, never passed on. Later the man with the snuff bottle pulled out a pipe similar in design to the one I'd seen the grandfather near Tseel using.

Some children, brimming with curiosity, as always, had followed us in. One of these, a girl of about eleven, her hair braided, wearing a short white dress and white tights, is strikingly beautiful. Her name is Otgontungalag (Youngest Bright). Another younger pretty girl with a white tuuz, or spherical ribbon of gauze, in her tied-back hair, wears a bright orange-red dress with white trim, its border not yet stitched, and white tights. The tuuz is a mandatory feature of Mongolian girls' school uniform.

22 - *At Batsuuri's ger, Naran Brigad*

The interview, which I conducted with Boldsaikhan's help, of Batsuuri, the shirtless man, was disappointingly brief. I might have gotten more information out of a tree, had there been any around to interview. However, some of his terse replies, I noticed in having them translated later, have a certain comic appeal.

"What is your name?"

"My name is Batsuuri" (Steady Foundation).

"How old are you?"

"Fifty-two years old." This was also Zayabaatar's age. I seem to have a knack for finding out fifty-two year old men in rural Mongolia to interview.

"How is your life here?"

"So-so."

"Do your parents and brothers and sisters live here?"

"They used to live here, but at the moment they don't."

"Did you lose a lot of animals last winter?"

"We lost fifty percent of our livestock." Another match-up with Zayabaatar!

"How did your life change after democracy?"

"Almost no changes."

"Are there any interesting historical monuments in this area?"

"There aren't any."

"What can you tell me about the history of the area?"

"This Naran Sum was once very famous among the sums of Govi-Altai Aimag, but then the population went off in all directions. The people took their possessions with them to Khaliun and Beger Sums. Now Naran Bag (Village) is subordinate to Tümen Taishir and Khesuun Bulag Sums."

"How do you celebrate weddings here?"

"They are celebrated widely here."

"How will you celebrate Naadam this year?"

"I will hardly celebrate Naadam this year."

"How do you get information here?"

"From the radio."

"What is your family's plan for the future?"

"Animal husbandry and agriculture."

"Have you seen any Americans in Naran? Where and when?"

"A few days ago I met two tourists from France. They were traveling by bicycle. When I was going to Ulaanbaatar, I met two students from America."

"Can you receive medical care when you want?"

"I can't."

"Can you tell me any local legends or anecdotes?"

"I don't know any."

Our visit at Batsuuri's ger over, we stopped at the village spring, with Otgontungalag and Bayaraa, one of the boys, escorting us to a rock-walled pool built into the bed. Our road bore left, ascending to mountains in the Khan Taishiriin Nuruu, and, about seven kilometers from the spring, was rejoined by the maverick line of telephone poles.

We reached a guanz Batsuuri had told us of. It had been open only a month, as long as the one we visited in Tseel. Boldsaikhan learned that the owner, a man in his late twenties named Batbayar (Strong Gladness), had been a classmate of our mutual friend Chimgee at the high school in Taishir, the next town north of Altai. His pretty wife, who wore a flowery purple deel, and a teenage girl, who played a cassette of Mongolian rock music while dicing the meat, prepared two large and heaping bowls of püntüüztei khuurag, store-bought translucent rice noodles mixed with fried mutton, potatoes, and vegetable seasoning. The couple's infant son played on the floor with two toy plastic trucks, one of them wheel-less. They were not homemade.

After leaving the guanz, we passed three gers where a man was shearing sheep, the white, spongy pile mounded beside him. I waved to the driver and passengers in a minivan that bounded past us heading south; they waved back. "From Khövsgöl," Boldsaikhan remarked. The unusual sense of affinity I felt in that brief moment of silent exchange seemed to augur my eventual arrival in that northern aimag.

The traffic was heavier than at any previous stretch of road since we were now approaching an aimag capital and this was the only route south over the range. Cut into the right wall of a ravine, the road climbed steadily to a green, upward-tilted bowl. A mountain wall descending to a smaller ravine just beyond this bowl showed an outcropping of red rock and another of white beside it—a striking juxtaposition. Ascending more gradually, we came within view of the ovoo at Dötiin (Short Cut) Davaa, as the pass is known locally. The blue, partly cloudy sky, green landscape, and three herdsmen in deels resting on the ground beside their horses at the ovoo completed a classic study in Mongolian picturesqueness. The giant cairn was stacked with large stones, interwoven with many blue silk khadags, and set with a stout slanting pole—like a harpoon stuck in a whale's back—thickly draped with more scarves. It would be our last ovoo before Altai.

As we sat with the herders, one vehicle, then another, stopped and the passengers, two families bound for Khaliun, poured out to take their three turns around the cairn. All at once, we found ourselves surrounded by a small crowd asking questions. A young man whom I recognized as the first shopkeeper who assisted us in Khaliun had apparently spread the word about our walk from Burgastai. He asked if I was tired and I answered "yes." For the first time I sensed that people were regarding us with admiration, rather than a combination of amazement and pity. I felt a surge of exaltation in the sudden consciousness of achievement. Dötiin Davaa was thus both a geographical and emotional high point, a "peak" not to be equaled until, after a long stretch of more or less desolate "plain," I reached the ovoo at Gants Davaa before Uliastai, capital of the next aimag, eight days later.

23 - Dötiin Davaa

After another twenty minutes of walking, we were within view of Altai, highest in elevation among Mongolian cities[19] and appearing about thirty kilometers away as short white horizontal lines on a mountain slope across the plain. A few kilometers later, around nine o'clock, we reached a spring that Batbayar had told us of and found a pleasant camping spot on a green terrace sprinkled with edelweiss upstream from the first gers. Lingering outside my tent after dinner, I was given a private viewing of a glorious sunset over the mountains where Altai stood: dark clouds edged with pink, yellow, and orange, sky between them pinkish-orange, distant mountains glowing purple. No—a young herder, returning with his flock to a ger downstream as I lay in my tent, must have also seen it. He sang a traditional-sounding song, the grunts of yaks providing a running base accompaniment.

※ ※ ※

Chapter 3
Temptations in the Desert: Govi-Altai Aimag from Dötiin Davaa to the Border

When you set out for Ithaka
ask that your way be long,
full of adventure, full of instruction.
The Laistrygonians and the Cyclops,
wild Poseidon—do not fear them:
such as these you will never find
as long as your thought is lofty, as long as a rare
emotion touch your spirit and your body.
The Laistrygonians and the Cyclops,
wild Poseidon—you will not meet them
unless you carry them in your soul. . . . (1-12)[1]

The next morning, cool, windy, and overcast, we set out northwest across the plain. Today we will reach Altai, our cherished destination for two weeks. We passed a herd of yaks, probably the same I'd heard last night. Later, small forests of Siberian larch appeared on the tops of two low mountains to our left. Like the green valley before Tseel and lush grass near the Tsagaan Gol canyon, these evergreen patches marked our advance, step by step, kilometer by kilometer, northward to cooler latitudes. It was also the first visible turning in the landscape toward the specific natural zone of Siberian taiga in Khövsgöl Aimag.

As we approached Altai that day, we may have crossed paths with Temüüjin, the future Genghis Khan, and his army, though seen only by the historic imagination now. It seems that Toqto'a Beke, leader of the Merkit people[2], and his sons Khudu and Chila'un, along with a few other survivors of the battle with Temüüjin at Saari Kheer in north central Mongolia, passed somewhere in the vicinity of present-day Altai in their westward flight. Pursuing them, Temüüjin spent the winter of that year, 1204, south of Altai. Toqto'a was joined further west by the Naimans.[3] Temüüjin defeated them at the mouth of the Irtysh River in 1205, the year before the grand assembly that acknowledged him Khan over all of Mongolia.[4] At about 3:00 pm we reached the outskirts of Altai, passing a brown, sprawling factory building. We aim for a light-yellow multistory building, the aimag hospital, behind which lies the residential area containing Boldsaikhan's cousin's ger. I kid him about our heading directly for the hospital; he has a stomachache and I heel blisters. After what seems an eternity, we have finally entered the gate in the board palisade and are walking across the dirt yard.

24 - A ger neighborhood in Altai

I have been imagining for some time now the look of bright-eyed admiration on his cousin's face when we appear, heroes of the desert, loyal to our word about returning on foot in two weeks. It will be a grand moment when, seated amid a crowd of rapt auditors, we retail the highlights and hardships of our rugged adventure. The door of the ger is locked on the outside and a large dog barks relentlessly in front. Tsetsegsüren and her family are away visiting another family in town, we learn from the only other person in the enclosure, a woman named Altantsetseg (Golden Flower) at the other ger. She admits us to the ger and fills in as hostess during my disappointingly brief stop there.

Shortly before we departed to find a hotel room for me, I made another visit to the fatal outhouse where I had dropped my GPS down the pit. Having forgotten to remove from my belt the plastic zip bag containing the flower samples and one or more stone flakes, I tucked it and my parka between a post and board on the inside edge of the palisade behind the john. When I returned, the bag was gone! Horrified, yet not quite believing it possible, I searched for it on the ground and on another part of the fence. When it was clear that someone outside the enclosure had reached in between the boards and taken it, I called for Boldsaikhan's

25 - Arriving at Boldsaikhan's cousin Tsetsegsüren's ger

aid in questioning two groups of children playing in the adjacent fields. I know the bag is gone, though, and as we are tramping around after the kids, I can't keep from bursting out alternately in shrill oaths and loud, ironic guffaws as though deranged.

The flower samples, maybe two dozen in number, so patiently gathered and dated for the record of my journey, and the last evidence of my finding the stone age settlements suddenly gone on a freak mischance: a thief happening to pass by at just the right moment to snatch what was so worthless to him or her but valuable to me. The incident wore an aspect of intentional malice on the part of Heaven, and I returned to my question after the accident with the water container on the very first morning: Is God or Fate against this trip? As we secured my room at the Altai Hotel and then bought groceries, I moved about in a daze. I was disgusted with Mongolians, with their self-defeating, petty regard for personal gain irrespective of the greater social good. I wanted to chuck the whole enterprise of the hike and promotional travel book. Why exert myself for such an ungrateful and undeserving people?

At the post office, my phone conversation with Enkhjargal, who had fortunately returned to Ulaanbaatar from her latest trip as a porter on the Mongolian Railroad, helped stem the tide of my rancorous, self-pitying monologue. There would be more flowers, she reminded me. Her aid in this crisis was a natural extension of that emotional and moral support I had found in thinking of her during the hike to Altai.

Returning to the hotel, Boldsaikhan and I separated our gear and supplies, including the cache of things we had stored at his cousin's, into what I would carry and he would take back to Ulaanbaatar. My damaged water container was exchanged for his good one. I also asked him to write down on index cards the questions he had used in inquiring about the route and location of water. He cautioned me to be sure of my next water source and not camp too close to the road, where I would be more vulnerable to molestation. As we parted at the door of my room, he made the slightest, almost imperceptible pause, his face expressing the solicitude and self-doubt of a mother leaving her child at school on the first day.

I slept poorly that night on account of a stomachache, probably caused by a can of fish I had bought at a delgüür in town. I accordingly slept in the next morning; it would be my third rest day.

The Altai Hotel on the main street in town provided a comfortable two-bed room with a bathroom and tub for 7,000 tögrögs, or less than $6.50. A large aspen tree stood outside my third-floor window, and it swayed and rustled in the morning breeze as I lay sleeping. One inconvenience during my stay was the routine electrical-power shutdown after dark, apparently to save energy. When I got up to use the bathroom on the first night, not being prepared for an unresponsive light switch, it occasioned panic and near disaster.

I managed in spite of my queasy stomach to eat the plate of eggs, mashed potatoes, and meat resembling large Vienna sausages brought up to my room for breakfast. At the Khaan Bank across the street I met Shawn, one of two Peace Corps volunteers who had completed half of their two-year teaching assignments in Altai. He said that a third volunteer had had to return due to heart trouble. I would not meet another American on my trip until a couple stopped on the road with their Mongolian driver on July 13th, about two and a half weeks later.

The service representative at the bank said I could not make a withdrawal because my account had been opened at the main branch in Ulaanbaatar instead of at the local one. I had prepared for this scenario, in spite of the assurances of the service rep in Ulaanbaatar, by arranging for the secretary at my college to call or visit the rep in the event of a problem. I went directly to the post office and phoned Baigalmaa.

"How is your trip?"

"Oh, it's been a very difficult trip. A lot of things have gone wrong. Right now I'm unable to withdraw money from the bank. Could you please contact Tsetsegmaa and explain the situation to her?" When I returned after the lunch hour at 2:00 pm, I had no difficulty withdrawing the 150,000 tögrögs I needed. The incident was repeated, in its essentials, the next time I tried to make a withdrawal—in Mörön about three weeks later.

My financial worries over, I visited the Govi-Altai Aimag Local Research Museum down the street from the hotel. It was a plastered building painted a dark salmon hue and had a pair of antlers mounted above the fluted square white columns of the façade. Among the most notable exhibits, besides the "automobile parts" display mentioned earlier, were two large genre paintings by B. Sharav (1869-1939), along with a photograph of the artist. A native of nearby Taishir Sum, Sharav collaborated with another painter on *A Day's Life*, a large, detailed collage of scenes, from mare milking to ger transporting, typical of nomadic life and executed in a lively, cartoon style. The work launched a major mode of genre painting that continues to flourish in Mongolia. One of the two canvasses in the museum showed scenes from daily rural life in the four seasons, represented in four horizontal bands. The painting was worthy of the National Modern Art Gallery in Ulaanbaatar.

After my tour I interviewed the museum's director, Tsend, forty-two, a town native. He referred to a local anniversary the citizens were busy preparing to celebrate in conjunction with Naadam, the national sports festival, next month. When asked about the availability of medical care, he said, "In our country we have both traditional and modern medical care. I can get medical care when I need it. In the recent past our aimag hospital was equipped with modern facilities. Sometimes, in very serious cases that we are unable to treat, we send the patient to Ulaanbaatar or to other cities." His testimony, then, corroborated, in essence, what Zayabaatar in Khaliun reported.

From the museum I went to the delgüürs on the tree-lined street a block south of the main street, its sidewalk set with green-and-white and red-and-yellow lozenges. The day before I had found a few twenty-four hour stores, a phenomenal discovery after Tseel and Khaliun. After buying groceries, I proceeded to the busy outdoor market bearing a slip of paper with a request written in Mongolian to direct the helpless American to the lip cream; one of the delgüür attendants had gone beyond the call of duty, instead of merely replying "baikhgüi," when I asked for this item. I ended up at the fatty tail of a sheep's rump in the meat market, a dingy, Tartarean hole in a building that would have enlivened the pages of Upton Sinclair's *The Jungle*. The sight of this room was enough to cure my lip blister for that day.

But there is much more to see: a large clothing section, each booth displaying virtually the same products so that one wondered how the merchants made a living; a hardware and automotive section accommodated in a row of the same kind of makeshift wooden booths used for displaying clothes; and a lot of stalls, usually selling delgüür items, operating out of the open end of shipping containers. I'd seen many of these so-called "container shops" in Ulaanbaatar.

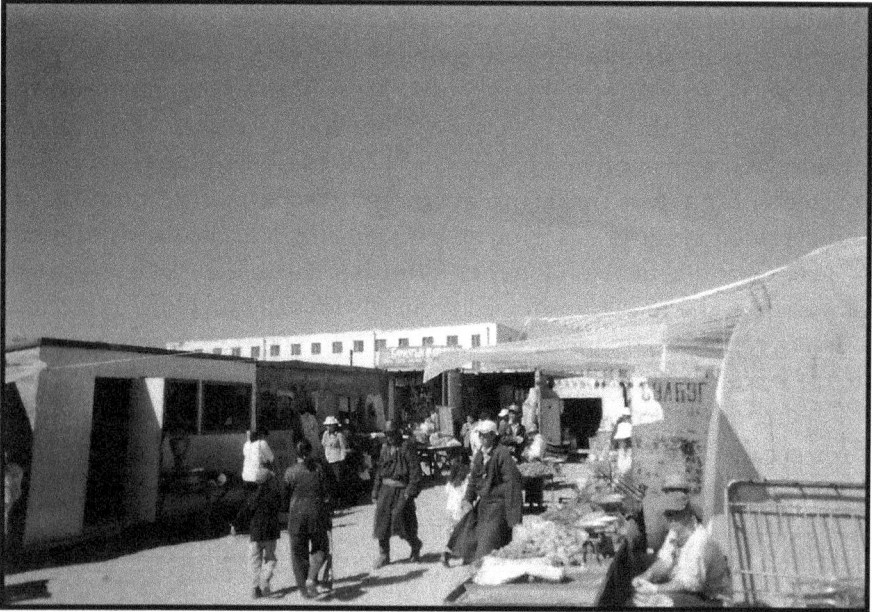

26 - Market scene in Altai

Taking in the colorful, diverse sights of the thronged labyrinth, "I can say I've lived if I've walked around in the Altai market," I thought to myself. It was the latest of several memorable marketplaces I had toured in my years in the Far East—the Naran Tuul in Ulaanbaatar, especially at its previous, unasphalted site in the Denjeen Myang district; the ancient Namdaemun and smaller side-alley markets in Seoul; a market near Session Road in Baguio City in the Philippines; and those in the shadow of the Forbidden City in Beijing. The efflorescence of raw goods, unpackaged and unscrubbed, so unlike the streamlined shelves of labeled stock in U.S. supermarkets, creates a holiday for the senses, a cornucopia of colorful detail and fugitive scents.

My last stop that day was the post office-telecommunications building, where I called Enkhjargal and finished writing and mailed a letter to her. In our phone conversation, I suggested meeting in Uliastai, the next aimag capital on my route. We arranged to discuss this further upon my arrival there in six days. The internet office had closed by the time I was ready to type messages to my father and a few friends. My luxurious hotel bed was rendered almost worthless again that night due to more stomach trouble. The likely culprit this time was some sausage links I had bought at the delgüür where my pass to the sheep rump was written. Once, on awakening, I noticed the bright oval moon near the horizon through the leafy boughs of the aspen outside my window.

ꝗ

The next morning, June 27th, relentless, monomaniacal announcements, which I later learned included minivan departure times, floated into my bedroom from the marketplace. They would have tempted me to return to Ulaanbaatar had I known at the time what they meant and what lay in store for me that day. As it was, I went to the market for shaving razors instead. I was passing back out of the gate when I suddenly heard, in waves of a flooding crescendo, the refrain of the female vocalist's hit song over an amplified radio.

> Eejiin mini,
> Eejiin mini,
> Eejiin mini. . . .

Oddly, I had also heard the song on the radio while sitting in Tsetsegsüren's ger shortly before our departure for Burgastai. Was the parting song with its repeated phrase referring to "my mother" a heaven-sent signal assuring me of my own mother's protection on this walking trip taken in her honor? Even if I'd known then that the song actually has four slightly different refrains, each indicating a different loved one, I could have hardly avoided the sense of her spirit guiding me.

I left town about noon, not forgetting to give the hotel attendant a copy of the summary of the Catholic faith, written in Mongolian, which I'd had prepared at my church in Ulaanbaatar. In distributing this literature on my journey—I had also left a copy with Tsetsegsüren after our overnight stay with her, at the ger in Bum, and at the guanz in Tseel— I was following, however remotely, in the footsteps of an ancient and venerable predecessor and namesake. William of Rubruck (c.1210-c.1295), a Franciscan friar probably born near Saint-Omer, France, was with Louis IX of France (Saint Louis) in Acre, Palestine in 1253 when the king commissioned him to visit the Mongol Empire.[5] Though Louis' motives seem to have been political, namely, securing an ally against the Moslems, William's were clearly those of a missionary. Leaving Constantinople on May 7th,[6] he reached the winter encampment of Mönkh Khan on December 27th. The friar accepted an offer from the emperor to remain at the winter camp for two months until the intense cold had passed and then accompanied him to the city of Karakorum, arriving on Palm Sunday.[7]

On the outskirts of Altai, a large sign bearing a road map with local destination points had a vertical line connecting Altai to Taishir Sum, forty-five kilometers to the north. I swayed under a cruel load of water; no water stops till then, Boldsaikhan had confirmed from locals the day before yesterday. Under a sunny sky dotted with cumulous clouds, I pursued my way over a gently rolling plain fringed with hills and mountains in the distance. It was indeed dry country; only one ger appeared that afternoon. The dusty road was frequently churned up by passing vehicles, including freight-bearing lorries, though there were occasionally intervals of up to an hour and a half between them. A jeep and a truck driver stopped to offer me a ride, but I rather peremptorily declined both times.

After crossing some hills, I entered an enormous plain, the largest I could remember seeing on the hike. On my third rest stop—and I seemed to be making fewer of them now that I was walking alone—I sat studying a stone that lay beside me, yellowish-white with part of its surface textured like a finely grained sponge or some other marine organism: a fossilized chunk from an ancient sea floor? Long afterward I happened upon a description of this peculiar rock in a geology textbook. It was oolitic limestone, which is created by the cementing of oolites, that is, tiny spherical grains of calcite formed in shallow, warm ocean water. The oolites' round shape results from the regular rolling back and forth under the impact of strong tides and, possibly, wave action, as they are being precipitated.[8] Though inorganically formed, the stone I had found was in fact part of the pavement of a shallow sea, probably the same one that covered most of present-day Mongolia up to about 250 million years ago.[9] That is why only one side of the stone was textured in this way.

I had not been long on the plain before I began to realize, with that nauseous feeling worse than any stomachache, that I was on the wrong road. This one had turned or continued to the right after leaving Altai, and I was traveling in an easterly, rather than northerly, direction. After depending on a guide for so long, I'd forgotten to check my GPS. The thickness of the vertical line to Taishir on the billboard map had led me to assume this comparatively busy road was the one to Taishir. How long had I been going the wrong way?

I tried sitting down to wait for a driver who could direct me to the turn off, but the intervals between vehicles had increased and, in any case, are always much longer if a passing driver is needed. I walked a short distance back to a small road that forked off in the general right direction. I stood there, telling myself I could take this road, checking my GPS frequently. In my dismay over the time lost, the impulse to hazard a shortcut was quite insistent. Marco Polo writes of the demonic voices and apparitions in the Desert of Lob, part of the Gobi in northwestern China, that beckon lonely travelers off the road to their death in solitary, waterless regions:

> It is asserted as a well-known fact that this desert is the abode of many evil spirits, which amuse travelers to their destruction with the most extraordinary illusions. If, during the day-time, any persons remain behind on the road, either when overtaken by sleep or detained by their natural occasions . . ., they unexpectedly hear themselves called to by their names, and in a tone of voice to which they are accustomed. Supposing the call to proceed from their companions, they are led away by it from the direct road and, not knowing in what direction to advance, are left to perish. . . . It is said also that some persons, in their journey across the desert, have seen what appeared to them to be a body of armed men advancing towards them, and apprehensive of being attacked and plundered have taken to flight. Losing by this means the right path, and ignorant of the direction they should take to regain it, they have perished miserably of hunger.[10]

While I was not prey to demonic voices or specters in the landscape, I was no less imperiled by mutterings in the recesses of my own heart. Had I given in to my inner compulsion at this moment, I might not have been able to turn back even after the road played out, as it was almost certain to do, and eventually found myself in a trackless, uninhabited waste, my water supply depleted.

"Why are you doing this—walking across Mongolia? It's dangerous. You don't know when you might meet up with bad people. What if your electronic compass breaks?" The rebuke of my friend Amar in Ulaanbaatar, which came back to me at this moment, might have been expressly designed for this crisis. I decided to exercise the self-control to endure the boredom and sickening regret that would attend each retraced step on the present road. It was possibly the first major turning away from the insidious impulse to hurry and save time in my foot journey, and it couldn't have happened at a better time.

Repassing the hills at the edge of the plain, I hailed an approaching truck to ask about the distance to the turn-off to Taishir but had difficulty framing the question in Mongolian, so I couldn't be sure of the driver's answer. Suppose my worst suspicions, that the road to Taishir was just outside of Altai, proved true? As I continued the trek back with my ponderous load, I vowed that if this sort of thing happened again I would sack the trip and return home. The toil and heartache simply weren't worth it. The image of the minivans with the placard "Ulaanbaatar" displayed in the front window that I had seen parked on the lot at the Altai market no doubt flashed across my mind once or twice.

As the evening wore on, I decided that since I had only enough water for the two-day hike to Taishir I would try to catch a ride to the turn off. The integrity of my walk across Mongolia would not suffer, I reasoned, since the road I was on was not part of the route. About 8:30 a gray minivan finally approached from behind and the elderly driver gave me a lift ten to twelve kilometers back to the turn off to Taishir, a road paralleled by telephone poles that I'd passed just after leaving Altai. It was the first time I'd been inside a vehicle of any kind in sixteen days, probably a personal record.

I cordially returned the greeting of, but did not stop to converse with, a group of men sitting beside their Zil 130 parked near the intersection. For about two hours I burned up the graded road, trying to get within a day's hike of Taishir before nightfall. Stopping on a hilltop, I picked out a camping spot a short distance down the slope out of view of the road, as Boldsaikhan had advised. As I sat in the dark eating my cold supper of crackers, chocolate bar, and orange Metamucil mixed with powdered cream, first one van, then another stopped on the same hilltop just above me. There had been almost no traffic while I was walking. That two vehicles should now happen along and stop at the very point on the road closest to my camp seemed an act of deliberate provocation by the Heavens, curious to see how much a mortal's patience could stand. After the lost-road adventure that day, I didn't have much in reserve for the stress of being alone at night in a remote place with a party of strangers. I fumed and raged—quietly—while my unsuspecting neighbors conversed. I had thought one or both vehicles would remain all night but, after many false slammed-door signals, first one, then the other, started up and shoved off. All that metaphysical ranting for nothing.

$$\approx$$

I rose early after finally getting a good night's rest. My stomach disorder had evolved into a case of diarrhea, however. Shortly after setting out, I discovered with the aid of my GPS that I was on the wrong road again. I backtracked to a likely road branching off to the right. Although the line of electricity poles, which I had been told extended from Altai to Taishir, was nowhere in sight, the position and destination icons on my GPS road screen were aligned.

As I continued over rolling fields and low hills, four gers appeared. I considered stopping at one of them to eat and ask about the route but decided not to; better to stick to the familiar track and comfortable habit, even if they may be leading me down the wrong road. For the first time on the hike, it seemed, the wind was against me, slowing my pace. This mischance, with my memory of several others still vivid, quickly thrust me back into my pose of questioner of the cosmic order. Adapting star-crossed Juliet's question, I kept repeating "What wind is this which blows so contrary?" somewhat melodramatically.

But I am not battling an implacable Destiny, it seems. At a turn where the road leads through some hills, I come to a well. The missing water stop between the towns, and at the ideal half-way point, is here after all. It must have been newly dug, for it was neither on the map nor known by Boldsaikhan and the two men he questioned in Altai about water. A young man who had come by motorbike from his ger confirmed that I was on the right road. Shaariibuu, as he calls himself, knows my guide and our mutual friend Chimgee, who were schoolmates of his in Taishir. He fills his plastic and metal canisters and pours water into the attached trough for his animals—several camels and cows and one yak—who have come to the well.

I empty my half-full, eight-liter plastic container, a heavy load carried more than thirty kilometers to no purpose, into the trough and, filling my drinking bottle half full, mix in two packets of Metamucil before drinking. Another, younger man, Batbaatar (Strong Hero), drives up on a motorcycle to collect water. He too knows both of my friends.

I have not been long on the road again before I reach his ger, one of two or three tucked under an outcropping of rock with a stone corral built into its face. A Zil 130 is parked on the premises. A girl and boy, then a young woman, come to the road from one of the gers—Batbaatar's wife and two of his children.

I understand the woman to say this is their permanent home site, and the corral, used in winter months, supports my interpretation of her words. It seems they do not migrate seasonally like most Mongolian nomads because the area provides sufficient pasturage year-round. Batbaatar comes now, holding an infant. Mongolian men are typically responsible fathers and often share the duties of child-tending with their wives. I learn that he raises sheep and that his parents live in a different locality.

After Batbaatar's ger, the terrain became more level and the horizon opened out to remote hills and mountains. On either side of the road were numerous white chunks of stone encrusted on one side with the same sponge-like matrix seen on yesterday's specimen. These, as well as brown stones with curiously dented and embossed surfaces, attracted my passing glance, cast in the hope of lighting on that stray shell or plant-stem impression left from the primordial ocean. I had not yet learned, of course, that the first kind of stone was inorganically formed. The second, I have since read, was a variety of bioclastic limestone consisting of cemented mud created by microscopic fragments of algae.[11] As noted earlier, I was right, nonetheless, in imagining myself crossing an ancient ocean floor. Among the living plants that turned up on this day's march was a small flower with yellow petals arranged in short, fan-shaped spikes at the top of its jointed, branching stem. It is the Limonium flexuosum flower, called takhir bereemeg in Mongolian.

The road passed through a dried salt marsh, a slight green-scum colored depression with delicate grass sprouting from the white earth. The terrain resumed its rolling character and eventually the road brought me to a view of a deep transverse valley, where the line of telephone poles to Taishir finally reappeared—a welcome sight. This was the valley of the Zavkhan Gol, a river that forms part of the boundary between Govi-Altai and Zavkhan Aimags.

Short-cutting to the left on a smaller road in the direction of the town, lightheaded from exhaustion and hunger, I finally got within sight of a picturesque collection of salmon pink, white, and gray-colored buildings: Taishir. I had survived my first solitary stage of the journey. I descended to the valley, crossing back to the main road on the right, where someone would be more likely to find me should I faint, and entered the town escorted by a boy whom I had picked up by a ger on the way in.

The central plaza and streets adjoining it were more deserted than one would expect, even for a Friday night.

27 - Town plaza with cultural center, Taishir

I've been told the population of the sum and its surrounding district had been steadily shrinking for the past three or four years. Each summer herdsmen and their families, sustaining heavy losses from unseasonably harsh winters and finding no employment in town, were migrating to the three largest cities of Mongolia: Ulaanbaatar, Darkhan, and Erdenet.

I entered a delgüür and almost immediately it became half-full of customers. Feeling a little dizzy, I leaned against the low glass display case that served as the shop counter, not unmindful of the histrionic potential of this gesture, and ordered bottled water with a few emergency high-energy rations like my usual crackers and chocolate bars. Turning back downstage before making my exit, I was delighted to see a familiar face in the audience—my friend Chimgee's little sister's. Sükhyanjin attended school in Ulaanbaatar and had made the minivan trip to Altai with Boldsaikhan and me on her return home for summer vacation. She was in town from her parents' ger in the countryside while being treated at the local hospital for an ear infection.

She, a girlfriend of hers, and a young herdsman who was apparently a relative of Boldsaikhan's escorted me to a nearby ger where I was told I could get gasoline tomorrow morning. The young man then accompanied me to the dirt bluff at the edge of town to point out the way to Uliastai—a route marked by a straight line of electricity poles that sprinted up the mountainside across the river.

I found a campsite in a pleasant grove of aspens beside the river and, in company with Sükhyanjin and her friend, who had seen me enter the grove, ate a large pot of rice cooked with chicken, tomato, and mushroom-flavored bouillon cubes. I was surprised to learn that Boldsaikhan was still in the locality, though I might have realized three days isn't very long to spend visiting the parents one hasn't seen in at least a year. The girls told me he would pass through town tomorrow morning to begin the trip back to Ulaanbaatar. Dinner over and my guests having gone back to town, I assembled my tent in the dusk. One or two pairs of black kites veered and tacked in swift flight and pursuit amid the trees of the grove, noisily tearing through the leafy walls.[12] The wind that blew so contrarý in the morning had died down.

I woke early amid the fury of a loud, violent wind shaking the grove and tearing at my tent flysheet. I wondered what invasion force had attacked with heavy artillery and aerial bombardment at dawn. I packed up quickly and, after washing some clothes in a backwater pool, returned to the delgüür that hosted last night's stage performance. It was closed, so I got gasoline from the couple at the ger and sat in the small, wall-less stadium off the town plaza to catch up on my diary. Boldsaikhan later informed me that his departure on the back of a motorcycle occurred around this time. Another shop opening first, I found two unpackaged items not on the store shelves in Altai—raisons and a kind of cookie resembling an oversized Fig Newton: a pastry square shot through with a hard, chewy raison jam.

Taking the girls' advice of the night before, I followed the river upstream to cross on the bridge—a new, modern construction of concrete with a "T.U.Ts." (acronym for "Quick Service Spot"), or kiosk, at the south end. Paralleling the bridge slightly downstream were traces of an older, simpler one. A point on the Zavkhan eight to ten kilometers upstream from Taishir was the projected site of a hydroelectric dam. Bids for construction contracts were apparently being solicited for the project, which was funded by the Kuwait government.[13] This bridge crossing was the occasion of one of my minor blunders on the journey. A large party in a minivan had stopped on the road after crossing just before me. By the time I reached the vehicle, many of the passengers, including all of the men, had gone to take a closer look at the river, so I decided not to bother with stopping to inquire whether this was the road to Uliastai. Had I done so and thereby learned it did, my walk over the next several hours would have been enriched by an interesting natural feature and probably less strenuous and troublesome.

I had read about a striking geological formation, an aggregate of hexagonal basalt columns, each two meters tall and ten to fifty centimeters wide, located about one kilometer north of Taishir.[14] I did not know that the approach to it was on this road. Picking my way back downstream on the opposite bank, stopping to fill my drinking bottle with the snow-fed water, I finally reached the electricity poles pointed out to me the night before. I called at a solitary ger to confirm the route to Uliastai. How much easier it would have been to ask the company at the bridge about the road. Two savage dogs surrounded me, and I yelled out in both warning and alarm while crouching, mostly as a feint, to pick up stones. I had given my battery-powered electronic dog chaser, which the ever-present wind seemed to render worthless on the one occasion I used it, to Boldsaikhan to take back to Ulaanbaatar and now carried his bottle of pepper spray.

But the young couple and their three small children have come to the rescue. Yes, this is the way to Uliastai. For this prize bit of information, I risked getting chewed up both approaching and leaving the ger—the dogs returning to the attack when beyond the reach and jurisdiction of the man's restraining call. I was also thrown off the trail to the ger of my friend Chimgee's parents', where I had hoped to make a pleasant stop; the man gave what proved to be inaccurate information, that it was on the hill back across the river, instead of near the route I was on. Ruff! Ruff!

It was a long stiff climb up the slope, with predominantly brown mountains culminating in 2,242-meter Ikh Nomgon Uul looking on from the left. In the heightened spiritual state induced by this physical ordeal, I prayed two Mysteries of the rosary instead of my usual one per day. Soon after conquering the slope and rejoining the road, which had made a more gradual ascent from the bridge, I came to an agreeable halting place beside an ovoo marking the pass.

I had not been there long, snacking and writing in my log, when a party in a gray minivan pulled up from the direction of Taishir. The late middle-aged couple with two young men, one in his late teens, the other in his twenties, made straight for me, who must have offered a most welcome, unexpected change from the tedium of road travel. The older boy, thrusting his face close to mine as he spoke, gave ample proof he'd been at the bottle that day. I calmly but firmly refused to relinquish my hold on the pocket notebook when he grabbed it. Skimping a little on my hard-earned rest at the ovoo, I soon rose to depart. He grabbed me. I mustn't walk to Uliastai; they were going there and I could ride with them. I shook him off and started out, but he followed and laid hold of me again.

"You're not going to walk; you're going with us."

I turned, backing away and, freeing myself angrily, answered again that I must walk.

"Hey! Call him off, will you?" I appealed to my gratefully diverted audience, standing off by itself, grinning. Soon after, I had wrested my arms from his grip a final time and managed to get off unstalked. The van passed me on the road and stopped. I suspect foul play, a show of physical violence for rudely rejecting their kind and sensible offer. But no one gets out or points a gun at me through the window when I walk past. The family is apparently so unused to the idea of someone walking by choice in the countryside, especially for about 150 kilometers, that they assumed I would change my mind after a little calm reflection. The driver starts off and passes me slowly a second time before leaving me to my fate.

As I proceeded up a rolling field with low mountains ahead and two or three gers, I had to quell, with firm footsteps and rallying words, the insistent voice of fear: "I am putting myself at greater risk, walking alone and unarmed in rural Mongolia, than I thought. I should have paid more attention to Amar's warning about bad people. No telling how often this sort of company, or worse, will turn up. I could get killed. . . ."

I did right in not giving ear to this internal lecture, though doing so seemed rather reckless at the time. While I was careful to avoid potentially dangerous situations—by camping well off the road, for example—my contact with the rural population during the remainder of my journey convinced me that they are a peaceable and non-threatening people, possibly more civilized and humane, in this respect, than the rural inhabitants of many other nations. I could consult drivers or herdsmen about directions on lonely, little traveled roads without fear of being harmed. When my campsite was found out by locals, I was never subjected to even bluffs of physical violence in fun. As I realized when time had given me some perspective on that day's incident, even the youth's misguided attempt to force me into the van stemmed from a genuine desire to be helpful and to save me trouble, rather than from any ill-mindedness.

The road gradually ascended across an upland plain all afternoon. I was approaching the border between Govi-Altai and Zavkhan Aimags at the pass on 2,419-meter Dulaan Khar (Warm Black) Uul. Among the wild plants I found on the plain were the speedwell, a perennial herb of the figwort family, having small blue flowers ranged in raceme fashion along the tip of the stem. The name certainly gave the huzzah to my general approach to the hike so far, though for inspiring my larger purpose, deacceleration of mind and body, "slowpoke" was what I needed. Another plant, called tarvagan shiir in Mongolian, had a yellow flower with folded or enveloped petals like the pea plant's.[15]

At one point the landscape changed to a deeper, more luxuriant shade of green, the feathergrass responding to the higher elevation. Above it stretched the cloudless, silk-blue sky—khökh tenger (deep blue sky), as the Mongolians call it—a scene that awakens vivid, plangent strains of Gershwin's *Rhapsody in Blue* in me. The familiar epithet for the country, "the land of blue sky," may owe as much to the intensity of the color on a day like today as to the large average number of sunny days per year—250.[16]

Two men and two boys riding up, I asked about the location of the next well. They hailed a passing truck. The driver was going by there and would take me. Fortunately, no one tried to force me into the vehicle this time when I declined the offer, and later inquiring of a family at a ger, I found the well after a few kilometers. One of the two mounted men who stopped earlier arrived about the same time leading two fine black ponies. He was clearly proud of the animals and probably chose to water them when I would be at the well to see them close up. I indulged him with a "saikhan mori" ("beautiful horse"). He worked the long, polished metal handle—I have graduated to pump wells—while I filled my water bottle and the eight-liter container to most of its capacity. I will have to carry my evening's supply of water until I find a suitable campsite. My helper's countenance bore an innocent, childlike expression that gave him a youthful air in spite of his apparent forty years or more. He was young in middle age.

The road to the pass became steeper after the well. My long, laborious uphill march with the replenished water containers was complemented for a time by a loaded lorry straining up a parallel road. Driven by my increased apprehensiveness after the incident with the youth today, I kept going until I reached the sheltering folds of the mountains bordering the pass. When I had found a campsite behind a stony hillock beside the road, I could command—rare privilege—a scenic view of two aimags, depending on which way I turned my head. To the southwest, far below me, set amid green shadowed hills, the upward-tilted green plain scored with the road I had just taken and the line of electricity poles, lay Govi-Altai; opposite, to the northeast, the land sloping down to a semi-arid, variegated plain stretching away to far-flung mountains, Zavkhan. I was being treated to a last, long, lingering look at the province I had spent more than two weeks getting to know as a foot traveler. Farewell to the huge, southwestern, Texas-like aimag of Mongolia, land of the stark beauty of stony desert expanses and bare, brightly colored mountains; the rare wild camel, Gobi bear, and saiga antelope; dusty, wind-swept towns subsisting on the government tax; the struggling herder family caught between summer's drought and winter's snows. At the same time, I was offered a preview of the province I was to sojourn in over the next week and a half. Hail to the composite, Mongolia-in-miniature aimag, Zavkhan!

The screened door of my tent entrance faced back to the land I'd been crossing. I suppose this was due to the lay of the ground, rather than any inclination of the heart; to sleep comfortably, I had to have the tent floor, if not perfectly level, then slightly sloped toward the foot. Still, as I lay down after eating dinner and reading a little from my copy of Laurence Sterne's *A Sentimental Journey through France and Italy*, I was delighted to be able to gaze as much as I liked, as if it were my front yard seen through the living room window, on the last plain of Govi-Altai growing dark in the dusk.

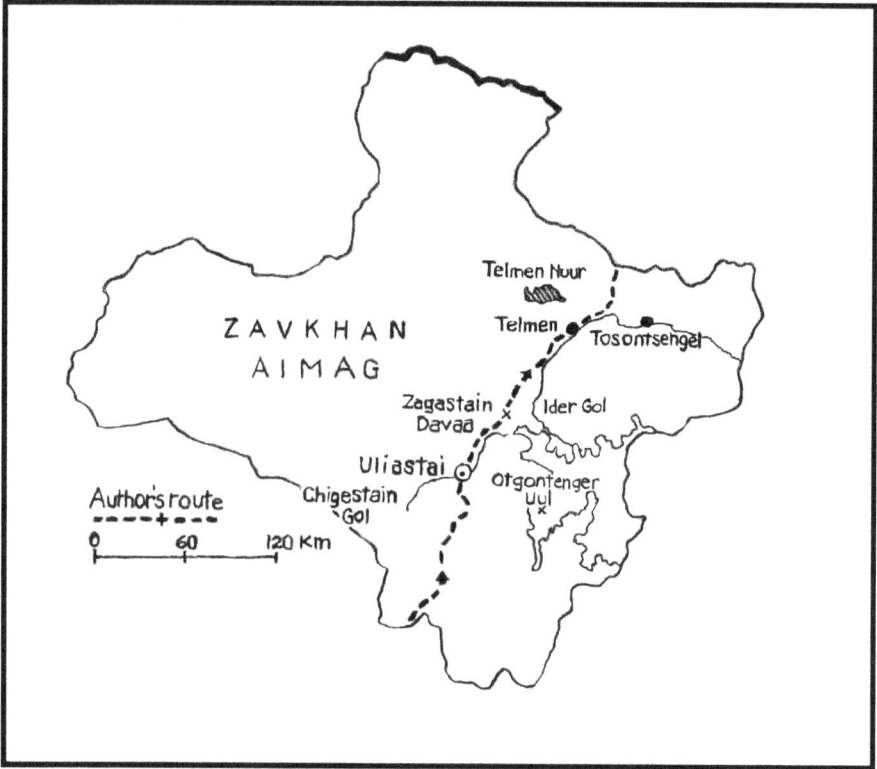

Map of Zavkhan Aimag

Chapter 4
The Mongolia-in-Miniature Aimag:
Zavkhan from the Border to Uliastai

Already how am I so far
Out of that minute? Must I go
Still like the thistle-ball, no bar,
Onward, whenever light winds blow,
Fixed by no friendly star? (stanza 11)[1]

The reference at the end of the last chapter to Zavkhan Aimag as a miniature Mongolia is explained in part by the shape of the province on the map: like Mongolia with its lobes, one on each of the four sides, but exaggerated as if in caricature. The chief reason for applying the term, though, is that all six of the natural zones in Mongolia are well represented: desert, desert steppe, and steppe occurring in the western part and mountain forest, high mountain, and taiga forest in the eastern.[2] With the six natural zones come the flora and fauna that inhabit them, of course, and Zavkhan is representative of Mongolia's exceptional biological, as well as geographical, diversity. The claims made in *Mongolia's Wild Heritage* for the nation as a whole can also be made for this aimag:

> Like few places in the world, Mongolia possesses a great range of natural ecosystems within its borders. It is a transition zone, where the flora and fauna of Siberia meet the very different species of the deserts and arid steppes of Central Asia.[3]

It was to be arid steppe that first day, Sunday, the last day of June, in Zavkhan. Breaking camp about 8:15 am, I reached a ger with a herd of horses grazing in the luxuriant feathergrass around. Should I stop to inquire about the distance to the next water source? I asked myself. I guess not—I'm already halfway past the homestead. Had I known that no water—along with no roadside gers and almost no passing vehicles to inquire about it—would turn up until evening, I might have checked my habitual haste and asked for information—or for water itself.

Sometime later I saw two demoiselle cranes, gray with black-and-white necks and heads, walking around atop a low granite ledge. The ground was riddled with holes, and little creatures that looked like field mice scurried into some of them against my approach. The fat, striped golio, or cicada, that I had seen on most of my walk in Govi-Altai had given way to medium-sized grasshoppers that sounded like tiny chirruping birds. Among the plants I found growing on the plain this day were the light-purplish sea lavender and light-yellow Panzeria lanata, which I had often seen in Govi-Altai. The Panzeria is often found growing near the barrows of mice or marmots, and, when young, is eaten by sheep, goats, and camels.[4]

There was a little breeze and the sky was overcast. The remote horizon before me seemed to promise something momentous and unprecedented in the landscapes I'd seen on my trek. Weren't those gigantic mountains that were taking shape out of the bank of clouded blue? I came to a crossroads that led on the right to Shilüüstei Sum, where I'd read there was an ancient ancestral-rite complex consisting of several deer stones, tall narrow slabs bearing stylized deer images. With the exceedingly scarce Sunday traffic, trying to hitch a ride to the site was out of the question. I considered taking the left-hand turn to a much closer sum, Tsagaanchuluut (White Rock), and arranging a ride from there, but the compulsion to keep logging kilometers on my trans-Mongolian route intervened. Like the decision not to take the side jeep trip to Eej Khairkhan, and, on two occasions in the last three days, not to stop at a ger for needed directions, I was influenced by what I saw as the special requirements of my journey—reaching a distant destination on foot. So the paradox of the rapid walking tour went on.

That afternoon I was briefly lured out of my way, however, by the prospect of viewing some unusual wildlife. As I was approaching two small ponds lying one or two-hundred meters from the road, about three dozen demoiselle cranes took flight and, giving their distinctive cry, somewhat like a cross between a raven and a goose's, circled aloft. Two ruddy shelducks—angir is the more onomatopoetic Mongolian name— and at least two gray and white hawk-like birds, presumably falcons, also flew up. After this sublime spectacle, I experienced a moment of bathos when the herd of animals, brown dots that seemed to retreat slowly up the hillside beyond the ponds as I approached, proved to be cows. I had grown unaccustomed to the sight of them during my two weeks in the Gobi.

The walk back to the road, which, as my link to traffic and towns, was my lifeline, took much longer than expected. "I must be careful when making side jaunts like this," I told myself. The plain had become increasingly dry and the spring that a jeep driver told me earlier that morning was fifteen kilometers ahead never turned up. I had less than a liter of water left. There was a moment of fear, a slight temptation to panic, as I thought of how my survival depended upon this repeated action of putting one foot in front of the other in recovering the road.

Once while crossing the plain that afternoon I heard, without seeing, a large aircraft pass overhead. The plane or jet, the first I'd encountered on my hike, must have been an effect of the law of compensation in the virtual absence of road traffic today. I finally crossed a low pass at the edge of the plain and entered a small valley bounded by green hills on one side, brown mountains on the other. Further left, or west, stood Bor Khairkhan (Brown Sacred), a 2,563-meter peak overlooking the village of Tsagaanchuluut.

Two or three gers eventually appearing, I approached them and found a stream bed with running water in it. It was now early evening and my carefully husbanded water supply was almost gone. How delicious and invigorating those gulps of cool, sparkling, spring water were! Three boys, including a mere toddler, came up, one of them bearing a metal ladle to make my task of filling both water containers easier. I returned with them to their ger to inquire about the next water stop. A girl, seeing me approach, walked up to the entrance to restrain the sleeping dog. The father being away, I walked past a high, squarish pile of dried dung to where the mother sat milking a cow. She was a stalwart, well-favored woman with clean, straight teeth. No water until Shireegiin (Table) Gol forty kilometers away, she and the eldest of the three boys reported. Thirty was the opinion of a jeep driver who passed on the road soon after. I would keep all of the water I'd collected, then, and look for a campsite.

I found one on the slope of a mountain on the right side of the valley, which had begun to narrow to Shandiin Dörölj Davaa. For the second night in a row I have a scenic lookout: a valley with a green, carpet-smooth floor before me and, to my right, a wall of splendid purple mountains where the valley veers to the left. I am now at the southwestern edge of the Khangain Nuruu, the highest mountain range in northern Mongolia.[5]

I pitch my tent near a marmot hole and prepare dinner while a hoopoe bird drones and one or two marmots chirrup outside their holes in warning to the colony. A lone herdsman stands beside his horse for a while in the valley far below, then rides away. Like last night there is no wind. At sunset, eating my Sunday dinner of powdered mushroom soup beside the smoking dung fire I've lit to ward off little black flies, I often look up from my reading of *A Sentimental Journey* to take in the lovely view. More vehicles, including a pair of heavily loaded trucks toiling up to the davaa, have begun to appear on the road.

🐏

I woke happy the next morning in a new day, a new month, a new work week, and a new province. As if echoing my mood, a cuckoo sang briefly. There was little wind. Descending the mountainside to the road, I found a hand-sized chunk of dark-brown volcanic slag—vesicular basalt—on the grassy ground. I started a large brown and white bird that held close to the ground as it glided off. A steppe eagle? Today would be an especially good day for finds and encounters.

Where the road paralleled a dry stream bed, I picked up a dark-gray stone chip about two and a half centimeters long in the sandy rut. Its sides and edges were gouged and scalloped somewhat too regularly for glacial abrasion to have shaped them. One edge had a narrow facet along it on one side that made it sharp. Long afterward I showed it to an archeologist I also consulted about the stones found in Govi-Altai, and he confirmed it was a rudimentary product of Middle or New Stone Age technology made of chalcedony.[6] The existence of a nearby settlement or campsite, which the chip points to, means that water must have flowed more regularly in the stream bed at that time.

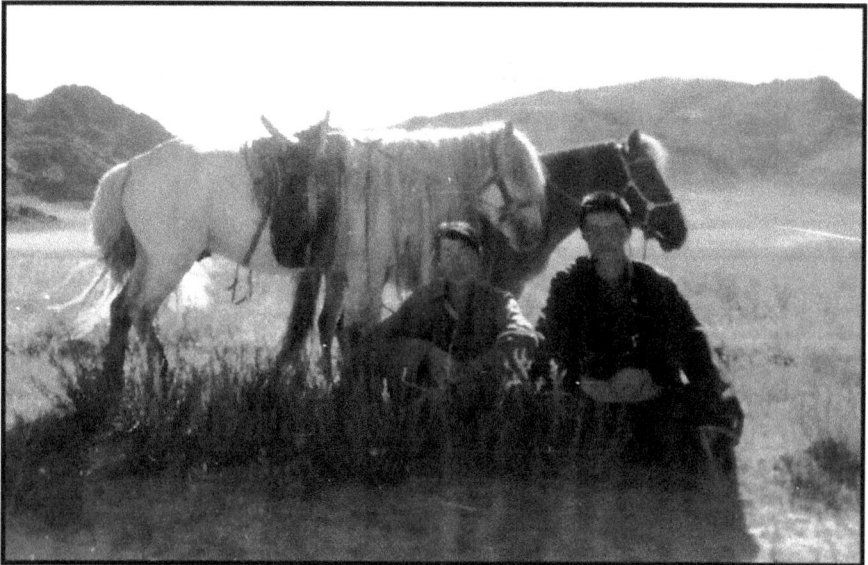

28 - Gantömör and Ankhbayar

A half hour after making this find, I was approached by two handsome young herders, one riding a white horse and sporting a gray deel, the other, a brown horse and purple deel. Both wore ball caps, one of them with the word "Champian" (sic) displayed in cursive script on the front. We sat down together in the sand near the stream bed. Both readily consented to an interview and one even extended an invitation to visit his ger, which, however, I declined.

"What is it like living here?" I asked Gantömör (Steel Iron), twenty-five, owner of the white horse.

"My life is OK here. I look after animals."

When I asked him whether his family had lost a lot of animals in the zuds, or heavy snows, over the last several years, he replied,

"Oh yes, a lot, a lot."

"Where did you camp during the zuds?"

"In the place which is called Temee Bökh (Camel Hump). . . ."

"How was life before the democratic revolution different from now?"

"It hasn't changed. No better than before."

"Are there any places of historical interest in the area that I should see?"

"Is it OK if I talk about a rock or mountain? . . . There is a big square stone that looks like a house."

"What can you tell me about the history of this area?"

"There is a sum called Tsagaankhairkhan (White Sacred) located north of our sum. Our sum and that one used to be one large sum in the area of the Tömörtiin Gol. Then our sum was created to the south at a place called Tsagaanchuluut. We will celebrate the fiftieth anniversary of our sum's founding on July 26-27th. We were given instructions on how to celebrate it." I had passed within about a dozen kilometers of the town of Tsagaanchuluut the day before.

"How will you celebrate Naadam this year?"

"Our sum will not celebrate Naadam; it will celebrate its anniversary. There will be a lot of activities, for example, an ovoo ceremony." In this religious rite predating Buddhism, locals offer milk products and money to the spirit of the mountain, and Buddhist lamas chant the prayers particular to that spirit, beseeching it for abundant rainfall, vegetation, livestock, and wildlife.

"How do you celebrate weddings here?"

"Each area celebrates weddings differently. To tell you how we celebrate, the man, accompanied by a few others, approaches the woman's family to ask permission for the man to marry her. If the family consents, the party returns in a few days to announce the day when they will come for the bride. The man must provide the ger. The woman contributes the bed and pillows, as well as the dresser."

The news was available from a local newspaper and radio station and from television at the sum center. "For the anniversary we will have a diesel-powered generator going twenty-four hours."

"What is your family's plan for the future?"

"There is nothing to tell you."

"What do you think about foreigners, especially tourists?"

"I have heard about tourists. They mostly hike. I'm glad to meet you here, traveling in this part of Mongolia. I hope that you will return for further travel in Mongolia."

"Are you able to get medical care when you need it?"

"Yes, I am able to get it. I can say that there is adequate access to medical care here in Mongolia."

"Can you tell me any local legends or anecdotes?"

"There was a good wrestler whose name was Arslan [Lion, the title given to the winner of a tournament] Choindon. Once, he said, 'I've claimed a new site for my ger at the summer pastures at Khyar (Mountain Ridge) and have put some stones around the site.' Then it was found that he had claimed the entire mountain slope! There is a big stone called the 'Cow Stone,' which was his chair. When he moved, he used to pack up his ger and put it on his back, then set his mother on top of the ger.

"I will now tell the story I heard about how he got the title 'Arslan.' Once he went to compete at the Naadam at his khoshuu [a term for an administrative district used between the 16th century and 1931]. In that khoshuu lived a champion wrestler who was attached to the noyon [a local nobleman in the feudalistic society of the 13th to early 20th centuries]. The officials had been looking for a wrestler who could compete with him. Choindon was discovered by a Manchu scout in the following manner. Choindon had reached the site of the tournament and lay sleeping in his field tent with his arm extended outside it. The scout passing by noticed Choindon's arm. 'This is a fine strong man!' he exclaimed. So it was decided that he would compete against the noyon's wrestler.

"In performing, with outstretched arms, the ritual devekh, or eagle dance, at the start of the competition, the noyon's wrestler made a show of his physical strength by holding a khunts, that is, a heavy box of tea, in either hand. Choindon, wanting to hold up something also, looked about but could find nothing. So he took up and held suspended in the air his and the other wrestler's zasuul [attendant, or second] while performing the dance.

"During the bout, Choindon caught hold of his opponent and was about to throw him over his back when he cried out,

'Please don't throw me down! Hold me! Hold me!' Then it was discovered that the wrestler's shin bone was broken. 'He won,' he admitted. 'Let him receive the prize.' But the judges [who, as friends of the noyon's, were reluctant to acknowledge the victor] gave him a white camel instead of the title 'arslan.' Then a hooligan in the crowd spoke up,

'Can you carry the camel?' he asked Choindon.

'Yes,' he answered.

'OK, then carry the camel to the tent pavilion where the noyan and his friends are and ask them, "Is this a camel, or is it a tevne [a large needle for sewing leather]?"'

"So Choindon carried the camel over to the pavilion and asked,

'Is this a camel, or is it a tevne?'

'Please stop, dear Arslan! Please stop, dear Arslan!' the astonished men exclaimed. In this way, he was given the title and rank of 'Arslan.'

"Later, Choindon was taken away to another part of the country. When, after several years he had died, a wolf was found living in his rib cage."

The tale is clearly in the tradition of the oral folk literature popular in the 18th and 19th centuries during the Manchu occupation, which poked fun at the oppressive aristocracy and Manchu overlords.[7]

Gantömör's friend, Ankhbayar, aged twenty-one, was far less vocal. He pointed to the spot in the valley where he had camped with his flocks during the zuds, or heavy snows, of the past three years, when many animals perished.

Riding their mounts, Gantömör and Ankhbayar escorted me a short distance on my way after the interviews. In finally slowing down my pace a little, I had made a couple of friends, not a bad trade-off for a few kilometers. The day, sunny and still almost windless, had turned hot when the road swung right and climbed steeply out of the valley to Daagatiin (Foal's) Davaa. It was an epochal point on my route, being the steepest that I had yet encountered and offering, like the roads through the green landscape before Tseel and wooded summits before Altai, a distinct departure in the character of the land. A large circling bird of prey with yellow patches on the underside of its wings, probably a vulture, looked on from high overhead, begrudging my progress toward a better-watered and more habitable natural zone.

Groves of larch, larger in area than those on the mountains before Altai, stood on my right. As I descended in the same northeast direction after the pass, the mountains to the north seemed higher and more majestic than those I was used to seeing. A plant familiar on my journey, the prickly pea shrub, grew much bigger here. The number of gers that began to appear in the transverse valley of the Tömört (Iron) Gol, the river mentioned by Gantömör, suggested a hamlet. Yes, this was certainly khangai, a term meaning a "mountainous and wooded country with abundant water and fertile pastures."[8]

Entering the valley, I stopped at one of the gers to inquire about the next water stop after the Tömört Gol. Two elderly men, the elderly wife of one of them, a middle-aged woman, teenage girl, younger girl, and small child all came out upon my arrival. Soon I had embarked on an interview with the patriarch of the household. He wore a shirt and trousers and a trilby hat after the modern, Western fashion. The younger of the two women read aloud for him my questions on the sheet of notebook paper.

Damdinjav reported a high mortality rate among the livestock in the "aimag," by which he may have meant "sum," during the last three winters, but said that he had not lost any animals himself. He estimated there were seven-hundred families and forty-thousand livestock in Tsagaankhairkhan, the sum I was now in. His observance of Naadam would consist of listening to the wrestling competition on the radio.

29 - Damdinjav with friend

"What is your family's plan for the future?"

"The plan of an old man?" he replied, personalizing my question. He was seventy-eight. "I hope that my children will be OK; that's all."

"What do you think of foreigners, especially tourists?"

"If I meet any of them, I'll tell them, 'May you arrive well and return well.'"

"Can you tell me any local legends or anecdotes?"

"Shall I tell him about Dambiijaa?" he asked the younger woman in a low voice. She gave a short laugh before replying,

"You can tell him about Vandanov."

"Vandanov! Vandanov!" the children chimed in.

"There was a man named Vandanov who was a White Russian and a Buryat[9] during the Mongolian socialist revolution in 1920-21. Someone from this area arrested him and took him away. I heard that he was killed. There was a man named Dambiijaa. He used to carry a gun about with him. He was a crafty one. That's all."

Dambiijantsan, called Ja Lama, is a legendary figure of the popular resistance movement against the ruling Manchus. After their expulsion in 1912, he became notorious as a cruel and seemingly invincible rebel leader seeking to establish a separate western Mongolian state.[10] Damdinjav's hesitation to speak of Ja Lama, though dead for as long as the old man had been alive, was eloquent testimony of the awe and fear this desperado must have inspired among the local population.[11]

After the interview I showed the stone chip I had found to Damdinjav and his wife. She quickly produced a file from inside the ger and was about to go to work on it when I stopped her. The same tool-making impulse of her immemorial ancestors who started the piece survived in her to finish it. When I was about to set out from the stream after filling my water bottle, two girls in the neighborhood arrived, each carrying a bundle of soiled linen to be washed. Otgontsetseg (Youngest Flower) spoke a little English, acquired in school in Uliastai. The other girl was named Nordogmaa.

The road became sandy as it continued northwest up the valley, where, in the bright green grass, yaks and horses grazed. A wide bridge with wooden planks and rails crossed the river in the bottom, the old, unused road leading up to it now almost obliterated by time.

A vehicle approaching from the opposite direction stopped. There was a Westerner in the passenger seat. He was the first I had seen since meeting Shawn, the Peace Corps volunteer, in line at the bank in Altai one week before and only the second I remembered seeing since leaving Ulaanbaatar. I must have been a rather exotic sight to him as well, though he told me in the ensuing conversation about an American acquaintance of his named Tony who had just finished a four-year English-teaching assignment in Uliastai. Another four teachers sponsored by an American college had recently come or were on the way, he said. Jordan, as he called himself, was a Bulgarian telecommunications specialist who had come to Uliastai in February or March. He was making one of his regular business trips to Altai. The remote rural setting of a lesser-traveled foreign country gave zest to our brief exchange.

Shortly after this chance roadside meeting, I noticed an unusual arrangement of stones near the road: low, bent-over slabs forming a rectangle with a large stone set upright in two corners. The stone rubble, sprouting large shrubs in the middle, made a slight mound. An ancient burial site? There appeared to be two more sites in the immediate area, one of them, on the other side of a dry creek bed further down the road, consisting of four small upright stones forming a rectangle. I hailed a party passing in a Zil 130, then two men on a motorcycle to ask about the first site. The former said it was a burial site but not old, the latter old but not a burial site. Not knowing which part, if any, of each report to believe, I later showed a photo of the site to archeologist D. Erdenebaatar of the Mongolian Academy of Sciences Historical Institute, who confirmed that it was a tomb from the Bronze Age, or about 2,000 to 1,500 B.C.

30 - Ancient tomb, Tömört Gol valley

He was less certain about the adjacent site with the four upright stones. If excavations there were to disclose straight walls of slabs connecting the stones, he said, the site was probably used for animal sacrificial rites in the Bronze Age or, much later, in the Turkic Empire period of the 6th to 8th centuries A.D. Few excavations had been carried out in western Mongolia due to the distance from Ulaanbaatar, he said.[12]

For a long time after these sightings in the Tömört Gol valley, complexes of stone posts were a fairly common occurrence. I saw another one or two likely ancient grave or sacrificial sites as the road turned northeast into the intersecting valley of the Shireegiin Gol. Other traces of the past as well would turn up during my sojourn in Zavkhan.

Across the valley of short deep-green grass, numerous gers surrounded by dark-brown board palisades and several larger plastered buildings soon appeared perched on a narrow shelf above the low river bluff and at the foot of the steep mountain slope behind it: Tsagaankhairkhan Sum. Leaving the road to enter the floodplain, I found a delightful halting place at two channels of sparkling, clear water flowing between grassy banks. I sat long, absorbed in the sight of the many small minnows—my first "fish" on the trip—darting about in the stream.

Continuing up the valley, one eye open for a good campsite, I saw a large dense clump of trees resembling, in shape and color, a shelf of gray granite. E. Ganbold of the Academy of Sciences Botanical Institute later informed me they were pea trees, a species related to the prickly pea shrub seen earlier today.[13] Two young boys rode up on horses after I passed a ger. One extended his hand, so I obliged him by stopping for a handshake and a question about his and his companion's name. He extended his hand again, this time with two briquettes of either cheese or aaruul, dried milk curds, but I have turned skittish and, already back in my comfortable stride, tell him that I have food of my own. It takes a lot of physical hardship and isolation on the road for a traveler to turn an act of kindness like this into a threat.

I gathered water for the evening where the road finally crossed the twin-channeled river, two tumbledown log bridges with only some of the board planking intact zigzagging their broken backs across. It was a picturesque spot where yaks, horses, cattle, sheep, and goats grazed in the lush green grass. The rousing note of a herdsman calling his flock gave an equally colorful dimension of sound to the scene. At least two gers, with folk sitting outside or milling about them, stood nearby, and many more gers were planted farther upstream. I would have to risk a less secluded campsite tonight; it was almost dusk and I was too fatigued by the day's walk in the heat to carry my heavy load of water far after crossing the river. The top of a rocky hillock overlooking the valley at the point where the road turned north would have to do.

A teenage lad rode up while I was cooking my pot of noodles, and two more boys while I was eating. They were far from posing any threat of violence or being up to pranks from idleness and boredom, though; they were herders out tending or rounding up their family's livestock. Most of the actual herding in Mongolia is done by children and youths. My unbidden guests, drawn to the hilltop by curiosity, as the herd of horses that gathered later on the slope were drawn by the grass, soon depart.

"Bayartai. Saikhan Amraarai." ("Goodbye. Have a good rest.")

ॽ

I am up at dawn, eager to begin the day's walk to Uliastai. I will take my next rest day in the aimag capital and stay in a hotel. Another early riser, a mounted herdsman I meet after regaining the road, blesses my undertaking with his smile and "Sain yavaarai" ("Have a good journey").

The dozen-kilometer haul up to Gants (Single) Davaa, elevation 2,502 meters, is slow and steady until, the slope steepening toward the top, the road enters on a long circuitous course for the benefit of motorized traffic. I decide, on the advice of a young motorcyclist I meet coming down from this stretch, to proceed straight, following the telephone poles. It is a formidable climb in the heat, but I am often regaled by the scent, as hearty as meat and potatoes, of a mountain herb, a plant that I was to encounter many more times on the journey north. But it is edelweiss, also known as lion's foot, that I want to find when I at last reach the ovoo at half past ten that morning. Taking the well-beaten path around the large cairn three times, I add a new petition, in unconscious defiance of the pass's inauspicious name, that Enkhjargal and I will marry happily. In the words of the Zavkhan poet Begzyn Yavuukhulan, I have resolved that

> To love only you
> I'll be beside you forever.
> To be loved only by you
> I'll keep you beside me forever. (15-16)[14]

A keepsake edelweiss, symbol of eternal love in Mongolia, would be nice to solemnize the occasion.

As one of its Mongolian popular names, uul övs (mountain grass), suggests, the flower is quite common here—unlike in Europe, where it grows in less accessible mountainous reaches[15] —and I had seen a lot of them on the final stretch of my ascent. I am disappointed until, looking for a place to sit away from the ovoo and arriving travelers, I find several growing. I select one to give her.

From my seat, which registers an altitude of 2,525 meters on my GPS, I can see Uliastai about a dozen kilometers due north deep in the next valley, its numerous board palisades giving it a purplish tint. At the sight of the long-sought Emerald City, the approximate half-way mark of my foot journey, my spirits soar higher even than the Alpine point they attained at the ovoo before Altai. For a moment I recapture the pride and self-confidence and jubilation from hard-won achievement, the zeal for yet greater triumphs, that I used to feel more intensely in my youth.

"This is such a wonderful trip!" I proclaim out loud. "I haven't done anything this exciting since the Appalachian Trail. I feel I'm alive again."

The road veered and descended to the left, following the base of a mountain on its right. The top of the mountain on the opposite side of the road was forested with Siberian larch. A ground covering of grasshoppers as thick as the eighth Egyptian plague made walking an act of cruelty. A man with a boy in the side car of his motorcycle stopped on his way up the road. The complexion of his handsome face was very dark from exposure to sun and wind. He was going to Tsagaankhairkhan, he said, to take this—and he raised the lid of the storage compartment of the side car. Inside lay a tangled mass of fibrous plant matter, like that used to make rope.

31 - Valley on descent to Uliastai

A young couple approaching on a motorbike stopped soon after. They were also going to Tsagaankhairkhan. She opened a large plastic bag of hard, wrapped candy, evidently intended for Mother, and invited me to take some. He raised sheep. When they learned my nationality, they spoke of their friend Tony, the American teacher whom the Bulgarian mentioned had just returned after four years in Uliastai.

The road ascended as it bore right, opening to view a deep majestic valley running transverse to the one I'd been descending. A pair of birds with brown heads and gray and black or dark-brown stripes on their backs darted from the outer edge of the road and sailed into the valley: great crested grebes.[16]

When I had made the long winding descent along the mountain slopes, I began to feel a little faint, so I stopped to mix powdered cream and orange Metamucil in my last half-liter of water. It was the hottest day of my trip so far, with temperatures probably in the 30s and almost no wind. The beverage and some of the raisons purchased in Taishir were sufficient for the home stretch—a straight, gently descending road—and the long dogleg route through town to the Uliastai Hotel.

The southern approach led through the industrial district, which dates from the 1950s.[17] The area appeared to be almost deserted and few factories showed any signs of activity. When I reached the Bogdiin (Holy) Gol, which seems to set off the industrial from the commercial and residential quarters, I had to walk to the east end of town to cross the bridge, picking up a couple of unusually tenacious, badgering children on the way. They were succeeded for a while by a gang of boys in their early teens. I turned to confront the boldest one in the lead, whom I suspected had designs on my pack. I was not in my best humor, thanks to tiredness, heat, and hunger, but my Emerald City was looking, close up, more like a place of brick and concrete.

I made my way up an aspen-lined avenue past several painted wooden kiosks bordering the sidewalk on one side of the street and two four-story soviet-style apartment buildings on the other. I had been looking for vestiges of the 188-year Manchu presence in Uliastai[18] when a woman coming from the opposite direction provided one in the form of a physiognomy that was undeniably foreign and, to my eye, Chinese. Like an archeologist uncovering a rare artifact, I was thrilled by the insistent actuality of the past. Her face was much more angular than Mongolians' typically are, having high cheekbones and jaws converging sharply to the chin. I didn't know at the time that the aspens, which are the source of the name "Uliastai" ("With Aspens"), were themselves a legacy of the Manchus, having been planted by them.[19]

The apartment buildings on the avenue gave way to a Petrovis company filling station, then to a row of small wooden shops with parked minivans and jeeps, as well as a billiard table, in front. I took the old ruinous log and plank bridge, now off-limits to motorized traffic, across the Chigestein Gol, which joins the Bogdiin Gol a short distance downstream. Skirting the marketplace and bus depot, I passed shops, restaurants, museums, a cinema, drama theater, hospital, and the town plaza area to the hotel. Though not emerald, with its painted plastered buildings in the sun's glare and combination of motor vehicles and horses, Uliastai now suggested a town in the American west near the turn of the last century. My mood must have improved.

The 6,000-tögrög, or $5.50, hotel room, though considerably higher than the cost indicated in the Lonely Planet guide, would answer my purposes quite satisfactorily, having, if not a shower, at least a sink with running water. The request of the attendant who registered me to leave my passport in the office and my refusal, however, augured trouble that would later cancel the blessings of my comfortable lodgings.

My first errand after securing the room was to phone Enkhjargal at the post office-telecommunications building on the nearby plaza. I was eager not only to share the news of the last stage of my journey and safe arrival in Uliastai, but also to find out whether there was a chance of our meeting here. It was too late to purchase a plane ticket, she said, and, in any case, she much preferred visiting me in Mörön, the next aimag capital. I stopped for dinner at the Khash quanz. After visiting several small delgüürs and kiosks along the street to replenish my stock of food, I returned to the hotel for the evening.

ௐ

The next morning began with an unpleasant exchange, or, rather, lack of exchange, with the attendant who checked me in the day before. When I asked her about getting some clothes washed, she virtually ignored me. I was going to let it go, but, seeing her in the lobby as I was on my way out to visit the museums, I repeated my question both there and, following her, in the office. I was completely ignored. Incensed, not realizing this might be poetic justice for recent occasions when I'd ignored others, I put up my microcassette recorder and walked to the Tegsh Hotel at the other end of town to inquire about lodgings there. I secured a beautifully furnished upstairs room for the same price as the one I'd left, though the bathroom was shared and had a water dispenser and basin instead of a sink with running water. The laundress was in.

I had stopped momentarily at the bench in front of the Uliastai Hotel after returning to check out when a young man came up and asked what country I was from. He was an Israeli and had arrived in town at 4:00 am that day. He and a female companion had walked from Tsetserleg (Garden) in Arkhangai Aimag to Terkhiin Tsagaan Nuur, a scenic lake roughly 175 kilometers to the northwest. They had stayed at gers, which was pleasant at the time, he said, but had resulted in his developing a stomach virus. He would have to postpone the bumpy jeep ride to his next stop, Khovd, capital of the Aimag of that name, in spite of scarcely being able to afford the cost of the hotel room here. The next morning I happened to see him, a pack on his back, walking toward the bus and truck station.

When I had finished moving into the Tegsh Hotel, I took up my recorder again and set out for the museums a second time. En route, I toured the outdoor market: lanes of shipping-container delgüürs and tables or booths displaying clothing, hardware, and wholesale food items. This market did not appear to be as extensive as Altai's. The merchandise in the Chinese trade quarter listed by Pozdneyev in the 1890s, suggests, in the number and variety of goods, that Uliastai had one of the largest markets in Mongolia back then. His list includes silk cloth, cotton goods, coarse American calico, Russian printed calicoes in assorted colors, Chinese jackets with or without sleeves, robes, caps for summer and winter, boots, silk tobacco pouches, brass and stone pipes, glass and stone cigarette holders and snuff boxes, purses, and chinaware.[20] I saw many large sacks of flour but, except for onions, no fresh vegetables. Pozdneyev identifies the following garden produce available directly from the farms: potatoes, carrots, black radishes, cabbages, pumpkins, horseradish, winter rape, onions, and radishes.[21]

The History Museum was situated between the Drama Theatre and the Museum of Famous Persons on the central avenue I'd taken into town. My guide for the tour of the second floor, Narankhüü, the museum treasurer, pointed out an oil painting by the artist Odon depicting a scene from the movie *Ulaan Dartsag* (*Red Flag*), based on a story or novel by Ch. Lodoidamba, a writer from Taishir. In "Navsai Damba and His Friends," a group of children lead a revolt against reactionary lamas. Here was evidence of three media supporting the former communist regime in Mongolia: painting, cinema, and literature. Another medium was employed in two photos of tailors from the Service Center who had distinguished themselves for their work in the outlying sums. At that time each aimag had a Center where essential services such as tailoring, shoe repair, and barbering were provided, and staff were regularly sent out to work in the aimag sums and brigads, or villages. Amid the welter of herders', soldiers', and lamas' paraphernalia in the museum was part of a wandering lama's backpack.

"The upright pieces of wood are made of tamarisk," she said. The lamas would put their mattress, blanket—all kinds of useful things—in the pack. It was so portable. They used to hike long distances." Perhaps the legendary Dambiijantsan, who had entered western Mongolia as a wandering lama, used a pack like this one. Had I come through the area a hundred years ago, I, too, might have sported a tamarisk-framed backpack.

After the tour I inquired about a jeep trip to Möngöt Khyasaa (Silver Cliff), site of a stone slab chiseled with four male figures. The monument belongs to the Turkic Empire period in the 6th to 8th centuries, though the slab itself may date from the Bronze Age.[22] The director of the adjacent

Museum of Famous Persons, Zavkhan Aimag's Hall of Fame, knew the location of the monument and offered to arrange a jeep ride there tomorrow for only 15,000 tögrögs, or less than $14. Tseveljid was a short gentleman with an intellectual physiognomy and quiet, composed manner. He agreed to an interview.

Fifty-eight, he was born in Urgamal (Plant) Sum in the western wing of the province. He expressed satisfaction with the changes, particularly the greater contact with the outside world, in the wake of the democratic revolution. Many places of historic interest in Zavkhan and throughout Mongolia were destroyed in the 1930s, he said. Today some nine registered historic sites in the aimag were under the protection of the government. His reply to the question about how weddings were celebrated contributed a few details to the picture sketched by Gantömör a few days before: Care must be taken to choose an auspicious day, according to the traditional Buddhist almanac, for asking the consent of the girl's family for the marriage; the wedding date must be announced at least three to four months in advance; and the wedding party celebrates first in the home of the bride's parents, then of the groom. "Our wedding celebrations are very elaborate affairs," he said.

He noted that, although a lot of tourists come to Mongolia, fewer visit Zavkhan due to the poor roads and distance from Ulaanbaatar. "A French student of Mongolian history and culture did his practicum here. Then the French ambassador to Mongolia came to our museum. Other tourists also visit. In this way, our country is being introduced to foreigners." He rated the province on access to medical care "very good," adding that both traditional folk medicines and modern, "European" medical treatment were available.

My guide at the Museum of Famous Persons was Gündegmaa, a research scientist. She systematically identified the celebrities and most if not all of their personal belongings—from TV set to wool-lined undershirt—on display in each of the three sections: religious, literary, and political. The literary room featured memorabilia of two writers from Zavkhan, the playwright and screenwriter Lamjaviin Vangan (1920-1958) and poet Begzyn Yavuukhulan (1929-1982) quoted earlier, an arrestingly handsome man of the race of large-eyed, ethereal-featured romantics founded by Shelley. Unlike the visionary author of "Hymn to Intellectual Beauty," however, he was a good accountant, according to Gündegmaa, having attended the College of Finance and Economics in Ulaanbaatar in his youth.

Back at my new hotel room that night, eating canned peaches and salted peanuts and reading *A Sentimental Journey*, I could reflect with satisfaction on the store of impressions and data I had gathered today by opening myself up to what this drowsy, obscure provincial capital offered. It was a moment of uncharacteristic unwinding from the border-bent attitude I'd slipped into. I could say with sentimental traveler Yorick:

> —What a large volume of adventures may be grasped within this little span of life by him who interests his heart in everything, and who, having eyes to see what time and chance are perpetually holding out to him as he journeyeth on his way, misses nothing he can *fairly* lay his hands on. . . .[23]

I was at the Museum of Famous Persons at the agreed-upon time of departure the next morning, July 4th, American Independence Day. Tseveljid invited me to sit in his office, where we would remain talking for an hour or more while the rusted and creaking machinery of a field expedition was slowly put into operation. I was introduced to Dorjkhand, a young woman who served as the English-speaking guide on the museum staff. Also accompanying me on the trip would be Gündegmaa, my guide on yesterday's museum tour, and Bayaraa, one of the History Museum staff. The driver, a man in his twenties, came, asking for the cash up front to buy gasoline. Only when he returned and we finally set out did I realize that the director would not be going along.

Crossing the bridge of the Bogdiin Gol, we turned left up the valley past truck farms of potatoes, onions, and probably other vegetables. Here was more testimony of an earlier day, for Chinese farmers had cultivated this same river bottom.[24] The valley narrowed to a gorge and the road closely followed the boulder-strewn river, clumps of large hardwood trees growing on the bank—a region that I wished I were walking through. The Bogdiin—as well as the Zavkhan—has its source on nearby Otgontenger (Youngest Sky) Uul.[25] Eternally snow-capped, 4,031 meters high, the mountain is considered sacred. The rare vansemberüü flower, a saw-wort found on its slopes, is celebrated in folk and popular culture, including a song with the refrain

> If I should see that divine flower,
> Though it were on the top of the highest mountain,
> I would carry my mother there on my back to show it to her.

Had I known that the mountain was only about fifty kilometers east of the monument on the same road, I might have added this worthy landmark to my itinerary that day. I may be the only tourist in recent memory to travel within a half-hour's view of Otgontenger and then stop. Credit for this dubious distinction must go to failure to consult my maps carefully when arranging the trip. Later in my hike, when I missed another opportunity to make a side jaunt there, it was largely due to my compulsion to keep pushing northward.

Our driver stopped first at a ger pitched next to the river, then at a gathering of men picnicking beside their Russian minivan to ask for "maslo," oil. No one seems to have any, but the search is dropped after one of the picnickers checks the oil gauge; apparently, we are good for one more day. The valley has widened. Where rounded hills hem in a small plain on the east side, a high sheer cliff of light-orange, yellow, and brown rock left by a shoving Ice Age glacier drops down to the river on the west side: Silver Cliff. We disembark and Bayaraa points out to me the unlikely object of our quest this morning, a light-gray stone post standing before the cliff across the river.

We try wading barefoot across. The speed of the current makes walking on the slippery stones too difficult, however, so we decide to cross in the jeep at a ford downstream. Standing before it at last, I find it to be a well-dressed, wedge-shaped granite slab about two meters high and running from about a half-meter wide at the top to about three-quarters of a meter at the base, which is encircled with river stones. I had read that noted Mongolian historian B. Ryenchin restored the fallen slab to an upright position in the 1960s. Delicately chiseled into the upper half of the flat side turned toward the east are two facing pairs of quaint human figures, one pair sitting cross-legged in the lotus position and the other standing beneath. Each figure has long braided hair and wears a deel and at least three of them have a moustache and bear a sword on their left side. Here, then, is another gathering at the river, one predating the picnic downstream by more than a dozen centuries. In addition to holding a sword on his left hip, the clearly defined figure shown sitting in the upper left held a drinking cup to his chest by his right hand. The picture resembles what is seen at many ancestral-rite complexes of statues called khün chuluu (man stone) in central and western Mongolia dating from the same 6th to 8th-century Turkic confederation era.[26] Archeologist Dovdoin Bayar suggested to me there are no other monuments from this period in which the figures are chiseled rather than sculpted statues.[27] As noted before, the stone itself may be a product of the Bronze Age.

32 - Monument with guides at Möngöt Khyasaa

When I had returned to the museum and bid my guides and the director goodbye, I stopped at the public library down the street. The same striking portrait of Begzyn Yavuukhulan, much enlarged, that I had seen in the museum greeted me when I stepped into the foyer. Finding the attendant of the department where English books were kept "baikhgüi" and the door locked, I left to begin my preparations for departure from Uliastai early in the morning. I called Enkhjargal, arranging to meet her in Mörön if I could arrive there within thirteen days, when she would still be on her summer vacation. I bought gasoline for my stove, taxiing to "First Company" filling station on the outskirts of town in order to buy the best grade available—number ninety three. I bought groceries, took a shower at the bathhouse on the hotel grounds, ate, and retired early.

ﾞﾞﾞ

Chapter 5
Spirits of the Valley: Zavkhan Aimag
from Uliastai to the Border

This poor soul cried, and was heard by the Lord,
  and was saved from every trouble.
The angel of the Lord encamps around those who fear him,
  and delivers them. (Psalm 34.7-8)[1]

The next morning, taking the road north through the ger suburb against a steady stream of people walking or driving to work, I reached Dechindarjaa Khiid, the town monastery, after about three and a half kilometers. It was founded in 1990[2] upon the arrival of democracy and the restoration of religious freedom.

33 - Dechindarjaa Khiid

As I stood before the locked board gate with the hours posted on it wondering whether to wait the hour and a half for the service to begin, the lay caretaker approached along the outside of the palisade and asked if I would like to tour the facility. Entering, we passed three gazebos containing prayer wheels, upright metal cylinders believed to multiply the supplicant's prayers according to the number of revolutions. Mongolians say that passing by a prayer wheel without using it is like neglecting to drink from a spring encountered in the desert. We went thirsty. With the gazebos was a khonkh (bell), a silver-toned metal tree about two meters tall, having three tiers of branches with bells pendant at the end and resting on three feet. Visitors stop to ring the bells and light incense in the burner. I understood my guide to say that the monks live in the single-story white building on the right side of the enclosure.

The interior of the temple consisted of a large, low-ceilinged room with four round red wooden columns, each entwined with the picture of a gold-colored dragon, forming a square area in the middle. Arranged in a row along the outside of these columns were low benches draped with rugs—the monks' stalls. Another table bore long narrow packets of sudar, Buddhist scriptures printed as xylographs in Tibetan and Mongolian. The Mongolian name is related to the sanskrit word "sutra," which, in Buddhism, refers to a discourse given by the Buddha.[3]

The rear wall was covered with icons of various sizes—statuettes and framed figures embroidered on cloth. Small metal cups on short stems used as votive lamps were set in a long row on tables against the wall. Empty now, on feast days and special occasions they are filled with butter oil and lit.

After taking in these and other features inside the temple and praying from my rosary on a bench near the door, I returned with my guide to the monastery gate to await the arrival of the lamas. Soon a young man wearing a gold-colored deel, tied with the usual orange sash, and a peaked purple and gold hat appeared, and I was invited to follow him back inside. He went to the rear wall and dusted the three tables, putting the votive lamps in a bag. I followed his instructions to imitate him—folding my hands and bowing before each table until my forehead touched the top. Taking an ornate metal pitcher from a table by the temple entrance, he bid me to take some holy water in my hand and wipe it off on my hair, as well as my sunburnt lower lip. I stopped short—not on religious grounds—when he told me to drink from the pitcher. I understood him to say the community numbered twenty monks. He was apparently not among the full-time members who lived on the premises.

There were only two, himself and a slightly older youth, at the prayer service that morning. Sitting in the lotus position on their rug-covered benches, they began a recitative chant in unison, the younger lama's voice pitched higher. The two made a not unpleasing stark harmony. The older had dispensed with the peaked hat, as well as with the purple tunic which his confrere was now also wearing. The younger rises to get a sudar. Their chant is punctuated once with brief handclapping and again with bells rung by the older monk. He yawns occasionally, gapping quite unreservedly. From my visitor's bench I contribute a silent recitation of the Joyful Mysteries of the rosary. Momentarily awakened to compunction over my ill-disposed manner toward unbidden, inquisitive locals, my prayers also have a penitential cast. The chanting is still going strong when I get up to leave.

Reentering the road, I pass a woman walking toward town. We stop to exchange a few words. Our brief conversation is spontaneous and cheerful—unlike the constrained dialogues I am used to giving and taking, if I enter into dialogue at all, on this trip. Had my visit to the monastery restored my sense of connectedness with others? It is an auspicious start to the second half of my journey.

I spent most of that day walking north up the valley of the Chigestein Gol. The traffic was much heavier than on most of the roads I'd walked so far. Where Khatavch Creek flowed into the river as it bears east, I noticed two small piles of rocks, each encircled by stone flags. Two upright stone slabs or posts stood on the circumference of one of the circles. They were ancient tombs.[4]

34 - Second man stone, Chigestein Gol valley

Less than an hour later I saw two more piles close together with a post at the edge of both. Coming around the first stone, I found myself face to face with a pudgy little man who gazed back at me ruefully. A man stone! "Khün chuluu" in Mongolian, man stones represent major political figures and were erected as part of commemorative sites during the Turkic confederation in 552-745 A.D.[5] The eyes were goggled, nose large at the tip, and lips thin in the broad face. A chiseled line designated the chin.[6] Like one of the figures I'd seen on the Turkic-era monument at Möngöt Khyasaa, his right hand clasped a cup to his chest. The other hand, which supported the right elbow, held a knife or dagger.[7] Mongolian archeologist N. Ser-Odjav's report on the site in 1970 measures the gray granite stone at eighty by thirty-five centimeters.[8]

Stepping over to the next post, I gazed, awestruck, upon a larger and much more complete and life-like specimen. The face stood out in greater relief from the stone. A deep groove above the figure's shirt collar ran around the stone, and a "V" in front delineated the shirt cleavage. The serene expression and what appeared to be wavy or plaited hair over the forehead suggested to my amateur's eye the influence of ancient Greco-Roman art.

According to N. Ser-Odjav, the monument represents a woman with a long braid of hair wound around the top of her head. Mongolian archeologist Dovdoin Bayar, who made a drawing of both stones in 1996, noted an object resembling a hairpin depicted on the slightly shaped back of the head. The eyes' oval was fairly large,[9] the eyebrows thin, neck thick, chin wide and double, and thick lips pursed. The ears were pierced with earrings with gem insets.[10] Like the neighboring stone, the figure held up the standard banquet cup with the right hand. Both figures, who may represent husband and wife, are thus apparently shown as if taking part in the ceremonial event that would have been held here in their honor.

The archeological sketch of the second figure in N. Ser-Odjav's study shows a bird suspended by a cord from the left hand, which also supports the right forearm. Two fish about a half-meter long, tails uppermost, are represented down the back of the torso, almost as though hanging from a string slung over the right shoulder. N. Ser-Odjav identifies the fish as an Arctic grayling and taimen. The height of the monument at the time of his measurement was 1.6 meters.[11]

The pair were oriented toward the east, direction of the rising sun, universal symbol of rebirth. Behind both was an enclosure, rudely defined by embedded stone slabs. The ground of the second figure's enclosure and, possibly, that of her fellow's, had been disturbed by misguided robbers.[12] They had assumed these complexes for ancestor worship include the remains of the deceased represented in the stone.

I am highly gratified to have finally added two on-site man stones to my stock of discoveries—and without having gone out of my way. And there is more. Less than two-hundred meters to the east stands a large rock mound with a fairly distinct ring of embedded stones forming a wide margin around it. Did the ancient nomads erect mounds over their dead? I had learned to associate mounds with grave sites from my knowledge of the burial practices of Mississippian Native American tribes. In fact, as D. Erdenebaatar informed me much later, such stone mounds, called khirigsüürs, mark Bronze Age tombs. Radiocarbon analyses from sites in central Mongolia revealed dates from 1,600 to 700 B.C. While the Celts were erecting Stonehenge, the Minoans the Palace at Knossos, and the ancient Egyptians the temple of Queen Hatshepsut, the early nomads of the Mongolian steppe were piling stone upon stone over their honorable dead.[13] A photograph that he showed me from the excavation of a site in Arkhangai Aimag suggests the border of embedded stones was a low wall gradually submerged to its top in wind-blown soil. Fanning out from the base of the pile to this wall were broad wedge-shaped walkways of stone flags.

At about 8:00 pm, seeing water in Khatavch Creek in an area between two collections of gers, I decided to set up camp a bit earlier than usual. This proved fortunate because a few hours were promptly taken up in fixing my stove, which had quickly sputtered out and refused to relight. The nerve-rending whooping and screeching of a group of men and boys who had just commenced horse-herding operations nearby, possibly to impress the foreigner in their midst, were almost as harrying as the malfunctioning stove. An older man from the group came to my camp on a ledge above the creek and sat down for a while. Later, all or most joined him. Working under their gaze, I was not equal to the occasion and politely told them I needed to be alone to concentrate. Two, irrepressibly curious, had returned when I finally got the thing going enough to boil water for instant noodles.

"Muu benzine!" ("Bad gasoline!") I remarked to them, being a bit more amenable to company now. Though I had purchased the best grade in Uliastai, after giving what remained in the bottle to the young motorcyclist I met on the ascent to Gants Davaa, the inferior gas bought in Taishir and Khaliun had apparently taken its toll on the stove's fuel line and jet. The rest of the hike was to be made under the shadow of greater or lesser uncertainty about my stove's functionality.

My two visitors remained, stretched out on the ground, as I ate my dinner at dusk. I mentioned the man stones and asked them about the large stone pile seen that day. There were more man stones one kilometer ahead, I understood them to say. The mound was not a gravesite. Time had eradicated not just the memory of the local Bronze Age elite interred here. That there had even been a burial at all or the practice of raising stone mounds over the honored dead had been forgotten. It was a sobering revelation. One of the classic expressions of hope in an earthly immortality, the noble words of the dying Anglo-Saxon chieftain Beowulf, now had a pathetic ring:

> "Command the battle-warriors, after the funeral fire,
> to build a fine barrow overlooking the sea;
> let it tower high on Whaleness
> as a reminder to my people.
> And let it be known as Beowulf's barrow
> to all seafarers, to men who steer their ships
> from far over the swell and the saltspray." (2802-2808)[14]

Dinner over, my guests depart "and leav[e] the world to darkness and to me." Not only "the rude forefathers of the hamlet," (4, 16)[15] then, but also the illustrious Hampdens, Cromwells, and Miltons eventually sleep in obscurity.

ƻ

I am up early and break camp in a cold, overcast morning. After about twenty minutes, I notice seven stone slabs or posts set in several circlets of embedded stones: three in one circlet, two in another, and one each in two more. Upright stones that appear to mark ancient burials continue turning up.

Early in my steady ascent to Zagastain (Fish's) Davaa that day, a lovely view offered on my right: a deep gulch with the Siberian larch timidly venturing all the way down the mountainside to level ground for the first time on my trip, thick brush and grass growing in the bottom where Little Khatarch Creek, running over stones, sparkles in the sun. I come upon a profusion of wildflowers of various kinds beside the road. They include knotweed; a white flower resembling Queen Anne's lace, or wild carrot; the sticky-stemmed catchfly, or campion, also called "butter and eggs" and obligingly like one of my favorite flowers, the snapdragon; a purple flower called nugiin shimteglei or myagmaisanjaa in Mongolian; and another that I'd seen by itself on previous days: the purple starwort, or aster

> –Fair as a star, when only one
> Is shining in the sky. (7-8)[16]

Zagastain Davaa has something for both the scientific and the poetic mind. It lies on the ridge that forms part of the Central Asian Continental Divide, chasing streams down the northern slope to ultimately empty into the Arctic Ocean and down the western to eventually steep some brackish lake[17] or expire in desert sands. Just below the pass, I stop to drink from a pool that appears to be the source of the creek. I am looking at the last body of water that drains west. From now on, most of the streams and rivers will be seen to flow northward. Those that are not, most notably the Egiin Gol at Khövsgöl Nuur, are merely adjusting to local terrain before settling on their true course. Zagastain Davaa, then, is another milestone, a geographical turning point, on my journey north.

And for the poetic temperament? The Polish-born scientist and travel writer Ferdinand Ossendowski reports the legend of the demon of the pass in his book *Beasts, Men, and Gods*:

> It was long ago, very long ago. . . . The grandson of the great Genghis Khan sat on the throne of China and ruled all Asia. The Chinese killed their khan and wanted to exterminate all his family but a holy old lama slipped the wife and little son out of the palace and carried them off on swift camels beyond the Great Wall. . . .

Pursued by three-hundred horsemen to Zagastain Davaa, the mother and child were about to be overtaken when she "lifted her little son toward Heaven and exclaimed: 'Earth and Gods of Mongolia, behold the offspring of the man who has glorified the name of the Mongols from one end of the world to the other! Allow not this very flesh of Genghis Khan to perish!'

At this moment she noticed a white mouse sitting on a rock nearby. It jumped to her knee and said:

'I am sent to help you. Go on calmly and do not fear. The pursuers of you and your son, to whom is destined a life of glory, have come to the last bourn of their lives.'"

When the mother expressed doubt that a small mouse could accomplish this, he jumped down and addressed her again:

"'I am the demon of Tarvagatain [local subchain of the Khangain Nuruu], Zagastain. I am mighty and beloved of the gods, but, because you doubted the powers of the miracle-speaking mouse, from this day the Zagastain will be dangerous for the good and bad alike.'

The khan's widow and son were saved but Zagastain has ever remained merciless. During the journey over this pass one must always be on one's guard. The demon of the mountain is ever ready to lead the traveler to destruction."[18]

Ossendowski heard the tale while traveling this same road over the pass toward Khatgal,[19] a town on my route to the border. The legend of the demon of the pass accounts for the mishaps that travelers seem to undergo with uncommon frequency there. He and his party made the ascent in a fierce wind and through deep snow. Losing the road, they were forced to spend the night in a small valley. The pass may lie buried in snow even during the summer.[20]

Nearing the crest, I tried to imagine the fleeing mother and child, three-hundred Chinese soldiers riding in close pursuit, on this very road. A cool wind blew—not a matter to cause alarm. I would stop at the top, snack on peanuts and a beverage of powdered cream and juice mix, work on my travel diary, and rest. I had not seen a vehicle in at least thirty, possibly forty-five, minutes. Maybe for once I would have the view to myself. . . .

I had just sat down at the iron picnic table when the dreaded sound of a motor began to grow on the wind. A yellow Russian minivan sprang into view and stopped. Doors opened and slammed shut. Suddenly, I am ringed round by a large staring family—several young and adult men and women, an elderly couple, teens, and children—my person, garb, and gear transformed into the materials of a live exhibit, "Westerner on a Country Ramble," at some Museum of Exotica.

"What's he got in the bag?" I hear a man ask.

"Peanuts."

Needled with questions, I feel like the stuffed macaw whose button is compulsively primed by visitors at the Science Center. Where are you from? Where are you going? What's in the bottle? Are you carrying a tent? Are you traveling alone? How old are you? Another driver, a well-fed middle-aged fellow who has arrived on the scene in time to hear the answer to the last question, stomps off in a comic display of alarm and self-deprecating disgust, as if to say, "A walk of that length at our age? Not me!"

Is this debacle the work of the merciless demon of the pass, who knows I would have preferred savage winds and deep snow? Maybe I should have circled the ovoo three times before sitting down, instead of postponing the rite for my departure. So it happens that, within hours of turning over a new leaf at Dechindarjaa Monastery this morning, I have flipped back to my old standoffish ways. If there was extra provocation for it here, it wasn't the white mouse of Zagastain that brought it on but

Nemesis for my wish to exult in the adventurer's exclusive mountaintop experience.

The patriarch of the extended family introduced himself. Yura, sixty, worked in the Telmen Sum branch of the state social security office. When I asked him about the next water stop, he reported that the road ahead crossed a river in about twenty kilometers. He and his sons asked if I was carrying a gun and not afraid of wolves, common in this part of the country. I answer "no" and let the cherished myth about the wolf threat lie undisturbed in their minds.[21]

Yura gave me his address and encouraged me to look him up when I reached Telmen about sixty kilometers away. After my secret peevishness during this roadside encounter, the friendly invitation and, as the men make for the van where the others are waiting, their "Sain yavaarai!" for a good journey feel rather like a heaping on of live coals.

Now deferentially circling the giant ovoo thrice, I descended the steep narrow valley of the Zagastain Gol, shortcutting to the next bow of the tightly meandering road—and inadvertently bypassing a roadside ger with a fiercely barking dog. After about eighteen kilometers the valley fanned out, displaying beautiful multicolored mountains at its far end. The landscape, moreover, had begun to turn from lush to arid, as if I were once again in the desert-steppe of the Gobi. At this juncture a road led east to Ider Sum on the river of that name. Roughly fifteen kilometers upstream from the village, in the shadow of Darkhan Uul, were the ruins of the Monastery of the Lama Who Separated Milk from Water. Chimedtseren, whose boyhood feat gave the monastery its name,[22] was among the monks featured in the Museum of Famous Persons I toured in Uliastai.

When, at intervals, water appeared in the bed of the Zagastain, it was either too far from the road or too close to gers, so I decided to wait until reaching the bridge mentioned by Yura before filling up and looking for a campsite. Hurrying to this site near the day's end, I passed another khirigsüür, looming off to the left, its neatly assembled stones apparently plucked from the hills lying well behind it. When I finally reached the bridge, I was astonished to find no water under it! What the devil? Had the river dried up since the family, who were apparently southbound, crossed it this morning? What earthly good did Yura think a dry riverbed would do me? Well, I would have to count on something turning up in the immediate stretch ahead. Night was coming on and there was no water I could now backtrack to within a reasonable distance.

Just afterward I came to a ger. Then there emerged from behind a low rise in the road, as if sprung miraculously out of the ground to rescue innocent fools beloved of God, a small building surrounded by a board palisade. The couple who owned the guanz and their two daughters, a young woman in her late teens or early twenties and a girl, appeared at the entrance. While the youngest took charge of my long-neglected water containers, I asked, still shy of meat after Altai, whether a bowl of lavshaa soup without meat could be gotten up. Their answer, a straightforward "no," probably appeared funnier to me when I recalled it later. I bought some crackers and, with my replenished stock of water, went a short way down the road where I was fairly well-concealed from motorized traffic. Soon I had settled down to the long wait for boiling water on the sputtering stove.

꒜

I was striking camp in the chilly morning air when a herder boy rode up. He did not seem to understand when I politely said I wished to be alone but sat on the ground and watched while I shaved. He did leave after this event, however. I decided to return to the guanz for breakfast. If lavshaa could not be prepared without meat, well then I would take my chances on a little of it; I had dined on instant noodles, the only thing my flagging stove was up to, the past four nights.

I asked the cook, the older of the two daughters, to prepare my soup with only "jijig makh" ("a little meat") and took a chair at one of two tables against the wall. A huge laminated poster of an ideal breakfast scene photographed in what looked like an English country house or luxury condominium in Florida hung before me. These slick banquets of Tantalus seemed to have a knack for showing up at my hungriest. I had been taunted with the same luscious fare in the kitchen of the guest lodgings in Tseel. There were three or four more specimens down the same wall and along the next one on the right, where a few of the family, including the father, lay snoring in bed.

The top of my table was scuffed from repeated use. Both tables had artificial plastic flowers stuck in a brown enameled clay vase molded to represent deer encircling the base of a tree. The vases were a comforting reminder of home, for Enkhjargal had given me the same one, for a pen and pencil holder, as a gift the previous winter. And now, as I sat reading *A Sentimental Journey*, "Lara's Theme" from the movie *Dr. Zhivago* played on the kitchen radio. A favorite tune of my mother's, our family had selected it for part of the background music in the commemorative video created for showing at her funeral. Here, then, was another expression of my journey's leitmotif, "mother," one which, like the song heard twice on the radio in Altai, took the form of music. I sensed in the concurrence of the vase and theme song the presence and protection of the spirits of these loved ones. I was reassured about reaching my goal. The stove would be fixed.

Meanwhile, for only a little meat, there certainly was a lot of chopping going on at the cutting board behind me. When the young woman flattened and sliced the dough to make noodles at the next table, we talked. Oyundari, the name I seem to remember her introducing herself by, was on vacation from school at a teacher's training college in Tsetserleg, capital of neighboring Arkhangai Aimag to the east. The guanz was a rest stop for international tourists en route to Otgontenger Uul. She listed no less than eight different nationalities in the catalogue of visitors so far: Chinese, Russian, American, French, Israeli, Polish, Tuvan, and Kazak. Whatever thoughts this list inspired about making a side trip were lost in my obsession with making it across Mongolia. I had just gotten another sign that the spirit of my mother was guiding and guarding me, but I still missed the irony in thinking her main objective was getting me safely to the border, especially if I was trying to get there as quickly as possible. Hadn't she prompted me to take the hike as a quest for freedom from rapid physical "motion" and its effects on the mind? Yet my overriding aim had become the border itself.

When my bowl of hot lavshaa was served I found it contained the usual proportion of meat—at least fifty percent. Had Oyundari understood "a little meat" to mean chunks cut in little pieces? The mutton bits did seem smaller than average thanks to all that chopping. That made twice today, once when I asked the herder boy for privacy and now in ordering my soup, that a request of mine had been misunderstood—and it wasn't even 9:00 am!

The sleepers, who weren't likely to have understood a request for privacy, were roused and the radio was turned up for Mongolian pop music. After finishing my breakfast of soup and milk tea, I bought more crackers and a chocolate bar. A party was now assembled at a larger table and other guests were coming in.

"Do you want a ride?" asked a man in Mongolian as I left the building. He stood in front of his vehicle with the hood raised.

"I don't need one, thanks."

About a half hour later the sky was clear except for a few clouds on its fringe and, even with a breeze, it was getting warm. The view across the plain to the left was incomparably lovely: a row of mottled mountains; green valley floor and lower slopes becoming light shades of red, yellow, orange, and green on the higher; shadows from some white, gray-bellied cumulous clouds scattered about the slopes; smooth blue sky above and between the clouds.

I made rapid progress on the unusually straight and level road, alive with clicking grasshoppers. By early afternoon there was a general cloud cover, tempering the heat. My feet were finally free of the moleskin and gauze patches I'd had to wear over aching blisters. I found myself thinking of my mother's last days, of her suffocation and near death, apparently from an accumulation of mucus in her throat, alone in a hospital room in Milan, Tennessee. I wept freely for maybe the first time since her death the day after the episode almost one year before.

The Ider Gol, emerging from behind the hills on the right, converged on the road; there was a steady line of gers marking it across the plain. In *Travels in Northern Mongolia*, Don Croner identifies the Ider as the first link in the earth's longest north-flowing system that empties into the Arctic Ocean. The Yenisei-Angara-Selenge-Ider system ranks fifth worldwide, being exceeded only by that of the Nile, Amazon, Yangtze, and Mississippi-Missouri.[23]

At one point on the six-hour stretch of arrow-straight, northeasterly road that afternoon, I was resting, exhausted, with my back against one of the telephone poles following the road when I heard the hoof beats of an approaching horse. I had not seen a herdsman or driver in some time, so the appearance of a visitor coinciding with one of my infrequent halts was exasperating. It was a boy, who, dismounting, began shooting the usual questions at me. After answering the one about a car, I told him I was resting and needed to be alone. I then tried ignoring him and, when he persisted, got up and started off. A rock bounding past me from behind, I turned to confront him and he rode off.

Shortly after, he returned with two companions. Keeping my pace and not trying to conceal my anger and irritation, "To Khövsgöl," I replied, tersely, to the older boy's first question and "I speak only a little Mongolian" to his second. Finding myself still accompanied, I gave them all a round bold stare. "What are you doing?" I asked them. I pointed to my little assailant. "He threw a rock at me. That one is bad." Just after, the older one, looking behind him, gave a cry and turning quickly about, galloped off, followed by the others. Apparently, some animals in their herd had gone AWOL.

Much relieved but half expecting a sequel to this incident, I walked a longer than usual distance at an even more rapid pace before my next rest stop. No one approached, however; nor, when I eventually looked behind me, did I see anyone following at a distance. A little reflection might have suggested that my chief enemy in rural Mongolia was my own irascible, paranoid self, driven by a fixed idea of personal achievement.

35 - First deer stone with rock mound in background

Shortly before reaching the village of Ögöömör (Bountiful), I noticed a tall leaning pillar of light-gray granite off to the right. Inspecting it, I found a four-sided stone with curvatures chiseled into its surface. I was looking at my first on-site deer stone on the hike.[24] Scholars believe that these tall narrow slabs bearing stylized deer images served as totems for the tribe, who would assemble periodically to offer sacrifices.[25] They are similar to the much later monuments of ancestral rites, man stones, in being oriented toward the rising sun and not marking grave sites. The images were indistinct after the weathering of more than twenty-five centuries, but the drawings in V. V. Volkov's study of Mongolian deer stones, first published in 1981, show three leaping deer down the length of the stone on one side; four smaller deer down one of the narrow edges; and a square shield bearing a chevron design, a belt beneath it from which an axe is suspended, and a deer's head on the lower half of the opposite narrow edge. The stone is just under two meters high, eighty centimeters wide, and fifteen centimeters thick.[26]

Thirty meters or more to the east I found another deer stone, its upper half broken off and lying next to the stump. Another hundred meters or more beyond it, I came to a large rock mound. A straight double row of embedded stones could be seen on two opposite sides of it; the stones on the other two sides were apparently below ground surface. Part of the khirigsüür had been adapted for use as a winter coral, the stones being pulled out and ranged down two sides to form walls. It was another lesson in the ephemerality of earthly grandeur.

In the vicinity of the mound were numerous stones set upright and circlets of flags. Excavations of such features at Urt Bulagyn, a khirigsüür site in central Mongolia, have shown that the upright stones mark human graves and the circlets contain interred cremated remains of animals.[27] Later I consulted D. Erdenebaatar, the project's co-director, regarding the purpose of the stone circlets. He suggested they contained the bone fragments of horses ritually slain and cremated for use in the next life by the deceased buried at the khirigsüür. Shamanistic burial practices, he said, typically involved interring the carcasses of domestic animals in association with graves.[28]

I soon reach the village of Ögöömör, where I will stop for water. But something is wrong. A hint of eeriness emanates from the rows of log huts and three or four larger buildings. Where are all the people? Surely not everyone is out with the animals? Is this a winter camp only? Two dogs bark menacingly from inside a salmon-pink wooden house near the road. Then a well showing signs of neglect suggests an explanation. In fact, as a resident in Telmen would confirm on the following day, the village's water source played out. Part of the string of gers seen along the bank of the Ider across the plain were the new homes of the Ögöömörites. The village, then, had not lived up to the promise of its name, Bountiful; I was looking at my first ghost town.

When, instead of bearing right toward the river, the straight road finally approached a hill, I hailed a fuel truck going in the same direction to ask about the distance to Telmen. I had very little water left and couldn't afford to take chances. The driver said he didn't know, an unprecedented answer that seemed to imply a considerable distance. He did indicate that a road along the telephone poles, now far to the right, went to Telmen, so I struck out across the plain in the direction of the road and river. Had I risked proceeding straight, I would have reached the town in about five kilometers, as I later estimated it. I might have stayed that night at the quaint-looking hotel that I discovered in passing through town the next morning. As it was, I had to walk at least eight kilometers to Telmen and go through all of the evolutions of finding and setting up an overnight camp. Is there a moral here? Probably nothing more, in a technological age, than "Always consult your GPS."

I crossed a no-man's land pocked with small bush-filled craters. It rained lightly before I reached the road and more heavily for a brief time after that. I soon found myself gazing at an idyllic pastoral scene: three bright white gers planted amid rich green grass sprinkled with edelweiss. I approached a corral of wooden rails where two teenage girls in deels were milking a densely packed line of goats, each turned hip to jowl to the goat on either side of it and with its horns joined to those of the next goat over on either side. Hoping to learn that the road crossed the river, my long-coveted water source, up ahead, I inquired at the corral. A boy was leading me off to the well when a thin man smoking a cigarette emerged from the nearest ger and told him to bring me some water from the plastic barrel inside the tent, explaining that the well water was bad. I drank two bowlfuls. The road and river met in one kilometer, he said. He seemed a little wary of me, possibly because I did not approach him first.

I made my way back to the road, which was now passing before a mountain bluff, and crossed a gorgeous patch of orange sand where tiny purple flowers of desert thyme bloomed in scattered clumps of green. Rounding the bluff, I noticed two places with large stone posts above the road. The river nearing the bluff soon afterwards, I descended to collect water for the night. A mounted herder boy on the bank looked on in silence as I filled the containers. I found a camp on the lee side of a rocky hill. As I began unpacking, a furry gray mouse appeared perched on a nearby boulder. A relative of the demon of Zagastain Davaa sent to help me? It had been my longest day's hike so far—at least forty-three kilometers, the length of a marathon. I was eager to eat supper and turn in. My stove refused to work at all tonight, however, so it would have to be a cold supper. Good thing I stopped for that bowl of soup this morning—and that it contained not "a little meat." Had my mother and Enkhjargal, whose intercessory aid I sensed at the guanz, something to do with my deciding to eat there?

At dusk I was entertained by the sight of a large herd of horses galloping down the hill to a few gers beyond the road, a long steady stream that passed by me, unseen, not fifty meters away. They, too, are eager for a night's repose.

꒳

I slept in a little, being tired out from yesterday's strenuous march. I debated whether to set out at once for Telmen or to invest some time first in trying to fix the stove. The thought that it was inoperable and that I would have to return to Ulaanbaatar would be sure to harass me all day if I chose the first alternative. Besides, the wind had died down since last night and it wasn't cold. Praying repeatedly, "Jesus, son of David, have pity on me," I began by cleaning the jet and needle. Finding the jet clogged, I applied the tip of a thin sewing needle from a matchbook kit that, by good fortune, I had not yet given away from my gift bag. Holding the tiny jet up and peering into it again, I now found that I could see the sky through a filmy veil. After filling the priming cup and igniting the wick, I found that the stove worked like new. God be praised! The inferior grade of gasoline purchased before Uliastai had apparently taken its course through the stove's system and the superior grade was now flowing unimpeded. Hopefully, I would be able to get more of the latter in Tsagaan Uul (White Mountain), the next sizable town on my route. "To Khövsgöl!" I announced out loud.

Nearby, larks warbled in their darting, swallow-like flight, as they had done the afternoon and evening before. On the road below there was a sudden halloo. Three boys racing on horseback followed by a slower horseman and barking dogs sailed into view. This was my first definite sign of the preparations for the children's horse race at Naadam, the national sporting tournament, just four days away.

Resuming my walk, I was surprised to find Telmen Sum only one to two kilometers down the road. The unprecedented wooden sign bearing the town's name was an overture of welcome. I passed a small spruce-looking stadium enclosed by board palisades, site of the upcoming wrestling competition at Naadam, and entered the town, escorted by a mounted gentleman dressed in a deel. With its trim plastered and wooden buildings of various colors and sizes, Telmen, formerly Ovogdii, was the most attractive town I had seen thus far. It wore the same old-fashioned, scrubbed, and orderly look that recreated frontier or western towns in the U.S. had, without any of their phony self-promotion and commercialism.

The museum in the central part of town was housed in a distinctive two-story, wooden, octagonal structure with a conical roof. Behind it were three statues, one of an animal that appeared to be a bull, another of a horse, and between them a silver-colored one of a girl holding a milk pail. It was closed, I soon learned, during the month of July and the proprietor was out of town. A small monastery stood at one end of the town.

Men were congregated at the open-air billiards table near the delgüür where my escort, who had never ceased asking me questions, obligingly led me. The small wooden building was unpainted except for the frames of the windows and door and the board that ran along the eaves, which were different shades of blue. When I had bought groceries, Nyamsüren, the woman in attendance, took me to a small pharmacy that carried the elusive lip ointment I had searched for in vain in Altai. After I had made this purchase, she complied with my request for an interview.

She was born in nearby Tosontsengel and her parents and other relations all lived there. She liked being in the countryside. Life was better now than it was before democracy, she said. Asked about interesting places in the locality, she mentioned "beautiful" Telmen and Büst Nuurs and the seven hills of sand. The sand from these hills is "so interesting," she tells me. "If you put it in your mouth, it dissolves!"

"How will you celebrate Naadam this year?"
"I'll just stay here and watch the wrestling and the fast horses racing."
"How do you celebrate weddings?"
"The man builds a ger. Then the couple invite parents, brothers, sisters, relatives, and friends. On the table there must be a sheep's back. It is a merry time for everyone."
"How do you get information?"
"Some of us go to the city. Those who don't, listen to the radio and watch TV."
"What is your family's plan for the future?"
"Our plan is to see that our children get a high level of education."

She indicated that it was difficult to obtain medical care. Asked what she thought of foreigners, she said that, although she had seen many, she knew little about them because of the language barrier. Nyamsüren related one local legend.

"As you continue on your way, you will see the mountain called 'Snake Stone.' If you climb the mountain, you will see a stone shaped like a crooked snake. In olden times, the hero of our region fought with and killed a huge snake on top of the mountain. He shot it with an arrow, slicing it in two. The lower, tail half jumped across the river, where it changed into a mountain. The upper half remained on the mountain we now call 'Snake Stone.'"

On my way out of town, I passed a large two or three-story wood-frame building with trees growing on the spacious grounds in front. A sign indicated the town hotel, an amenity I did not think Telmen offered. I winced with regret at having just missed an opportunity to stay overnight in this picturesque building. A few boys recognized me from Zagastain

Davaa; they were Yura's grandchildren. Our meeting was hardly remarkable given the size of the extended family in that van. The boys pointed to Yura's house nearby, but by now my habitual eagerness to be moving had returned. I told them simply to give him my regards.

36 - Nyamsüren with daughter Dolomaa and company

I had traveled only a short distance, though, when I noticed people and vehicles ahead: a small crowd standing or seated around a yellow minivan with the red, white, and blue Mongolian flag suspended on a pole next to it; blue Zil 130 truck; red car; and several motor bikes. A man's voice blared over the loudspeaker mounted on the van. Riders, men and boys, were going to and fro. Off to the right were many saddled and unsaddled horses tethered to poles. To the left, a red flag was posted at the base of a hill on which were a few small groups of men or boys with their horses. A practice race for the local Naadam was in the making. In spite of the general excitement over today's event, it didn't take long for a gathering of curious boys to form around me after I sat down. Zorigoo (Courage), Enkhbold (Peace Steel), Nyamochir (Sunday Thunderbolt), Gantulga (Steel Hearth), and Davaasüren proudly pose with their horses for a group photo. As preteens, all are eligible Naadam jockeys. The race is scheduled to begin at 4:00 pm. For the second time this morning, I excuse myself.

37 - The five Naadam jockeys outside Telmen

Seven kilometers north of town I came to a guanz I had been told of in Telmen. It was a plain, unpainted shack with a table and bench, large bed in one corner, and stove. Gray bags made of plaited plastic strips, the kind I'd often seen used for transporting coal or kindling in Ulaanbaatar, had been cut open and tacked to the ceiling to hold the insulation in place. Next to the guanz was a small wooden building used to store animal hides and sheep wool.

Being very tired, I was invited by the proprietor to rest on the bed while my soup was prepared by his wife and teenage daughter in a ger next door. For the next half hour or so I lay listening to the noises of children playing outside. My bowl of lavshaa was served with a metal jug of unsweetened cranberry juice, a pleasing extra that suggested I was entering a region of more natural abundance. My host, I learned in a brief interview after the meal, was Sanjmyatav, aged thirty-six and born in Telmen. He made his living growing vegetables. "My life here is neither bad nor good," he reported. This year's local Naadam would be an especially good one, he said.

Setting out after thanking him and his wife and daughter for their hospitality, I passed a large fenced-in vegetable garden, Sanjmyatav's work site. It was the most extensive area under cultivation I'd seen since the grove outside Khaliun in Govi-Altai. Shortly before reaching the guanz, I had filled my drinking bottle at an artificial channel that had been cut from the Ider and crossed the road to irrigate this garden.

Rain clouds had blown in during my lunch and the weather was now cool. Later that afternoon, a thundershower threatening, I took shelter in a tumbledown wooden corral beside a house that appeared to be abandoned. As I sat snugly watching the rainfall, though, a herdsman rode by in the direction of the house, then repassed before my view wearing a slicker.

About 7:15 that evening, as I was crossing the Khüren Tal (Dark-Brown Steppe), a wide plain where the Ider Gol bends to the east toward the Selenge, I saw my first airborne plane of the hike. The modest size and altitude suggested a domestic craft, though it did not have the color of the MIAT (Mongolian Airlines) fleet. It was flying east, in the direction of Ulaanbaatar. If the airport at Tosontsengel to the immediate east, a popular fueling stop for MIAT planes traveling from the western aimags to the capital, serves other aircraft as well, the plane may have landed there first.

In the valley at the end of the Khüren Tal, the road diverged, the right branch steering toward Tosontsengel on the Ider, the left, Mörön by way of Tsagaan Uul. Two vehicles entered the first branch just before I arrived at and discovered the fork. Had I come fifteen minutes earlier, I might have hitched a ride and toured Tosontsengel and some of the scenic attractions in the area. I had only a liter of water left and did not know where the next water source on my road was. I also wanted to buy more ninety-three grade gasoline, which I had been told was available at Tosontsengel, and to call Enkhjargal before her next run to Beijing regarding our plans for meeting in Mörön. Finally, I was beginning to see the advisability of a half, or even full, day's rest.

I walked up the right-hand road leading to the town for at least three quarters of an hour without encountering any more vehicles. About 9:30 I pitched my tent on the back side of a small hill near the road, intending to try to hitch a ride in the morning. As I might have known, though, the next day I would end up waiting only a brief time for a vehicle before cutting across the valley to the other, Tsagaan Uul road. And so the irony continued: a foot journey, conceived as a way of slowing down, a crusade against the tyranny of speed, conducted with all dispatch.

After dark it began to rain. I got out of the tent to put stakes down on either side of my flysheet, making it taut, and brought my pack inside. Lying there with webs of lightening flashing above the hills in the vicinity, I returned to the petition I had repeated in the stove crisis that morning, making a frame around the day: "Jesus, son of David, have pity on me!" My tent, with its metal poles was in an exposed, elevated place, and the rocky hill itself might attract and conduct a bolt. After the storm passed, I became more conscious of an aching in the lower half of my tired legs.

ॐ

Rising early, I heard from opposite sides of the valley two songs, a herder's and a hoopoe's. The first, which came from a homestead across the valley from my camp, may have been a gingo, an anthem sung daily while leading the horse slowly around the hitching post in the final weeks before Naadam. Gingos are believed to inspire horse and rider to their best performance.[29] The second song was much nearer at hand. Just before I broke camp, a hoopoe alighted close by on a stone ledge, its alert head facing the general region of the sunrise, as if it were eager to plunge into the bright new day. Instead of continuing to moan out its soothing name, it began emitting a short rasping sound as soon as I saw it. Like other artists, it seems, the hoopoe requires retirement and self-effacement in the creation of beauty. The bird is said to resemble a giant pink, black, and white butterfly when it takes flight.[30] Not knowing this at the time, I did not see the butterfly when it winged away.

I am back out on the road to Tosontsengel, waiting in vain for the glint of an approaching vehicle to appear down the valley, when a truck coming from the opposite direction stops. Several men, one very Slavic in appearance but speaking Mongolian with the others, disembark. Thirty kilometers is the consensus on the distance to the next water stop on the Mörön road, too far to attempt on what is left in my bottle. When they offer me a half-liter of water, though, I accept it and am once again on my way, crossing the field toward the Mörön road.

Bypassing a second chance that morning to visit Tosontsengel when another, intersecting road turns up, I have soon gained the quiet rural road that leads up the narrow valley of the Khürdetiin Khooloi. The air, slightly chilled from last night's rain, is filled with the song of larks and a delicious herbal scent. The wet ground is crowded with grasshoppers. My route today will take me through the Bulnain Nuruu, part of the larger Khangain and, as I will realize much later, on the border between Zavkhan and Khövsgöl Aimags. The change in topography is welcome after the three days of wide, flat land in the Ider valley and Khüren Tal. After entering the Khooloi, I pass a burial mound of stones somewhat smaller than those I am used to seeing. It is enclosed by a square of stones buried up to their tops.

After not seeing anyone for a few hours, I met a middle-aged herdsman in a deel driving a cattle-drawn wagon up a parallel road. We sat down to talk. I was anxious to get off my feet, for a slight catch or jabbing sensation had developed in my right knee. My roadside companion expressed unfeigned, child-like delight in our chance meeting. His lively, cheerful manner put me in mind of Wordsworth's type of the contented, hearty, virtuous peasant fostered by the natural setting he has grown up in:

> Fields, where with cheerful spirits he had breathed
> The common air; hills, which with vigorous step
> He had so often climbed; which had impressed
> So many incidents upon his mind
> Of hardship, skill or courage, joy or fear;
> . . . .
> Those fields, those hills—what could they less? had laid
> Strong hold on his affections, were to him
> A pleasurable feeling of blind love,
> The pleasure which there is in life itself. (65-69, 74-77)[31]

Were the siblings he told me about who had moved to Ulaanbaatar as happy and healthy as he? Before we parted he urged me to visit his family's guanz in a ger not far down the road.

When the Khürdetiin Khooloi widened, I noticed an unusual pyramidal concrete ovoo atop a hill on the opposite side of the valley. Arriving at the ger-guanz, I ordered my usual bowl of lavsha, a pan of which already stood prepared on the stove. It was the first time I had set foot inside a ger since my return visit to the home of Tsetsegsüren, Boldsaikhan's cousin, two weeks before. My host, a thirty-three-year-old man named Bayarbat (Happiness Strong), resembled the man I met on the road and may have been a cousin. He was shirtless and shoeless and wore lavender slacks. Two young men were playing cards at a small table when I entered the ger. The illustration on the deck was the same U.S.-currency, Ben Franklin face that I saw on the two sizes of playing cards in the billiards hall at Tseel. Also present were three girls aged about eight to ten.

Later, Bayarbat's wife, Baigalmaa, and a man named Bold-Erdene (Steel Jewel) with two boys arrived on a motorbike. She was dressed in a silver-blue silk blouse, dark slacks, and boots, he in a dark-blue woolen deel, trilby hat, and boots. The quanz had been in operation for one year. In interviewing my host and hostess after the meal, I was told that the area was called Shumuultai Khüree (With Mosquitoes District) and that the pyramid-shaped, concrete ovoo I had seen that afternoon was known as Dund (Middle of) Shumuultai Khüree. An ovoo ceremony had been held at the monument seven or eight years before.

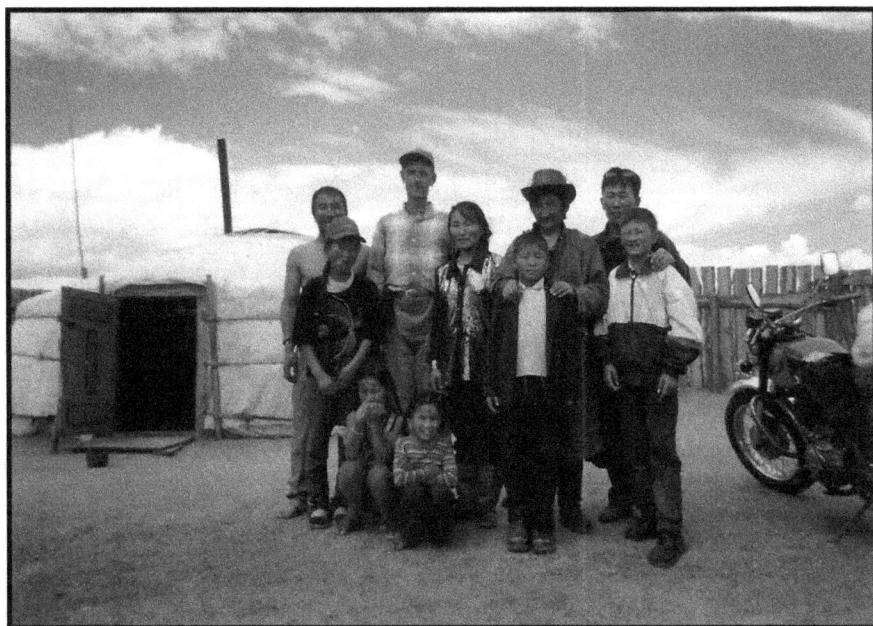

38 - The author with Bayarbat (left), Baigalmaa, and company at ger-guanz

The sky gradually became overcast, wrapped in white and gray cumulous clouds, and a cool wind blew as I made the ascent from the guanz to Khalzan Sogootiin Davaa. Sitting at the pass, I was struck by the sight of a Siberian larch forest on the adjacent hills' slopes, the turning towards a northern clime I had first noticed when in view of Altai town. The trees' sudden appearance here was appropriate for a pass at the entrance to Khövsgöl Aimag, the most heavily wooded in Mongolia. Only twenty years before, almost forty percent of its total area had been covered by forests.[32]

That I was about to enter my third and final aimag, the name of which I had used since the Gobi to answer the inevitable question from locals about my destination, was entirely unappreciated at the time. Khalzan Oogootiin was indeed another Simplon Pass; like Wordsworth crossing the Alps, I had reached the long-anticipated moment without knowing it. Though aimag boundaries were not indicated on my 1:500,000 scale map, they were on the cut-off section of the 1:2,500,000 that I also occasionally consulted. How ironic to have missed this milestone when, instead of the journey-in-progress, I was focused on making progress and reaching my journey's end.

☙ ☙ ☙

Map of Khövsgöl Aimag

Chapter 6
Rain, Rivers, and Wrestlers: Khövsgöl Aimag from the Border to Mörön

. . . The cottagers,
Who ministered with human charity
His human wants, beheld with wondering awe
Their fleeing visitant. (254-257)[1]

Most of the descent of about fifteen kilometers down the wide gully of a creek to the village of Sogoot (With Doe) was made in the company of a swarm of black flies; along with more trees, the cooler and wetter climate of this northern aimag also meant new pests. I thus saw my first Khövsgöl landscapes through the green fog of a mosquito-screen hood. Near Sogoot, a truncated rainbow appeared in the sky as rain clouds threatened. I passed, then walked back to, a charming little guanz, a painted wood-frame house with one or more small larches in front. It was a considerable advance, in outward appearance, at least, from previous establishments, beginning with the converted animal-hides warehouse in Altai village. I would order a meal and, if the rain persisted, ask about lodging. The rain cloud that was at my back looking, like most fears, less formidable when I faced it, however, I decided to turn around again.

At the edge of the village I crossed the creek to a spot that seemed relatively isolated but upon reaching it discovered a ger in my immediate neighborhood back on the other side. It had been hidden by a low hummock or fold in the terrain. Oh well, then, let the whole village stop by for a chat; I wasn't going to look for another camping spot tonight. My first visitor, who came as I was in a reclining position testing a spot for my tent, was a girl from the nearest ger on my side of the creek. Shortly after, two young men, flagged, no doubt, by my now assembled tent, made their way over from the road on a motorbike.

Bilgee wore sunglasses and Western clothes and did most of the talking. He introduced his companion, Damdinsüren, a big fellow dressed in a deel, as a champion of the local Naadam wrestling competition. Having resigned myself to social interaction this evening, I decided to make an opportunity of necessity and ask if I might interview them.

Twenty-nine, Bilgee lived with his parents and siblings in Sogoot. "The life of cattle-breeders after democracy was very good," he said, "but right now things are difficult because in the tsagaan zud during the last two winters we lost a lot of animals. Also, it's not raining now so there isn't enough grass for them. The grass is yellow and dry."

He mentioned two places of interest in the area: Khüree Asga (District Rock) and the Gav, a long fissure in the ground left by an earthquake in 1905. I had read about the second attraction, known as the Bulgan Fault, and planned to take it in on my way out of Sogoot the next morning. Running nearly four-hundred kilometers, slicing across northern Zavkhan Aimag to the west, it is supposedly the world's longest active fault line. Measuring between 8.2 and 8.7 on the Richter Scale, the quake left fissures sixty meters deep and more than ten meters across.[2]

Bilgee would celebrate Naadam watching the wrestling on TV and enjoying a meal prepared khorkhog style. Khorkhog is a way of cooking meat using fire-heated stones. The red-hot stones are placed in a lidded pot containing the meat and a little water. Information was available through the newspaper and television; subscriptions and satellite disks were both available here. He remarked that he and his fellow countrymen and women liked "the foreigners who come to do research about our country and its climate," adding, "It would be nice if these people gave us practical advice based on their findings." As far as medical care, there was a doctor at the center of Soogot Brigad. The care was OK. When asked about local anecdotes or legends, he referred laconically to a demon that people said inhabited the area.

Damdinsüren, twenty-eight, lived with his father and seven brothers and sisters at a place named Khökh Tenger (Dark-Blue Sky). He said his life as a herdsman was "very good," but when I asked him pointedly how many animals he had lost in the tsagaan zud he said, "So many. We had one-hundred cows; now we have five." Mongolians typically withhold the truth if the standard, sanguine replies to questions like "How are you?" don't cover the actual facts. For Naadam, he would go to the sum center at Tsetserleg to take part in the wrestling competition.

> "I'll try to win," he said.
> "Is it difficult?"
> "Yes."
> "How many wrestlers will compete?"
> "One hundred and twenty-eight."

Following Bilgee and Damdinsüren's visit, a girl from the neighboring ger across the creek came carrying a liter bottle of juice and a kettle of tea. I accepted the juice, pouring it into my drinking bottle, but, as I had no cup, arranged to stop by for tea in the morning. Finally, a young couple, the wife bearing her tea kettle, and another man showed up. I learn that two American travelers passed through Sogoot recently in the direction of Telmen. The woman is about to set off for her ger for cups when I decide things have gone far enough. I was only joking when I said, "Let the whole village stop by"! I manage to buy myself off with a pledge to try to come to the couple's ger for tea in the morning. The two leave on their motorbike, the wife, tea kettle in hand, seated behind, and the man walks away.

Before turning in I witnessed an extraordinarily beautiful sunset: orange, pink, light blue, and gray spread on and around two bands of cumulous cloud. To use the jurisprudential metaphor, it was the first of many occasions in this aimag that would gradually redistribute the weight dragging the "endurance" pan in the scales of my experience of the hike to create a more just balance with the "enjoyment" one.

I hadn't slept well when I got up early to bathe in private. Rain had fallen briefly after I turned in and the night had been cold. After my ablutions in the icy stream, I was forced to lie down in my sleeping bag to warm up before proceeding to pack. It was almost mid-July, but the town with the lowest recorded temperature in Mongolia by that time— Tosontsengel at -52.9 degrees Celsius in 1969[3] —was only about sixty-five kilometers away. Striking my tent and tumbling everything into my pack, I hurried with aching fingers across the stream to the ger, where, fortunately, I had promised to stop for morning tea. A short, attractive, middle-aged woman admitted me. Her name, I soon learned, was Choijiljav Oyun. Besides her daughter, Khulan, the girl who had brought juice and a kettle of tea to my camp, two other women were inside. Oyun's elderly mother, Sodnompil, and a sister, Oyuntsetseg (Wisdom Flower), a beautiful teenager who was not much older than the daughter, promptly dressed when I came in.

The interior of the ger was simple and, instead of being mounted on the usual circular wooden pallet, rested on the bare earth. The small tin stove was stoked with split wood, however, a major improvement over the dried brush I was accustomed to seeing used in Govi-Altai. Oyun and Sodnompil served tasty homemade brown bread with the milk tea.

"Will you take our picture?" they ask after breakfast. With much ado, the two arrange themselves in their best deel, one of deep green silk for the daughter, brown silk patterned with large gold medallions for her mother. The group poses in front of the ger. I request an interview of Oyun.

39 - Oyun (far right), daughter, Sodnompil, and Oyunstetseg in Sogoot

She was born in Nuur (Lake) Brigad in Telmen Sum of Zavkhan Aimag. Her parents were among the founders of Sogoot Brigad, and her father, two older brothers, and a younger brother also lived in the area. Like the wrestler Damdinsüren, she, along with her mother, brothers and sister, and the children, would be going to Tsetserleg for Naadam. Oyun gave me a somewhat different report from Bilgee's about the availability of medical care. It was difficult for locals to get proper treatment, although her case was an exception, she said, without making it clear why. The medical staff were probably personal friends of hers.

A persistent question at the back of my mind during this visit— "What have you done with the men?"—is only partially answered by the arrival of a middle-aged representative of the male sex during the interview: he is one of Oyun's brothers. My visit at the Ger of the Family of Women concluded, Oyun and Khulan led the way to my next social engagement that morning, tea at the ger of the young couple who had also brought their kettle to my camp.

He was standing outside holding his infant child as we approached. My brief perfunctory visit unexpectedly yielded one tantalizing bit of information about the area, whether from its history or folklore, or a combination of both, I haven't been able to learn. During our chat indoors, my host told me—in spite of his wife's attempt to silence him with the words "Don't tell what you're unsure about!"—that Genghis Khan had once fought at Khüree Asga, gaining followers among the local people. This was one of the two local places of interest mentioned by Bilgee.

On my way once again, having faithfully discharged my social obligations in Sogoot, I walked down the road past the delgüür and a few other small buildings in town in the bright clear morning. Before leaving the village precincts, I was forced to make one more ger stop, this time for the humbler purpose of asking directions to the road to Tsagaan Uul. The horrendous episode when I lost the road to Taishir outside of Altai was no doubt still fresh in my mind.

After a brief consultation with a man outside this ger, I set off on the road that ran east along the northern base of the Bulnain Nuruu, the range I had crossed the day before. In my preoccupation with finding the road, I failed to recognize any traces of the Bulgan Fault trench, which, according to my 1:500,000 scale map, also followed the base of the Bulnain. A ditch that I remember briefly scrutinizing was probably a dry gully created by seasonal run-off.

Someone is calling me. I sit down to rest while the man who gave me directions catches up. He points out the way again. Still not clearly understanding, I ask him to walk to the road with me and he complies. It is much farther than I expected. In our steady stride—he is probably in his late twenties—one, two kilometers soon separate us from the road we were on. I begin to grow uneasy. What if this is a trick? He stops, takes out his small field-glass piece and scans the landscape around. As we continue, I half expect at any moment to see his arm reach around from behind and to feel a steel blade in my belly. Trying not to betray any alarm, I slow my pace a little to keep him abreast and more fully in view. Another kilometer or so passes. No, we are getting too close to an enclave of gers up ahead. If he were planning to murder and rob me, he would have done it by now. Thus does the guileless plain-dealing Mongol herdsman send back, like a clean mirror, a true picture of the modern Westerner's complicated, mistrustful mind. It was the classic wilderness experience of self-confrontation, that walk with my guide in the corner of Shavar Türüü (Mud Ear of Grain) valley. Before he continued on alone to the gers, I gave him 3,000 tögrögs, about $2.75, and asked his name. "D. Gunaabazar," he told me. Of all the villages and towns I visited, and would visit, on my journey, Sogoot easily bears the palm as the friendliest. God's blessings on this gentle community at the entrance to Khövsgöl.

Coming over the hills, I startled two mounted huntsmen, who rode by carrying rifles. A solitary foreigner walking this lonely road is not exactly an everyday occurrence. I descended to a road bordered by a telephone line at the edge of the wide Jarantain (Sixty) Gol valley. The upper end of the valley, where I am headed, is known as Khurimtiin Tal (Wedding Steppe).

During this afternoon's walk I would leave Tsetserleg and enter Tsagaan Uul Sum. These and a third sum, Bürentogtokh, which I would pass through on my way to Mörön, were the focal areas of present-day Khotgoid culture in Mongolia. The Khotgoids were a tribe occupying the area between Lakes Khövsgöl and Uvs to the west. Chingüünjav, leader of the mid-18th century rebellion against the Manchus, was a Khotgoid prince.[4] I would later visit the ruins of his fortress near Mörön.

I entered an area of numerous freshwater ponds, pools, and streamlets bordered by tall, lush vegetation. It was a new environment, my first bona fide riparian landscape on the hike. Feeling very tired and not knowing when I would find water again today, I decided to rest and cook an early dinner on the bank of a scenic pond. Two ducks repeatedly dove under water to hide whenever my approach to the water's edge or movements on the sand bar alarmed them. But the rain that created this lovely setting soon threatened to spoil my picnic. I had to hurriedly eat my pot of soup and pack up for fear of my gear getting soaked. The rain dissipated shortly after I was once again on my way.

Now the road, leaving the row of telephone poles, bore left across a wide newly constructed bridge over a small river, probably the Tes. This is my most dreaded scenario. Which route do I take? The road's direction is not in line with the next wayside point on my GPS, but the roadless way along the telephone poles, which is almost sure to lead to Tsagaan Uul, will be more difficult walking. I decide on the latter. With the benefit of hindsight, I would have been better off taking the road. I was navigating too precisely and should have read the wayside point beyond the next one.

Those varieties are lost sight of at a little distance, at a little height of thought. One tendency unites them all. The voyage of the best ship is a zigzag line of a hundred tacks. See the line from a sufficient distance, and it straightens itself to the average tendency.[5]

Just beyond this point I noticed a large flock of white and gray birds somewhat larger than a pigeon scattered on the adjacent hillside. Without knowing it, I was looking at my first specimens of a waterfowl that would later become very familiar on the hike: seagulls. They were probably black-headed gulls, a species common on Lake Khövsgöl.

I soon realized that I had landed myself on the wrong side of the river. Ahead the telephone poles veered left across it, standing amid the channels with the impunity of flamingos balanced on one leg. I would have to wade across after removing my boots and socks. But with the active stream distributed over two or three channels, the water was only knee-deep at most.

The rain had started up again when, stopping at a ger on the other side of the river, I confirmed from an elderly woman in the yard that the telephone line indeed went to Tsagaan Uul. As I was passing the ger next door, a woman standing with a girl in the doorway motioned me inside.

"It is raining," she said.

"I'll be all right," I replied and kept on with never a hitch in my stride.

The rain was falling more heavily when I passed two gers soon after. Two persons stood outside, one of them watching me go by. The rain increased and the cold wind, rising, drove the drops sharply into the back of my neck and left side. Glancing over my left shoulder occasionally, I saw an even darker shade of the blank gray wall that almost completely ringed the horizon round. My hands ached with the cold.

I was unprepared for rain like this, never having witnessed a protracted summer rainstorm in Mongolia. Still, I kept going. Once, when the wind picked off my ball cap and hurled it, rolling, along the ground, I turned to face the wind and sky, shouting, "So, what is going on?" A timely thunderclap boomed in answer. I kept on. My clothes and gear became soaked, making camping out tonight out of the question. With evening approaching and little prospect of encountering a ger on this solitary roadless route, I began to think I might die from exposure if I didn't turn around and retrace my steps to the last ger. Turn back? I couldn't afford to lose so much time. Besides, how unmanly! . . .

Recognizing my mania for what it was, I forced myself to stop and go back. Walking more rapidly against the wind and rain than I had with it, I reached the two gers in about forty minutes. I would learn on the following day that at the point where I turned around, I was still about four kilometers, or an hour's walk, from the next gers. My destination-driven approach to the journey was not only costing me many rewarding experiences; it was proving dangerous.

The woman at the first ger directed me to the second one, and I was promptly admitted. I shivered so violently as I stood before the stove that I could hardly hold and drink from the bowl of tea I was served. I removed my boots and, pouring the water into the metal catch basin, set them near the stove. Two short clotheslines had been rigged up between the two bagana, or central posts supporting the roof, using a pair of all-purpose orange deel sashes. Soon my socks, shirt, rain jacket, and, later, sleeping bag and half-mattress were hanging up on display for the family to see.

My hostess is Pürevsüren, a pleasant-featured and slightly stout matron. There was also an elderly woman, Pürevsüren's mother or mother-in-law, wearing a tattered deel; a teenage girl, who, I was told, attended school in Tsagaan Uul; a boy named Bayaraa in his early teens, whom I had met out herding earlier that day; and several children. A small kid goat brought in out of the storm was secured by a cord on the other side of the room.

To my dismay, the precious hearth flame soon began to flicker and fade, and my hostess was nowhere in sight. I risked the impropriety of suggesting to one of the family members present that I stoke the stove myself. Then Pürevsüren returned and rigged another clothesline for me, behind where I stood by the stove desperately trying to make my skimpily clad 1.8-meter (5-foot, 10 ½-inch) frame inconspicuous.

An elderly gentleman came in and sat down near me on the metal box used for storing firewood. We conversed a little. The rain stopped. I declined Pürevsüren offer of dinner, saying I had already eaten. At this point, it was about the only way I had of not being intrusive. Nonetheless, she served me chips of aaruul, the dried milk curds,[6] which I spread with khailmag, a yellowish paste made by adding flour to boiling cream and sprinkled with sugar.

During my long vigil that evening, most of which was spent with my eyes bent on the stove, I got a close-up view of the process of making tea: Put water in a large basin and set it on the stove to boil; toss in bits of dried tea leaves; add salt, pour in milk, and stir. More interesting, though, was the sight, stolen across the ger, of the grandmother rolling her own with the leaves of an old coverless book. I would have liked to know what creative use the hard front and back covers were put to. At bedtime, my vestal-like watch over, I spread out my now dry mattress and sleeping bag on the floor and, tucking my still wet passport under the mattress, lay down to sleep. More people arrived, but after so much walking outdoors and standing indoors today, I had little trouble falling asleep.

श्

July 11th, the one-month anniversary of my setting out from the southern border and the first day of the national sports festival of Naadam, I rise early with the first light showing through the toono, or circular skylight. My boots are a little damp inside, but my woolen socks are virtually dry. The family is soon stirring. Today they will go to Tsagaan Uul, Pürevsüren's hometown and the administrative center of the sum. I ask Bayaraa if he will be in the horse race, betraying my ignorance of Naadam customs: Participants are normally between the ages of five and nine.

For breakfast my hostess prepares the delicious gambir, or fried sweetened bread, that Boldsaikhan used to make for us. This is served with milk tea and more of the tasty aaruul chips with khailmag and sugar. I include a few items from my gift bag, a wooden pencil, matchbook sewing kit, and pair of plastic sunglasses that might be useful for taking in the athletic events, with the 5,000 tögrögs that I give as a freewill offering for the night's lodging.

"I almost died!" I can't resist adding, somewhat melodramatically, in thanking my hostess before departing. My experience as a guest at Pürevsüren's ger at Khujirt (Salt Marsh), the name of the immediate locality, provided further support for a working hypothesis of mine: Pick a ger at random anywhere in rural Mongolia for requesting food and a night's lodging and you are sure of being received hospitably. Alexander Michie, who traveled by camel caravan from China to Russia across Mongolia in the mid-19th century, wrote, "The cardinal virtue of the Mongol tribes is hospitality, which is as freely exhibited to perfect strangers, as to neighbors, from which a return might be expected."[7] James Gilmour, a missionary in Mongolia from 1870 to 1885, explains that "intercommunication is difficult, and is carried on mostly by verbal messages conveyed by chance travelers. . . . A traveler is in some sense a newspaper and a postman."[8] It seems that rural Mongolians' access to information through newspapers, radio, and TV, repeatedly mentioned in my interviews with locals, had not yet eroded their celebrated hospitality.

The morning was cold, windy, and overcast, and I took the half-dozen or so kilometers along the telephone poles to the next gers with the hood of my jacket up. I crossed patches where my boots plucked up the skin of the earth in wet clayey blocks. As I neared the hill at the end of the plain, I saw a flock of about two dozen demoiselle cranes in flight. Approaching a ger settlement, I inquired of a friendly mounted herdsman about the location of a spring and the road to Tsagaan Uul. Not finding the spring amid the herd of grazing yaks he pointed to, I climbed the slope of the hill to one of the gers to get second directions. One or two of a group of children at play near the ger conducted me to the door, where a comely young wife invited me in for tea.

Her year-old child was inside the simply furnished ger, and in the course of my visit she dressed baby in a tiny brown deel for the holiday. I noticed the customary wall apron with pockets for toothbrushes, bars of soap, and other toiletries hanging in its usual place to the immediate left of the door as one enters. Near it on the floor before the first bed along the wall was the herder's leather tackle. My delicious tea, which appeared to contain an extra measure of milk, was served with bread slices with öröm, the cream made from a boiled mixture of milk and flour, and a cup of sugar for sprinkling over the cream. Like a lot of those who extended hospitality to me on this trip, she was pleased to have an English teacher in Ulaanbaatar as her guest. Teaching is one of the esteemed professions in Mongolia, though the deplorably low salaries of native teachers at all educational levels belied this fact.

I wished her a "happy holiday" before taking my leave. She handed me from the clothes dresser at the back of the ger a new shirt, still in its store packaging, and offered wrapped hard candy and a cache of dried cheese wedges as well. I had to decline the nice shirt and all but two pieces of cheese, explaining that I couldn't afford the additional weight. I gave her a potpourri of scented, colored wood chips in a small net bag and two-hundred tögrögs. Outside the ger I asked her and a young woman who had dropped by if some stone posts beside the road marked an ancient burial site, but they didn't know. I would pass several spots with upright stones and one Bronze Age khirigsüür that morning. I was well down the road when the two women called out to me to stop. "What is this bag of wood chips used for?" my hostess wanted to know. The question didn't seem to warrant detaining me in this way until she added, "Is it for soup?"

The road proceeded through a much smaller valley at roughly a right angle to the line of telephone poles I had followed down on the plain. Still in pursuit of the elusive spring, I stopped at a ger sporting a satellite dish and a small windmill. The white dishes had become a fairly common sight during the past few days, but windmills to generate the electrical power for them were a novelty. A short man who wore an amused puckish expression on his face appeared with several youths in the doorway and escorted me to the local water hole, a shallow-walled pit incised in the black earth.

The pass at the end of the valley, like the one before Sogoot, was wooded with larch. This time, however, the ovoo itself was of wood; the dead tree branches and trunks of saplings stacked pyramid-wise would be typical of ovoos in Khövsgöl. I found a pleasant sequestered spot on the spongy forest floor and boiled a pot of noodles in the event of rain that night. The springy moss-topped soil was an effect of the accumulation of rain and melted snow above an iron-hard permafrost block. Mongolian forests contain the world's southernmost permafrost, a forty to four-hundred-meter deep layer of perennial ice left by the Ice Age.[9] Because the ice layer also prevents trees from sending stabilizing roots deep into the soil, some of the larches stood at tilted angles. A further indication of the underground ice sheet may have been the two salt lakes that I would pass that afternoon. Unable to drain into the soil, the salts in the rainwater and melted snow accumulate on the surface and gradually create salty soil;[10] the lakes were apparently created by annual run-off over such soil.

I experienced one of the happiest moments of the trip till then as I descended the pass across the hilly undulating plain. After Tsagaan Uul, just thirty-five kilometers away, there was Mörön, which I was now hopeful of reaching by the day prearranged with Enkhjargal. The sun had finally come out again, and in the quarter of the sky that the wind was proceeding from were white, instead of the earlier dark-gray, cumulous clouds. The large gray cloud that could be seen over my left shoulder didn't bother me.

I rested again in view of lovely Tunamal (Transparent) Nuur, the largest lake to appear along my route so far. The white hills on the farther shore were variegated with patches of larch. Except for one or two gers near the right edge of the lake, there were no signs that anyone was—or had ever been—here. This struck me as strange for such a beautiful setting, even with the saltwater, on a summer's day—and on a holiday at that. But Mongolia, I then recalled, is a large country with a very small population. In a region almost three times the size of France,[11] there were about two and a half million people. Besides, Naadam is traditionally observed in towns and cities, and camping out was not a popular form of recreation in a nation of mostly tent-dwellers.

Soon after passing Tunamal, I reached another salt lake, Gashuun (Bitter) Nuur, which was smaller and lay nearer the road. An enormous flock of small black-and-white ducks and a covey of white waterfowl flew up from the shore as I approached. There was also a small flock of honking ruddy shelducks. The male sports a black neckband during the

40 - Tunamal Nuur

mating season,[12] but I am too late to observe this, for there are several ducklings swimming amid the group. The bird is also known as the "lama duck" because its rusty brown color and paler head suggest the garb of Buddhist monks of the Yellow Hat sect.

I have come to the lakeshore not to watch birds, however, but to shave, having skipped this part of my morning routine as a guest at Pürevsüren's ger. I couldn't have chosen a worse place for this. Had I been more proficient in Mongolian, I would have been warned off by the lake's descriptive name. The saltwater seemed to fortify the hair sprouts on my face, the way a saline-based fertilizer might garden plants, making them harder to cut. At the same time the cold water made it difficult to form lather with my bar of hand soap, and as soon as I did manage to lather up a little the cold wind coming off the lake dried my face. With the wind also creating waves, I had to waltz on the shore to get a cupful of water without submerging a boot. After futilely raking my face for a while with the cheap razor I'd gotten at Altai market, I returned to the road, glad to have my bitter experience at Bitter Lake behind me.

I kept up a stiff pace, in spite of aching tiredness in my legs, well into the evening. The tyranny of speed that I had intended, crusader-like, to conquer, seemed more established in me than ever. My solitary walk—

even the road was unoccupied today—eventually brought me within the compass of several scattered gers about 10:30. I found a camping spot in the fields as far as possible from neighbors on both sides. The wind had finally stopped and the pursuing gray clouds had decided not to precipitate in rain today.

July 12th, Enkhjargal's birthday and the second day of Naadam, I wake jubilant under a clear sky. I am succeeding in my enterprise! I will reach the Russian border! Who would have thought it possible? And I will get to Mörön by the 17th, in time to meet my sweetheart there. As I begin preparing for departure, however, I notice a soreness in my left ankle. Then I remember the unusually loud popping sound it gave out when I rotated my foot while lying in the tent last night. Well, the soreness is bound to pass after a bit.

The pain increased, however, as I walked to Tsagaan Uul, which appeared after a turn in the road. I begrudged even these few kilometers, knowing that I should not be walking on what felt like a sprained ankle. In fact, I had a budding case of tendonitis, as I would find out much later. It would have been difficult to stay and rest at my camp, though, with less than a liter of water left and a good halting place so near.

I passed a sign bearing the name of the town and, outdoing the sign I had seen at the entrance to Telmen, an illustration. At an outlying filling station I got the standard "baikhgüi" reply when I asked about the ninety-three grade gas that I had put off getting at Tosontsengel to save time. Had I not been in such a hurry but taken at least a half-day's rest there, I might not have been forced now to make do with both the stove-clogging seventy-six grade and a game leg. It was the first major reckoning on a trip that I had been consistently pursuing in a manner contrary to my set purpose: learning not to rush. I was told by the attendant that there was a hotel in town.

Inquiring of some of the many pedestrians in the streets and lanes of a residential district about the location of a guanz, I bore right, passing the high white-washed wall of the Naadam stadium. The top of the posts in some of the board palisades in the neighborhood were hewed into ornamental spheres, a novel architectural flourish. As in Tseel, the low-lying residential area was dominated by an "acropolis" with plastered public and administrative buildings, here white or light yellow in color.

The consensus about the best quanz seems to be one in a row of kitchen gers erected in the shadow of the stadium wall to serve the holiday crowd. The felt walls are rolled partway up for better ventilation, exposing the wooden lattice work. Two or three tables with the conventional short square ger stools are set up on the grassy earth inside. On the stove in the middle is a large basin of mutton soup made with long translucent rice noodles, called püntüüz, and potatoes—French fries cut with serrated edges like the packaged frozen variety sold in U.S. supermarkets. I was served a similar dish at the guanz before Dötiin Davaa in Govi-Altai.

Other guests come in as I eat, reading *A Sentimental Journey*. A dog outside sticks its head through the lattice to sample the potato salad from a basin in the kitchen area. The cook quickly shoos it away and moves the pan further inside the ger. The cost for two bowls of soup, each with a slice of bread, is 1,000 tögrögs, less than a dollar.

Being told the hotel was closed because the proprietor was away—though "away" turns out to mean "not on the premises"—I limped into the stadium. There was no admission fee. Small tents with beverages and snacks spread out on the ground in front ran for a short distance along the inside of the wall on either side of the entrance. Beyond the tents on the right side was a two-tiered pavilion flanked by a short segment of bleachers. A row of spectators sat out of the sun on the first level. Seated behind a green wooden railing on the second tier was a smaller group, which included the announcer. It was a day for flags. On the ridge of the green metal roof flew three small ones, a blue with two reds on either side of it. Several meters in front of the pavilion, the red and blue Mongolian flag waved atop a tall larch pole, and at its base were planted two red and two blue flags.

Hundreds of spectators, dressed in deels or Western clothing about equally, were seated on the four-tiered bleachers that lined the inside of the wall across the stadium from the pavilion. More sat on the grass in two semicircles that marked the immediate central wrestling field. In the wall of the stadium directly opposite the pavilion there was a side gate and, next to it, a shed where the wrestlers awaited their turn. Mounted on the shed roof were three large paintings on wood, each illustrating one of the three "manly" sports: a wrestler poised in the ritual eagle dance, a jockey on horseback, and an archer shooting.

Competitions are typically held on the first and second of the three-day festival. I have missed the local horse-racing event, which took place three days before. Such departures from the official days of observance are common in rural Mongolia. I was later told the competitors were divided into five groups, depending on the horses' ages, which ranged from one to six years,[13] each being assigned a certain number of kilometers on the racecourse, which would have been open terrain. The contestants ride barebacked.

But now it's time for the wrestling tournament. I am sitting in the bleachers with the crowd as the first elimination round gets underway. The two wrestlers perform the eagle-imitation dance called the devekh,[14] running with outstretched arms in patterns of short circles to opposite sides of the playing area while a man in the pavilion chants. They are wearing peaked hats, jerseys with no front, blue briefs, and the high-topped leather boots with upturned toes worn by Mongolians year-round. The blue hat and red jersey of one wrestler is countered by the red hat and blue jersey of the other. Prerecorded urtiin duu, or long song, a distinctive alternation of rolling high and low notes faintly resembling a yodel, plays in the background as the men fight. Long song is said to represent the sounds of nature: wild animals, running water, rushing wind.

Two more contestants emerge from the shed and, after the preliminaries, settle down to their bout. One fight is over quickly. To win one must make the other man touch the ground with his back, elbow, or knee. The victor raises his right forearm—normally the entire arm—for the loser to walk under, a ritual called takhimaa ögökh,[15] (to give up the knee joint in wrestling), and stoops before his second, who restores his hat, which was removed before the bout began. The loser dons an ordinary ball cap, the kind that, regrettably, I am wearing. The winner then runs, eagle-dance fashion, around the flagpole before going to the pavilion to receive a handful of granular dried milk curds, a type of aaruul known as khorkhoi (insects) because of its small spherical size and shape. The wrestler tosses some of this aaruul behind him high into the air a few times as he runs back to his second on the sidelines to share some of the granules with him. He then leaves the playing area. One variation on the follow-up ritual I noticed was stopping to honor some of the spectators by handing them granules before leaving.

Since there is no time limit, some of the bouts that afternoon were quite long, one lasting about three-quarters of an hour. There were pauses where contestants stood casually watching the fight going on next to them. Sometimes when the two bent-over figures were locked in a mutually supportive embrace, the second of one of the wrestlers would slap him unceremoniously on the rump to try to speed things up a little.

During intermission between the first and second rounds, I sit quiet and reserved amid the bustling crowd in the bleachers. I am in an ill humor on account of the sore ankle, which may interfere with my plans

144

to reach Mörön by the 17th, if not to get to the Siberian border itself. Children jostling against me on the crowded bench and some occasional light artillery discharged against my person from behind do nothing to improve my mood. Still, the leg injury does seem remarkably well-timed, allowing me to recuperate while taking in a major exhibition of national culture. Before this, I was always back in the States for summer vacation by Naadam.

41 - The Naadam wrestling competition, Tsagaan Uul stadium

By intermission after the second round I have moved to a more remote, less crowded area of the stands. It is time for the closing ceremonies of the horse races. With a shout, one of the five competing groups of young jockeys, led by a mounted man wearing a brown deel and cowboy hat, rides into the stadium from the side gate. Each holds onto the same long rope. Some are wearing a brightly colored, numbered jersey and an ornamented cloth hat, others a ball cap with either a deel or Western style clothes. The group proceeds to the pavilion, where a bowl of milk is taken up and passed around. The man in the brown deel chants a song on the microphone, praising the physical characteristics and merits of the winning horse. The song is performed in a yodeling chant in the manner of long song. In composing it, the singer has at his disposal formulaic passages like the following refrain:

the horse which doesn't stumble over round stones,
which can't be overtaken by the eagle,
which doesn't slip on smooth stones,
which can't be overtaken by its enemies.

Also attended to at this time was the bestowal of prizes on the winning horse. The most common prize at a rural Naadam is a saddle blanket. The horse's owner may give a gift to the jockey later. The man leads the troop, hallooing in chorus, back out of the stadium and another group of riders with their leader enters. The entire procedure is repeated several times, presumably once by each of the five groups of contestants. In some of the groups, the chanting was done by one of the boy jockeys.

By the third elimination round of the wrestling, I was beginning to feel uneasy with the sense of wasted time, so, despite of my wish to see whether a certain late middle-aged fellow named Batchuluun (Strong Stone), who appeared to have many friends in the audience, would prevail, I left the stadium to find the hotel that someone had told me was now open. The Arslan (Lion), or winner of the contest, I later heard, was one Myagmariin (Tuesday's), a student at the Wrestling College in Ulaanbaatar.[16] A drop of water brushed across my face as I passed before the general area of my first seat in the bleachers. A parting shot from my behind-the-back assailant?

I went up the hill and found several delgüürs, where I replenished my supply of fruit-juice mixes, one-minute noodles, macaroni, crackers, chocolate bars, and dried-banana packets. After a brief wait in front of the hotel, I was admitted by the proprietor, a young man just returned from the stadium, into a dark and surprisingly large front lobby. The walls were hung with several huge custom-made paintings, in one of which a woman welcomed the traveler by holding out a bowl of milk with a khadag, the blue silk scarf, draped across her two outstretched arms.

Intensely curious about my trip, my host plies me with questions for several minutes at one of the tables before showing me my room. As the staff are off duty for the holiday, he is attending to me himself. Batsükh (Strong Axe), director of Badral Company, which owns the hotel, is a portly broad-shouldered gentleman with a florid, beaming countenance and closely shaven head. I accompany him up a flight of ancient, creaking stairs painted the same gaudy orange used on woodwork inside gers. The two wooden second-floor hallways, which form a "T," have a quaint antique flavor from the innumerable undulating lines of boards in the wall and floor. We enter a room with a brightly patterned carpet where another young man sits on a sofa watching the end of the two-day wrestling tournament in Ulaanbaatar on television. I follow Batsükh through a doorway into the second, also carpeted, inner room, where I deposit my backpack. There are two beds, a short table spread with a white cloth, another smaller table, and a cushioned stool.

The man in the first room is about to leave, but I invite him to stay until the event is over. Two pairs of contenders remain, including Sükhbat, who was the Arslan of last year's tournament, and Bat-Erdene, winner of an astonishing ten successive tournaments up to last year's. Batsükh joined the man on the sofa and I occasionally interrupted my perusal of *A Sentimental Journey* in the bedroom to ask questions about Naadam. Bat-Erdene falls. So does Sükhbat. A new star blazes in the firmament of the Mongolian wrestling empyrean: Ösökhbayar, the Arslan, is now receiving the benediction in the form of a proffered bowl of either airag or milk from President Bagabandi and the First Lady, who are seated in state at the stadium pavilion.

A plate of dinner was brought up to me from the kitchen. Batsükh also surprised me with a mound of dried cheese chips wrapped in two sheets of scrap office paper, the printed side out. Later, sitting up in bed with my book while light scattered sounds of voices and vehicles from the village street below entered through the window, I considered how, if one were ever stuck in rural Mongolia, fate could certainly do worse than the Tsagaan Uul Hotel: a quiet room with good service and a friendly host for 3,500 tögrögs a night, food included. The thought of a few long summer days spent reading in this pleasant retreat complicated my interior debate about whether or not to stay put for a while in order to rest my sore leg.

❧

Up early before the house was stirring, I tested my leg, which had swollen above the ankle, while unsuccessfully trying an outside approach to the row of outhouses in an inner yard of the hotel building; the door to the lobby, which led to the inside route, was still locked. The pain warned me off from walking today. But finding it less when I had laced up my boots and taken more trial steps, I decided to gamble on the leg's being on the mend and the pain going away. If it does persist, I told myself with a sly wink, I will return to the hotel.

My decision, influenced by my desire to see Enkhjargal in Mörön, was reinforced by a further consideration: If I set out today, the anticipation of our meeting will give wings to my feet on the final 130 or so kilometers there, compensating for any possible physical inconvenience. If, on the other hand, I lose the chance of seeing her by recuperating here, my walk to Mörön will be insufferably tedious and probably take longer, even with a sound leg. So my chronic urge to get to Russia was still unsubdued by my present visitation from Justice. Would I come to my senses anytime soon?

I recrossed the same valley I had entered the town through. As the road climbed a hill that jutted into the valley, I could see below on the right a small pretty lake, Ulaan (Red) Nuur, supposedly rich in fish. It was a cool morning with high cirrus clouds. My ankle continued to ache with each step but the pain was bearable.

After passing over the hill, the road rose and fell along hilly terrain in a scenic lonely region. Then the dreaded diverging of telephone poles and road occurred, leaving me uncertain about my course. After deciding to keep to the road, I found the road itself, in monstrous, hydra fashion, suddenly forking. Dashdorjyn Natsagdorj in his poem "My Native Land" celebrates a "Country where all may ride and drive at will." (38)[17] The dark side of this peculiarly Mongolian freedom is a maddeningly branching rural road system that is the bane of the unaccompanied foreign traveler. There were virtually no vehicles on the road, the final day of Naadam being generally devoted to socializing and vodka drinking, so I could not consult drivers about the way. Nor was my GPS, which I had bought precisely for this kind of situation, very helpful. The road I had used in creating my landmarks must have been an old one, for I was not headed in the direction of my next two wayside points, though I was on course for the third one. After about two hours, I prayed fervently to Jesus that a vehicle would come and the driver confirm that I was on the right road. With my sore leg, not losing the way had become more critical than ever.

Not long after this, a family in a jeep approached from behind, and the driver stopped to my signal. Yes, this was the road to Mörön. Then, down in the next valley I saw the line of electricity poles I had lost earlier. Inexpressibly relieved, I made sincere vows to the Lord in gratitude for His Providence. With a clearer perception of my folly in setting out this morning, I might have thanked him for His Mercy instead.

Continuing over the same jagged terrain the rest of the day, I finally reached a high pass above the village of Bürenkhaan (Completely King) lying in a beautiful, green, bowl-shaped valley. The elevation of the right-hand peak bordering the pass was 2,192 meters. After making the descent, suspecting that the bed of the stream intersecting the road up ahead was dry, I crossed to the village to inquire about water. It was built largely of logs, like an early colonial settlement in New England. Even the palisades enclosing the houses were of upright logs rather than the usual boards.

A boy directed me to the stream, which flowed through the village. So, it wasn't dry after all. I filled both containers before realizing that I could make my camp beside it downstream. I decided to carry the water with me regardless and, walking northwest past the road until I was out of view of any traffic, pitched my tent in the field close to the stream. It had been my longest day's effort so far, about fifty kilometers. My argument for not remaining in Tsagaan Uul, that I would make better time on my journey, seemed valid.

After a hearty meal of macaroni cooked with some of the cheese chips that Batsükh gave me, I went to wash my pot and spoon in the stream and—wonder of wonders!—found most of the water gone. Wild hypotheses—lunar gravitational pull, nightly operation of a flood gate by the Bürenkhaan Brigad Water Division—flashed through my mind. When I returned to the dribbling creek to take a sponge bath before bedtime, the water had ceased to flow and I had to resort to standing pools that were sinking fast. Revenge by the river god for assuming that the bed was dry at the road?

A boy returning on foot to the village stopped by. He asked several questions but didn't linger. A herd of horses, nervously whinnying, galloped about near my camp. They seemed to regard me as an interloper. A few camels grazed in the distance.

I rose the next morning with dawn richly glowing above the mountains. Later, a full distinct rainbow, with a thinner, hazier echo of it, straddled Bürenkhaan across the plain. In my anxiety about my sore leg, I interpreted the spectacle, with the help of the Biblical passage, as a token of divine reassurance. I also noticed that the swelling above my left ankle had gone down a little.

And I found the stream flowing again! The uncanny erratic flow was given a plausible explanation by an American tourist I met soon afterward: the pattern of recent rainfall in the area of the stream's source, which is apparently in the mountains north of Sangiin Dalai (Treasury Ocean) about thirty kilometers to the southwest. Apparently, rain had fallen there a few days ago and again last night. I could now take my first full bath since my two-bit shower at the Tegsh Hotel in Uliastai ten days before. Heraclitus was right, fortunately.

I am sitting at the pass leading out of the valley a few hours after breaking camp. Sticking to the long upward march in spite of the pain in my ankle has amply rewarded itself, it seems, in one of the loveliest mountain prospects of the trip so far. Under a partly cloudy sky, a steep mountain of pink and light purple descends to a narrow valley with a river twisting through it. Another mountain, of the same color but less steep, stands behind it. In this visual parallel of the double rainbow seen near sunrise, I find a restatement and confirmation of the Heavenly sign. Swelling in broad pools in places, the Delger-Mörön, a name that means "Abundant Large," appears not only wider and deeper than rivers seen before; it is also bordered by trees, now on one side, now the other, in alternating stretches. Another gradation in my march north. The banks of previous rivers were generally treeless.

42 - The valley of the Delger-Mörön

The confluence of the Delger-Mörön and the larger Ider is the beginning of the Selenge link in the earth's fifth longest river system[18] referred to earlier. The ovoo at the pass is a large mound of stones surmounted by a pyramid of sapling trunks, a transitional form between the southern stone and northern timber ovoos on my route. Other new features are the surrounding single-rail log fence and wooden shrine.

Despite the favorable omen in this scenic outlook, the pain in my leg was more acute on the descent. Then, the walk up the winding valley on the level riverside road, a backpacker's dream, was spoiled by the stabbing sensation that accompanied each step. After a few log cabins, apparently designed for tourists, I came to a guanz set up in a ger. I considered stopping, for a light rain had begun. Pushing on, I passed a second guanz in a log house where the proprietor, standing with children in the doorway, beckoned loudly and long.

The trees along the river were aspen interspersed with some small willows. One large shrub with rather small light-green oval leaves and small purple berries was probably a cotoneaster. After the rain passed I made a longer than usual halt, lying in a shady spot near the current flowing swift, wide, and clear. Apart from some of the mountain passes, I could not remember stopping in a more beautiful setting, though I probably made between six and ten stops a day. Later I passed a pair of ruddy shelducks honking their brood of seven ducklings out of harm's way into the middle of the river.

Unlike the scenic hike along the Tuul Gol near Ulaanbaatar that I routinely took in the summer, this river route was unmarred by litter and land development. I was probably about two summers ahead of the contractors, picnickers, and campers. Once, though, while I sat resting beside the road, a jeep stopped and a party of youths with a volleyball came bounding out in my direction. I immediately got up and, giving a few sullen replies to their questions, set off down the road.

Blocked by a cliff at the river's edge, the road ascended steeply to the top of a low mountain. Before me to the east lay a long and wide stretch of the Delger-Mörön valley and there, at the end of its forty-odd kilometer extent, was the miniscule shape of a shining white city. I wept with relief at the sight. That must be Mörön! My long-awaited milestone. Surely, no matter how painful the swelling in my leg becomes, I will be able to cross that final plain.

After the descent, the village of Bürentogtokh across the field on the left presented a picturesque front: a line of low buildings of various colors interspersed with aspens along the river and backgrounded by silver mountains. As I followed the road east after bypassing the town, the late sunlight, focused and trained on the mountains beyond the river by the rain clouds suspended over them, created a dazzling display of subtle, interwoven colors on the barren slopes. One mountain was distinguished from the rest by its predominantly silver tone. The sum district is the site of a group of five deer stones and an associated burial complex.[19]

When I got to within a day's walk of Mörön and could see no gers in the immediate vicinity, I cut across the plain to the river. There was an inviting grove of sheltering aspens, which, however, proved to lie on the opposite bank. Directly across the river lay a quaint pyramidal rock hill. Finding a spot on the bank free of the debris of one or more former ger encampments, I finally set down my pack about 8:30. Some rapids a little upstream made a soothing clangor. There were few insects. I rejoiced at having found a campsite that was practical, sequestered, and scenic.

These were the circumstances, or at least those I was aware of, in my selection of a camping place on the evening of July 14th. A subsequent discovery requires adding another factor unperceived at the time. How could my usual criteria of water availability, privacy, attractive surroundings, and distance to water or a town on the following day alone account for my having chosen to camp, beyond any conscious suspicion of the fact, within a kilometer of the former site of a palace of Mönkh Khan, a grandson and successor of Genghis Khan? The palace had stood on the plain almost directly across the river and in the area behind the pyramid-shaped hill, called Altan Gadas. Had I come 750 years earlier I would have had to pick my way through innumerable gers and buildings forming part of a small city, Erchüü, seasonal capital of half the known world. It is also possible that Altan Gadas was the site of the royal court where William of Rubruck first met with Mönkh Khan and resided in the winter of 1253-54 before accompanying him to Karakorum. Intending the figurative sense of following in his footsteps by distributing the synopsis of the Catholic faith along my route, I may have stumbled upon the literal one as well.[20]

I had read of the site of Erchüü in Arbulag Sum, but since my maps showed only the sum center northwest of Mörön, I didn't know that the river marked the sum's boundary and I placed the site much further north than it actually was. I am forced to assume that the place held a latent magnetism that my long, solitary, ascetic foot journey had made me susceptible to. The spirit inhabiting it or the souls of its former occupants had whispered to me, unusually attuned by now to the Mongolian landscape, beckoning me from the road. A curious incidental detail that later came to light is the meaning of the name Altan Gadas: North Star, the lodestar that guides voyagers. I would learn about the proximity of my camp to the palace site a few days later on a tour by car to historic sites in the Mörön area.

I am off at dawn, my earliest start since the day I reached Uliastai. Helping me rise at the first light were not only my eagerness to get to Mörön, but a wriggling under the tent floor on the spot where my hand lay. The head of a small rodent? While packing, I discovered a toad in my camp, probably the first I'd seen in almost four years in Mongolia. Covered with brown spots, it was a female Siberian sand or Raddes toad, the most common species in Mongolia. The male is a light-green and grayish color.[21] I am going without having eaten a cooked supper last night, for my stove refused to run on the inferior seventy-six grade gasoline I was forced to buy in Tsagaan Uul. My ankle feels worse than ever, but the thought that I will reach Mörön today buoys up my spirits and impels me forward.

The level plain, sprouting clumps of feathergrass, as well as a species of bluegrass, Poa sibirica, was broken by a succession of hills that blocked the view of the city. Soon, however, I was sitting at the top of the last one, eyeing the coveted golden goal. Feeling, with my injured leg, a bit like Moses sighting atop Mount Pisgah the unattainable Promised Land, I thought of a poem that my mother, bedridden a few years before her death, had asked me to find the text of for her. She knew only the opening lines. Without recourse to the internet, I was able to track down the poem, which I seem to remember was a narrative piece by Thomas Babington Macaulay. I recalled how at that time my mother's request suggested to me that she identified with Moses in the poem; some cherished dream was eluding her. And now, it suddenly occurred to me that the dream was the Ph.D. referred to near the end of the autobiographical sketch, apparently a project from her graduate studies in the 1980s, which I discovered among her papers and read at her funeral. "I guess my ultimate goal is for my children to be able to refer to me as 'my mother, the doctor,'" she had written.

As far as any resemblance between my situation and Moses', if the ankle problem posed some threat to my reaching Mörön, I was nonetheless more confident than ever of getting there now. Still, with the pain in my leg at its worst, and other, unexpected obstacles arising on my march this day, it would seem as if Heaven begrudged my attaining the goal. It was easily the hottest day of the trip so far. Breezes visited only occasionally and then very briefly. Although there were plenty of clouds in other quarters of the sky, I had to wait, it seems, until 7:45 pm before the sun was finally obscured for a while. A more formidable foe than the sun, though, was the river.

After crossing the last hill, the road proceeded in a direction well to the right of Mörön. Seeing a few vehicles on other roads to the left, I abandoned the main road to take one of these. Later, a herdsman standing on the roadside confirmed that this was the way to Mörön. Soon after, however, the road ended abruptly at a deep narrow stream channel. Why had the fellow answered "yes"? He couldn't possibly have misunderstood my question. Did he hate foreign tourists? Disgusted, I leapt the channel, hoping to find another road beyond it. Instead, I found a bog which cut me off from the main road when I tried to return to it.

Seeking out the drier patches of ground, I went forward until I had no choice but to slog through the marsh in the direction of some gers along the road. Hot, tired, hungry, wincing with pain at every step, I lost my patience. I wanted to pitch the whole business of the walk and travel book. Mongolia, represented at the moment by one ignorant or malicious herdsman, didn't deserve so much of my time and attention. It was another occasion of serious reappraisal, like that after the incident of the stolen flower samples in Altai and of the lost road on the first day en route to Taishir.

The main road, which I had now recovered, staged another demoralizing deception an hour or two later. After rounding a hill, I saw, to my utter stupefaction and dismay, the road making a long serpentine detour at the base of the hills to the right in order to avoid more streams of the river bottom. I was being led in a half-circle dance around one side of the city, instead of being allowed to walk straight to it. I capitulated, plopping down beside one of these streams. Yet out of my despair, new wisdom arose, for failure is a readier teacher than success.

On Being Somewhere

Pushing for eleven days to get to Mörön,
limping with the town in view the whole of the last day,
I dropped down, defeated, on the grassy bank
of the marshy bottom where the road began
another murderously long meander to avoid the water.

Under the boughs of aspens and gray willows
on the green island across the stream,
a herd of horses, brown, black, and dappled white,
grazed, scratched themselves against the glossy wood,
or stood together resting, tails swishing, in the shade.

Head lying in my elbow's crotch, close to the sod,
I saw Mongolia from a different angle:

detached, luminous, frozen, entire—
horses ranged with interlocking boughs on an island grove,
idle bank of clouds piled in the shimmering blue—
and rested at my deferred destination.

It was my undue insistence on the goal, to the point of neglecting the way, the enjoyment of the scenic landscapes, clean air and water, healthful exercise, society of friendly country folk offered by the journey, that the sore ankle and other hindrances on this day's hike were designed to correct. My leg injury and the bog episode were, in fact, direct consequences of my goal-centered mindset, which drove me to over-exert myself and take shortcuts. Not only was I learning that hurrying to get "somewhere" could, paradoxically, slow one down, I had also discovered that the experience of the journey itself was my true "destination."

The wisdom arrived at in that moment of despair by the road and expressed in my poem was shown by my mother when she realized her health would fail before she could earn the Ph.D. At the end of the short autobiography, after referring to her "ultimate goal" and expressing concern that time is running out, she alludes to a statement of Goethe's to the effect that "the journey is far more important than the arrival." By being more concerned with the journey-in-progress than with making progress on the journey, I could also finally begin to fulfill the mission my mother had inspired me with on the day of the wake: Slow down for the sake of recovering from a motion-centered mindset. That would mean real progress. Maybe all of the times I'd sensed her guidance and protection on the hike were not for the sake of reaching the border after all but for remembering this original healing purpose.

I met with one further obstacle after setting out again: a roadblock and patrol post at the bridge over the Delger-Mörön, the first I had seen on my hike. But no doubt because the earlier impediments had accomplished their purpose, at least temporarily, in a new mental outlook, I was immune to this one and passed through as freely as the prime minister himself, who, incidentally, had visited Mörön within the week, I later heard. I simply kept on walking, twice looking up boldly at the patrol house, past the parked vehicles of other travelers.

An unusually large number of drivers, including motorcyclists, passing me on the road after the bridge stopped to offer me rides, which I turned down. As I neared the city, I met two girls named Binderiya and Tserennadmid, each carrying a bag and offering me several briquettes of aaruul from them. I took one from both bags. The friendly reception I was getting seemed auspicious. At the edge of town, a young woman who stood at the roadside holding an infant invited me over to her ger for tea, but I declined, explaining that I must find the hotel.

I came to a gas station which sold the elusive ninety-three grade. Another young woman whom I asked for directions to the Delger-Mörön Hotel in the central part of town escorted me there. I secured a room with a bathroom that included a sink with running water for 3,500 tögrögs, just over $3.00, per night, meals not included. When I sat down, exhausted, on one of the two beds, I felt like a 19th-century subequatorial explorer just returned to civilization after a long and perilous sojourn in the jungle.

⁂

Chapter 7
A Stage in Mörön

To take to your use out of the compact cities as you pass through,
To carry buildings and streets with you afterward wherever you go,
To gather the minds of men out of their brains as you encounter
them, to gather the love out of their hearts. . . . (stanza 13)[1]

At the Khaan Bank the next morning, July 16th, I found the service counter besieged by a mob in the manner of an Ulaanbaatar concert-hall cloak room after a performance in winter. Many of the patrons appeared to be government employees, for they would hand an official-looking booklet to a woman behind the counter, who, entering information onto a ruled sheet of brown paper, would return it with a modicum of cash. Also behind the counter were two women binding sheaths of tögrögs and putting them in large stacks. Nearer the back, three women worked around a squeaking printer, one of the few mechanical devices I saw in the room.

When I was finally attended to, it was the same story I'd gotten in Altai: I could not withdraw money here because I had opened my account at the bank in Ulaanbaatar. The sequel, too, was the same. I phoned Baigalmaa, whom I again found at her post at the International College, and asked her to notify Tsetsegmaa, the central bank representative, about the problem. When I returned to the bank in the afternoon, I was able to make the withdrawal with little trouble. I had taken one extra precaution this time, though, that may have helped: praying the Joyful Mysteries of the rosary at my hotel room between the two visits.

As I was leaving the telecommunications building after my phone call to Baigalmaa, a tall, alluring young woman whom I had seen inside approached me.

"Are you going to. . . ?" she asked, naming an out-of-town place unfamiliar to me.

"No, I'm resting here in Mörön for now."

"Where are you staying?"

Moral instincts in full vigor after my eleven-day march in the wilds, I felt repelled. "I am staying where I can rest my leg, which is sore," I replied, pointing down at my ankle.

My strategy in making this disclosure, to diffuse the predatory impulse in her by arousing the maternal one, worked. "Oh, I see," she said, smiling.

I limped off, inadvertently headed in the wrong direction to my hotel. In retrospect, I can see that she was probably nothing worse than a canvasser seeking new clients for a local tourist agency. I had forgotten that I was now in one of the prime regions of Mongolia's tourism industry.

According to my hastily made agreement with Enkhjargal over the phone in Uliastai, she was to buy an airplane ticket to Mörön—to be reimbursed by me as a birthday present—and I would try to arrive within thirteen days, by July 17th. If I didn't she was to cancel the ticket. I had come with two days to spare. When I phoned her yesterday evening, she told me she had not purchased the ticket partly because her attendance on a dying relative prevented her from going anywhere at present. Seeing my disappointment, though, she thought over her situation and decided to try to get away for a few days. She told me on the phone today that she'd made arrangements to fly to Mörön tomorrow afternoon. Excellent! I would be at the airport waiting.

Standing on the asphalted east-west thoroughfare down the street from my hotel the following afternoon, I caught a taxi in the form of an old Volga with springy seats. The driver agreed to wait at the airport until my party arrived. The domestic MIAT plane was a little early, though scarcely early enough for me. And now my lovely Mongolian friend, beaming, dressed in a black pants suit, was standing before me, was within my arms again! But who is the elderly lady friend she has brought with her?

"Bill, this is Mary. We met on the airplane."

Beside her stood a Western woman who appeared to be in her late 60s or early 70s, spectacled, sandy-haired, and sporting a leather visor. She was wearing shorts and carried a bulging orange backpack. I invited her to ride with us to the hotel, where she could find lodging. Mary Richards was an American from Traverse City, Michigan on the fingertip peninsula of northern Lake Michigan. Apparently taking her cue from the town's name, she had most American tourists beat by a couple of continents, if not circumnavigations of the globe. Wielding a calling card with the professional title "Professional Bum (Life is an adventure for those with the courage to explore!)," she had already been to Helsinki and St. Petersburg this summer and would visit the Ukraine, Greece, and Paris after Mongolia. But she was no mere "frequent-flyer" customer, and she took the word "traverse" in its earlier sense of "to go against" also. For example, she had recently co-piloted a sailing boat across the Atlantic.

Enkhjargal and I were given a tour of the local museum by the man in charge of acquisitions after she and Mary registered at the hotel. Sereenendorj was a thin, bespeckled gentleman of middle age with a brisk, enthusiastic manner of address. When we had completed the tour, we confirmed the arrangement I'd made with him during a visit to the museum that morning to meet at 10:00 am tomorrow for a tour of Mönkh Khan's palace and other local sites. In the early evening Enkhjargal and I dined out with Mary, ending up, after a long circuitous walk, back where we'd started in the neighborhood of the museum at one of the few restaurants still open. The matinee hours of most of the shops and restaurants in a town on the foreign tourist circuit came as a surprise. It was probably during that first night in Mörön that Enkhjargal told me she'd had a dream recently in which I returned to Ulaanbaatar from the hike on August 10th.

Sereenendorj met the three of us in his old gray Volga at the appointed time at the museum the next morning. We took the airport road and entered the Delger-Mörön valley, which I had passed through two days before but on the other side of the river. At a point fifteen kilometers west of town, at the north end of the Uushigiin Övör (Lung's Front Side) valley, we came to three rows of more than a dozen deer stones, the largest collection in the aimag, as well as several small khirigsüür mounds.

The tall and columnar stone of gray granite at the southern end of the third row, where we began our tour, was distinguished by the lifelike representation of a man's head in relief. Russian archeologist V. V. Volkov, whose study on Mongolian deer stones includes this site, indicates that the stone represents an actual central Asian man who lived 2,500 years ago.[2] The lips are pursed and protruding,[3] the nose long and thin. Both ears, which are clearly defined, have two earrings, one a large pendant and the other much smaller and clipped to the top of the ear. The large earrings are a clever adaptation of the sun's disk traditionally represented near the top of deer stones. The addition of a human head to this stone also makes the conventional "necklace" near the top of many deer stones and the "belt" with crossed diagonal lines in the middle actual articles of jewelry and clothing. Implements suspended from the belt include a war axe with a small square hole cut in the blade, hook, and knife. Instead of the usual crowded placement of leaping deer images set diagonally within the separate sides of the stone, on the upper half below the head the images are horizontal and wrap around two or more sides.[4]

43 - Deer stones at Uushigiin Övör

In 1999 D. Erdenebaatar and Japanese archeologists excavated one of the fifteen khirigsüürs found at the site. That there were also fifteen known deer stones lent support to the theory that, where khirigsüürs and deer stones occur at the same site, the mound marks the grave of the person worshipped at a particular deer stone.[5] However, the Mongolian archeologist would conclude from his joint excavation with Russian archeologists here about ten years later that deer stones in central Mongolia served as cenotaphs and, where they occur in association with khirigsüürs, the

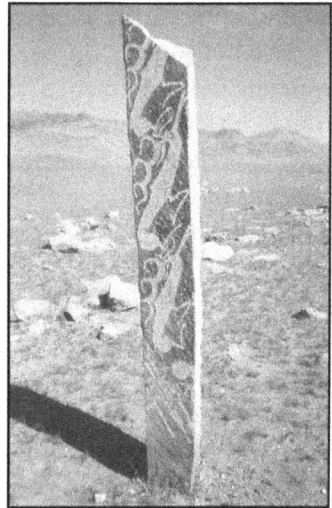

44 - Reverse of nearest deer stone

persons they memorialize are not buried in the mounds. Several new deer stones or fragments were found.[6]

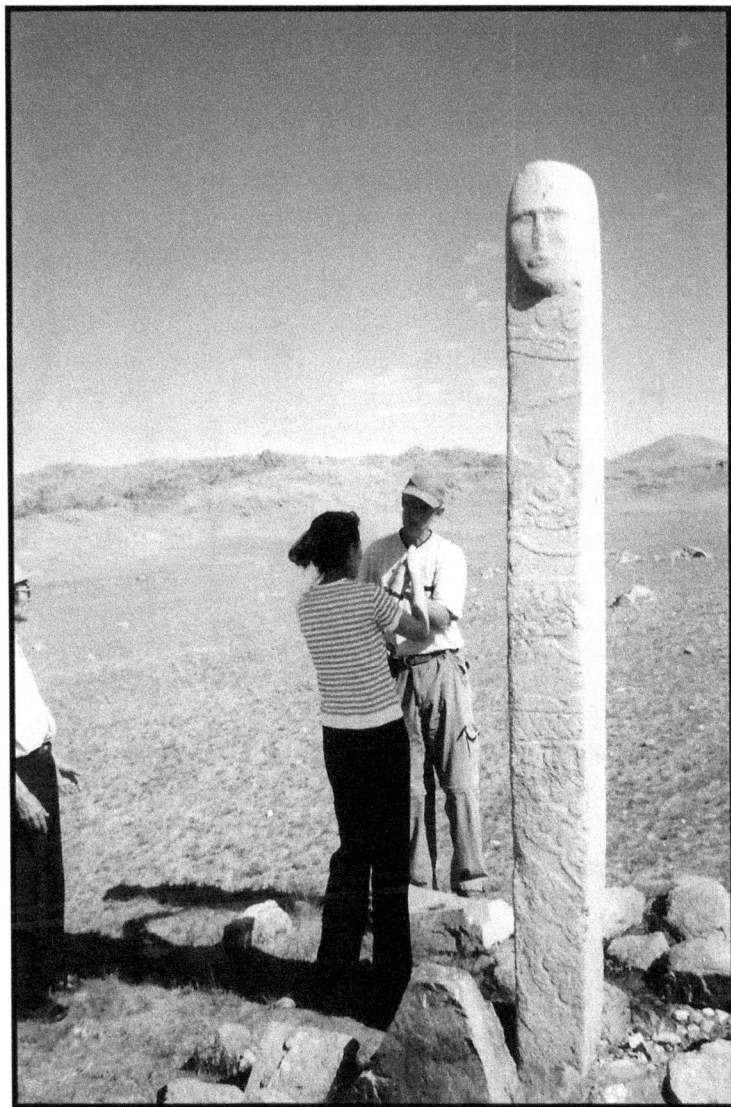

45 - Enkhjargal and author with Sereenendorj at Uushigiin Övör deer stone

Our visit to Mönkh Khan's palace and the city of Erchüü farther west in the valley within Arbulag Sum was enlivened by the discovery that I had camped in the area. The trip was made difficult, especially for an automobile, by a recent heavy rain that had deepened the runoff stream channels bitten into the roadbed, scattered a lot of stones over the road, and created patches of sodden, muddy ground. After stopping several times to build ramps of rock against the walls of the deeper runoff ditches or to map out the driest route across a field, we were forced to halt within a few kilometers of our destination, visible in the plain north of the Delger-Mörön and south of Delger Khan Uul.

Enkhjargal and Mary agreed to wait in the car while Sereenendorj and I completed the trip on foot. Amid fields stubbled with clumps of feathergrass, I found a reddish stone, roughly the size of a brick and flat on one end. My guide said it may have been made by human hands. Reaching an unpainted wooden house, we were invited in for tea by the head of the household, a buck-toothed man named Bazartsog who turned out to be an ex-student of Sereenendorj's from the grade-school class he had taught in 1980. His wife, also buck-toothed, served the fried-pastry cubes called boortsog and curdled cheese for dipping it in, with milk tea. The couple had two boys with them. Strings of meat were drying from the long horizontal beam of the ceilingless roof. Unfolded chocolate bar wrappers, pages torn from magazines, and other paper scraps were tacked to the upper wall area as insulation and, possibly, pop-art decoration. There was a stack of folded felt, lattice work, and other ger parts on the floor to one side of the single room.

We set out on the last stage seated behind Bazartsog on his motorbike. When we had passed the distinctive pyramid-like hill or rock, Altan Gadas Uul, that I'd seen across the river from my campsite four days before, the driver stopped beside a low, flattened mound of sand. This, I was told, had been part of the palace, which covered an area thirty meters square. At the base of the mound was a square granite block with a charred bowl hollowed out of the middle: an incense burner. Ascending the mound, we found a flat, square stone with a disk embossed in it, apparently the pedestal for a column. I picked up to examine a small piece of clay rubble like a fragment of thick earthenware but with an impression like that left by burlap on one side.

Excavation here had revealed foundation work consisting of upright slabs of shaped granite and trenches where other slabs had been. At the corners and midway on two of the thirty-meter walls were six large shaped-granite blocks on which columns once rested. A lot of brick rubble and enameled and unenameled clay shards were found. Bits of charcoaled wood mixed with fragments of plaster and chalk suggested there had been a fire.[7]

Sereenendorj called my attention to a string of piles of small stones that seem to have marked one of the four one-hundred-meter walls that surrounded the city of Erchüü, of which the palace was the center. The foundations of many other buildings were found within, as well as some others without, the city walls. Excavations have shown that the locale included a residential area; districts for trade, handicrafts, and blacksmithing; a military garrison; and a temple for prayer.[8] Some thirty or forty meters beyond the west wall of the city we found a pile of large stones with a thick scattering of the same kind of small clay shards that I had found a specimen of on the mound. It seems that archeologists had found fragments of brick, tile, and enameled and unenameled drinking and eating vessels here.[9]

When Sereenendorj had finished pointing out the few features of the site, we hopped back on the motorcycle behind Bazartsog and rode a short distance to a mound or low hill of sand back in the direction from which we'd come. A gray granite stele bearing the date 1955 and inscribed with traditional Mongolian script down three sides stood on the hill. It read, "Mönkh Khan's monument was found here." O. Namnandorj, while doing field research in the area in 1950s, was told by locals of a monument called "Chingüünjav's Chair Back," an epithet suggesting that it provided inspiration and moral support for the 18th-century hero in staging his revolt against the Manchus. The archeologist excavated here a 144 by 78 by 20-centimeter stone slab resting on a shaped stone block.[10] The stele is now in the National Museum of Mongolia in Ulaanbaatar.

Some scholars have claimed that it was erected by Möngke's daughter Isiji and her husband Tavnan while the khan was campaigning against the Sung State in southern China in the late 1250s. The face of the monument is engraved with three vertical rows of Mongolian script and twelve rows of Chinese characters, as well as an ornamental image of horns. It reads: "May Mönkh Khan live from generation to generation ten thousand ten thousand years, so that happiness may reign until the raising of the tiger flag."[11] He died, probably from dysentery, in China two years after the monument was erected, having reigned for only eight years. He was around fifty. After his ascendency as khan in 1251, this Christian-era Ozymandius—the original of Shelley's tyrant-emperor reigned in the 13th century B.C.—massacred the inhabitants of the regions occupied by his rival cousins' families.[12] According to Marco Polo, when Mönkh Khan died, twenty-thousand men—all of those encountered as the body was being conveyed through the countryside to its final resting place—were slain to provide the deceased with servants in the next life.[13] This, incidentally, was the general practice upon the death of a great khan and was also designed to keep the burial site a secret. The exact locations of Genghis Khan's and his immediate successors' tombs have yet to be discovered.

A landmark from Chingüünjav's revolt was the third and final stop on our itinerary. Sereenendorj had pointed out its general location at the base of a forested mountain across the river from the palace site. I was in the vicinity without knowing it when I passed Bürentogtokh four days before. The ruined fort stood within the arc of three mountains: an enclosure maybe two-hundred meters around with thick walls of sandy earth tapering toward the top and roughly two meters high. Passing through a wide gap in the wall facing us and crossing to the middle of the rear wall, we came to a modern stone monument bearing the inscription "Khotgoid Chingüünjav's Memorial."

In October of 1756, he came here with about five-hundred soldiers. Another five hundred or so, fearing the army of the Manchu general at Uliastai, had deserted. This was apparently the site of the munitions plant, where guns and other weapons were manufactured using the coal and metal mined in two mountains our guide had pointed out en route to the deer stone site. There was no siege or battle here.[14] The uprising ended the following month with Chingüünjav's capture.[15]

After our tour, Enkhjargal and Mary arranged with a local agency a trip to Lake Khövsgöl the next day. It had been Enkhjargal's dream for many years to see this natural wonder, arguably the most scenic place in Mongolia. Although the lake was on my route north, I decided to join them. A dry run trip would provide an opportunity to identify potential water stops and inquire about a boat ticket back down the lake after completing the hike.

The next morning, the glittering blue expanse of lake bursting into view after our ride through rugged, forested country reminded me of Lake Baikal, which I'd seen recently on a trip to Moscow on the Trans-Siberian Railroad. I had little success with the boat ride query but, in addition to noting water stops, scouted out a lodging place in Khatgal at the lake's southern tip. I also made tentative arrangements for a short trip by horseback to visit a Tsaatan, or reindeer-herding, family upon reaching a camp on the lakeshore. That evening at the Delger-Mörön Hotel, I exchanged with Enkhjargal my surplus gear and supplies for several items I'd asked her to bring, including razors, muesli, and light plastic to protect my pack from rain.

As we sat with Mary in the airport lobby the following morning, I promised Enkhjargal that I would call her from Mörön a week from tomorrow, Sunday, the 28th; she would be returning from one of her bi-weekly runs to Beijing that day. I did this to ensure that I would not resume my hike before the ankle healed. There were times when I would regret making this promise.

One of these occurred that very day as I sat in my hotel room writing a poem on the occasion of the first anniversary of Mother's death. Titled "A Minute's Worth," it begins by referring to a promise I'd made to her at her deathbed to use my remaining time on earth well. Then, evaluating my present hiking exploit in terms of this promise, I recall the moment when the words "I accuse you of motion" leapt out at me from the flashcard at her wake. "Have I done wrong to measure time in milestones?" I ask. The poem continues:

> I think of all the minutes sacrificed—
> in playing back old rock tunes in my head,
> mouthing fingered strings of "Hail Mary"s,
> retailing scenes of past accomplishments,
> or just chewing the cud of consciousness—
> to making another mile on the map.
> And how, for the sake of the last two hundred,
> I'll spend two weeks of minutes like
> I did the thirty or so before this one:
> walking to three restaurants on different streets
> to find all of them closed, then to a store—
> the only one still open—to buy hand soap
> they didn't carry, back to the hotel room
> to swat and sweep the latest batch of flies
> bagged by my window curtain and call in
> the attendant to look at the broken commode.
> Yes, in the minute, I stand accused of motion.
>
> What was that closing reference to Goethe
> in the autobiographical sketch found
> among your papers and read at the funeral?
> Something about the journey being more
> important than the goal? Mother of five,
> you entered late on the path to a Ph.D.,
> yet, long before an illness crippled you,
> attained true wisdom: learning is its own end.
> Never so happy as when you sat absorbed
> at your books—Herder, Hauptmann, and Von Kleist,

a Dickens novel or a Sayers mystery—
you ceased racing against time to finish
the courses, conference papers, articles—
means for attaining scholarly distinction—
but set your own deadlines and lived each minute.

Teach me, then, Mother, from this minute, to stop
trying to be first, go out of my way
to be in the middle, in the minute, as
I journey sitting still at this hotel—
reviewing my *Mongolian Phrasebook*, reading—
and, later, stand upon the road to watch
the shadows galloping up stony hillsides,
broom grass rocking across windy fields,
hear the past echoing in empty spaces,
the open message spoken by the dawn,
savor the scent of wild thyme in the air,
feel the surrender of the setting sun.

The poem returns to the realization in "On Being Somewhere," that I was privileging the goal at the expense of the journey. I wasn't rushing through the countryside now—thanks to an injury brought on by rushing—and, in deciding to remain at the hotel for another week, I was in a sense opposing the speed mentality in myself. Yet, because I was resting here in order to be able to get to the border, I was also still attaching too much importance to the future achievement and not enough to the present experience. Staying in Mörön, where I would soon run out of sightseeing options and reading matter, would mean sacrificing time that could have been used more enjoyably and productively in Ulaanbaatar. As my injured leg improved from day to day, though, my healthy regret for promising Enkhjargal I would wait here and call in another eight days took a turn for the worse, becoming an unhealthy regret at the delay in my pursuit of the border.

Several days after Enkhjargal's departure, I did manage to improve the time by seeking out miscellaneous places in Mörön to tour or conduct an interview, usually with the help of an interpreter. Nergüi (Nameless) was a small, pretty, young woman of about twenty with a soft voice and shy, shrinking-violet manner that sometimes compromised her effectiveness. During the school year she studied English, German, and Russian at a university in Erdenet, a city 421 kilometers to the east.

Khövsgöl Flour Foodstuffs was a large sprawling compound that included some tall smokestacks, a narrow six-story yellow building, and another fairly tall white building. The sign at the entrance to the mill read, "We are our customers' reliable partner. Our products are dependable and of good quality." This text was accompanied by an illustration depicting a woman holding out a bowl of milk in one hand, draped with the blue silk khadag—the same iconography of welcome recently seen in the hotel in Tsagaan Uul.

The director, a stocky gentleman with white, closely cropped hair, was seated behind his desk at the far end of a large room. A newspaper lay before him on the desk. His straw hat and what appeared to be a dictaphone were placed on a small table or desk to his right. There was a calendar or poster with the title "40 Years Mörön" in English on the wall behind him. Khövsgöl Flour Foodstuffs Company was founded in 1961. On the same wall was a framed colored drawing of Sükhbaatar, the popular hero of the 1921 revolution that established the socialist Mongolian People's Republic.

"Why do you want to know about the mill?" he asked me, referring to my request for a tour.

"I am writing a book in order to make Mongolia better known so that more foreigners will visit."

He said it was impossible to provide a tour, as everything was locked up now and the mill was not operating. When I asked him about an interview, however, he consented and invited Nergüi and me forward to sit at the long shiny conference table that filled the middle of the room.

The director was fifty years of age and born in Galt Sum. He referred to three main divisions of the physical plant: the grain storage area, the flourmill proper, and the maintenance shops. The entire milling process involved some forty steps. I later learned that the wheat is conveyed a distance of eight kilometers within the mill during processing.[16] During the 1980s Khövsgöl Flour Foodstuffs operated the best flourmill and one of the best food-producing industries in Mongolia, he claimed. The mill was awarded the golden prize from the Central Committee of the Union, a national workers' rights and compensation office, and took first, second, or third place in many competitions. Since the coming of democracy and privatization, the mill had fallen on hard times. Here was evidence of the depressing effects that could result, in the industrial sector, from the nation's transition from a planned to a market economy. With less grain being produced in Mongolia and little working capital available, the mill operated only one to three months out of the year, utilizing just five to ten percent of the physical plant. The eighty or so workers must seek other employment during the off season.

"When will your mill begin operating this year?"

"That's a difficult question. I told the Minister of Agriculture and Prime Minister about the lack of adequate circulating capital and grain production. In their party's platform during the election campaigns, they pledged themselves to support national grain production, but they haven't provided us with any real assistance. If we have the circulating capital and our financial capability improves, we are ready to begin working at any time. If we receive ten-thousand tons of wheat this year, we will be able to continue our usual operations in the future."

Khövsgöl Foods, a combination bakery and distillery, was one of the largest private companies in the entire aimag at the time of our visit.[17] Leaving the driver and car in the lot, Nergüi and I enter the large compound through a metal gate. The director is "baikhgüi," having left his office a few minutes before. Inside, a sign over his door reads, "Those with initiative seek opportunities while those without it seek excuses." Seeking opportunities, we inquire of office staff about his whereabouts and are directed to the company cafeteria. A man sitting at one table isn't him.

We proceed to the construction site of a large factory building, where we have been told he has gone. We don't find him there, either, so we take advantage of the opportunity to look in at the vodka distillery and bottling plant next door. A truck is unloading plastic crates of empty vodka bottles—as commonplace in Mongolia as sheep dung—outside the small building where women clean the bottles with a scouring machine. A woman on the assembly line next door loads empty bottles into, and removes them full from, a vodka dispensing machine, the humble descendant of the silver-tree liquor fountain at Karakorum during the Mongol Empire.

We were taking the initiative to visit the bakery—a long, single-story building across the open central area of the compound—when some workers sitting near the entrance guardhouse stopped us with the warning that we weren't allowed there unaccompanied by the director. Determined to the last to seek opportunities, rather than excuses, we asked a baker making his way over to the cafeteria if we might interview him. As a final flourish, told suddenly that we must leave the premises, we asked him if he would mind being interviewed outside the gate. Our visit to Khövsgöl Foods was a regular initiatives tour de force.

Gonchigjav, a fifty-four year old who had been employed at the plant for thirty-one years, baked bread. He wore a white uniform and hat on his shaven head, and his face beamed with benignity and cheerfulness. There were about fifty employed at the plant, he said. When asked about changes since the democratic revolution, he referred to how the company used to have to set their production goals for the next five years. Making the Five-Year Plan was one of the soviet government's numerous mandates designed to stimulate economic productivity.

46 - Assistant director, Mörön power plant

Among the other stops I made alone or with Nergüi were the Khar Zakh, or black market, where I found the *Mongolian Phrasebook*; a shoe repair shop, little bigger than a kiosk, on the main north-south road; a sawmill, where we were turned away[18]; Danzandarjaa Khiid, where the young monk I interviewed explained his call in terms of a desire "to do something beneficial for people and animals"; a small, privately owned seamstress's shop; and the diesel-run power plant, where the friendly assistant director answered my question about conditions since the advent of democracy, "Even though this society calls itself democratic, life is bad today."

᚛

About a week into my stay in Mörön, I also called on a retired physician at his home. Though much improved, my ankle was still sensitive, and this particular doctor, whom Enkhjargal had located for me during her visit, was reputed to be a good one. The two-room wooden house had a large sapling, draped with drying socks, in front. The doctor was in. He sat shirtless in the middle of the floor, a pot-bellied older gentleman with a closely shaven head. His wife sat in the room working a sewing machine. There were several children around.

After hearing a brief history of my complaint, he asks me to sit down on a short stool. I am facing the wrong direction, he tells me. I must sit with my back to the middle of the room. I'd never heard of this bit of guest etiquette but assumed it applied to rare cases when the visitor was a patient. When I have removed my left boot and sock, he grips my ankle and leg in several places between his forefinger and thumb, keeping the cigarette he is now smoking between his lips. He assures me that nothing is broken; the swelling is caused by the accumulation of blood vessels in the swollen area due to over-exertion. I must return the next two days for massage therapy. I pay the fee—eight-hundred tögrögs, less than a dollar—and leave.

I came for only one of the follow-up treatments since my ankle was considerably better the next day and he told me then that I could resume my hike. The ankle wasn't broken, as he said, but the report of accumulated blood vessels? Like many of the herders I consulted about directions, he may have thought wrong information more helpful than a blunt "I don't know." He was right in this case. Nor would I have been as hopeful of recovery had he used the clinical term "tendonitis," my actual condition as I learned later.

On the Friday of my second week in Mörön, I took a test walk, with my loaded pack on, to the market and back. The sensitivity in my ankle was gone. During a phone conversation with Enkhjargal after her return home, I had hedged a bit on the promise I made to her at the airport, telling her it was just possible that my ankle would heal soon enough to make it impractical to stay in Mörön through Sunday, the 28th, the day I had told her I would call. It was beginning to seem that way now and I was tempted to depart early in the morning on the following day or Sunday. On the other hand, it also seemed bad luck to break the initial agreement—my unsettled brain now prey to superstition. Besides, there was a show at the town concert hall on Saturday night. I would wait at least until Sunday.

The drama theatre-concert hall, a white building with a decorative device of abstract, modern art in relief high on the façade, was on the west side of the town square. A sign posted in front read,

> Youth without dreams
> Are like birds without wings.

I am the first audience member when I enter well before 7:00 pm, the announced starting time. Trained by some memorable experiences in four years of concert going in Ulaanbaatar, I have come early to be sure of a seat. The name of the singer, Kh. Bolormaa, is, of course, unfamiliar to me, but professional live entertainment is about as rare in rural Mongolia as the endangered snow leopard or wild boar, and after almost two weeks in Mörön I am not a picky customer. The cozy auditorium is quite attractive and well-maintained. The inner edge of the stage's proscenium is inset with the interlocking square design I had noticed, most recently, on a ger wall partition being stitched in the seamstress's shop on my town tour. The backdrop of the stage represents a landscape of multicolored mountains and white clouds with a gigantic lake— Khövsgöl, no doubt—crossed by flying birds in the foreground. Suddenly, as if a line had been forming for a while outside, a group enters and sits down. As the hall fills to about eighty percent of its capacity, I learn from those seated near me that the singer is from Govi-Altai.

At 7:40 we are still waiting for the show to begin. The audience has resorted to rhythmical handclapping. Finally, the young female moderator walks on to be followed soon after by the star herself. Bolormaa is about twenty-five, though she looks scarcely over twenty, and quite lovely, wearing a low-cut yellow-and-gray evening dress and a white necklace. Like the songs I had heard in the concerts of veteran pop entertainers in the capital, hers are of the pop variety blended with the stately steppe-imbued traditional type. Her voice is strong and clear, her stage manner confident and professional, in spite of the frequent opening and closing of the auditorium door near the stage. There are no missed notes. Bolormaa is very good.

She sings a song about her mother. For another song, having the repeated phrase "eej mini dee" ("mother of mine"), she descends from the stage and mingles with the audience. She addresses her mother again with "minii eejii" in the next song. This is followed by yet another mother song! The confirmed theme of my hike was proving to be a theme of the concert. The audience is much quieter and more attentive than the jaded concert crowds in Ulaanbaatar. Another difference from performances in the capital is the absence of the touching ceremony in which a member of the audience, usually a small dressed-up toddler representing his or her parents, bestows a bouquet of roses or other flowers on the singer at the conclusion of a song. The lack of flower shops in Mörön would neatly explain this local idiosyncrasy.

After the second intermission, Bolormaa emerges in a red silk dress. As the concluding song of the concert gets underway, two men, probably staff, appear in the doorway, suddenly intent on the program. And now the audience, myself included, is singing with the artist, who holds the microphone out to us from the stage:

> Eejiin mini,
> Eejiin mini,
> Eejiin mini ner buten baivaldaa,
> Enekhen nasnii mini gantskhan zaya yum uu daa.
> (My mother's,
> My mother's,
> If my mother's name is honorable,
> That is my crowning achievement in life.)

It's that song again! First heard on the trip as I was preparing to leave Altai to begin my hike; next, exactly one month ago today, June 27th, while about to set out from Altai to begin walking alone; and now, heard live near the time of my departure from Mörön for the last stage of my journey. I was not aware at the time of the pattern—the consistent association of the song with a significant departure—but merely wondered at how it kept turning up and how I was probably hearing it sung by the artist herself. This was enough to convey a sense of my mother's continued guidance and protection. The impression was strengthened when, in my room the next morning, I heard the hit song again on the radio in the hotel lobby and then confirmed through the staff that the singer was in fact Bolormaa. I wept thinking of how the song that had come to represent my mother's involvement in the progress of my journey had, in a remote part of Mongolia, been sung to me live by the artist.

Eager to complete my walk across Mongolia, I had considered the day before leaving early this morning. I now decided to stay put for another day and fulfill my promise to call Enkhjargal. It was fortunate I did so, for a heavy thundershower fell in the late afternoon; I might have gotten very wet had I left today.

Chapter 8
On the Trail of a New Self: Khövsgöl Aimag from Mörön to Khatgal

This page of life
Which man writes
At his every step
Is his biography
Which bears a true witness
To who he was in this varied world.
They say,
As you wear out the saddle stirrups
You should understand this world better
And you should become a more thoughtful man
And turn to look back at your tracks. (12-22)[1]

Monday, July 29th, I wake, glutted with rest, in the early morning darkness and eagerly dress and finish my packing. At about half past five, I am standing on the front porch of the hotel, clear of the door, wriggling into the arm straps of my pack. One of the men who were clamoring to be admitted when the attendant unlocked the door to let me out offers his assistance, but I decline with a "Zugeer" ("That's OK"). I notice alcohol on his breath. One or more vehicles are parked in the front lot; the men appear to be staff getting ready for a lake tour.

Under a high moon more than half full, I walk north up the lane and turn right on another to the main, north-south street. Here is the little shoe repair shop where I interviewed the proprietor, Pürevsüren. I go north on the main road, strewn with puddles after yesterday's rain, past the white well house where I used to collect drinking water and the lane I would take to the market. The neighborhoods of small wooden houses and yards surrounded with board palisades are dark and silent. The stench of outhouses hangs in the air. Dogs roam about.

It is beginning to dawn as I clear the town. The fragrant scent of an herb has replaced the stench. Large white moths like stone arrowheads turn up often on the dirt road. Their hour in the summer's sequence of ephemeral insects must have arrived while I was abed for two weeks. I would see colonies of them along most of the west shoreline of Lake Khövsgöl.

Afoot and light-hearted I take to the open road,
Healthy, free, the world before me,
The long brown path before me leading wherever I choose.
(stanza 1)[2]

In addition to the Whitmanesque excitement of setting out on foot once again, I feel a strange physical sense of euphoria as the colors of the ground and surrounding landscape deepen in the progress of the dawn. It's as if I had died and were walking in a resurrected body on a new earth. I attribute this uncanny sensation to my long convalescence and lighter and more comfortable pack; I overhauled and repaired it in Mörön, greatly reducing the pull of the load away from my back, and, after leaving some of my gear and clothing at the hotel, besides what I gave to Enkhjargal, am carrying only the essentials.

I take a right-hand road toward a deep mountain gap. Then, when it begins to turn more sharply to the right toward a cemetery, sit down to await a man leading a bicycle down from a small collection of wooden buildings at the foot of the mountain. It's the old crisis of losing the road out of town, repeating itself in spite of my recently having traveled the road by jeep.

"By the telephone poles?" I ask, after the man's reply to my initial question about the location of the Khatgal road.

"Yes."

But after resuming my walk, I find there are two telephone lines. "Which one?" I should have gone on to ask. A jeep that I signal on the road beside the first line doesn't stop. It is feeling like the same old earth now. I pass the cemetery, its closely packed headstones scintillating with metal fixtures, on the lower slope of the mountain to my right. If this cemetery was like one I'd seen in Ulaanbaatar, the metal included tin boxes for oil lamps or incense burners and fans from old motors mounted on the headstones. The blades turning in the wind are believed to multiply prayers in the manner of spun prayer wheels. It was, strangely enough, the first modern cemetery I remembered seeing on the hike and would be the only one.

Soon after, a boy approaching on a bicycle from the opposite direction assured me that I was on the right road. I was resting beside a dry ravine after entering the gap when a young woman came down the slope from a wooden house. Otgoo, as she introduced herself, wanted to know whether I would drink tea at her home. I was already on my feet—I must have sensed this was coming.

"No, I must be going. Thank you."

The road ran up the slope a short distance and I could see Otgoo off to my right walking back to the house. At a sign "Airag Zarj Baina" ("Airag Sold Here"), where the road turned away irrevocably to the left, I changed my mind. "It's not what you do, but what you don't do that you regret." The counsel of a wise old Jewish woman, once repeated to me by a mutual friend, came to mind. There was also the fresh lesson from the traumatic final day's walk to Mörön and tedious two-weeks' recuperation from an injury caused by hurrying. Even now my troublesome left ankle was aching a little. Making an about-face, I routed the enemy of hastiness within. Like the moment when I viewed the scene with horses on the river island, accepting Otgoo's invitation to tea was a major victory in that crusade to conquer the demon speed and recover my unhurried mindset. I was learning the nature of true progress, whether in journeying through Mongolia or life itself—appreciation for the all-important present.

Her house was a small plain building of hewn logs. Another structure with the clay plaster dropping off the lattice work stood beside it. Inside, the house was ceilingless and the long horizontal beam below the exposed rafters was hung with strings of drying meat, which had turned gray and looked leathery. Sheets of newspaper completely covered the walls of the attic for insulation. Folded felt and wooden parts of a ger were stacked on the floor not far from the entrance and beside this stack were some large cooking basins. On the other side of the room, a butter churn stood next to a table. Beds and couches were ranged along both long walls and an infant lay in the bed nearest the table and churn. In the shrine area before the short wall at the far end, there was a large black-and-white photograph of a late middle-aged man and a box of Buddhist sudar wrapped in the usual yellow cloth. If other families had the scriptures out in their homes, I didn't notice it.

Otgoo's husband, twenty-five years old, namesake of the military hero Davaadorj commemorated in a statue on the square in Mörön, was working on a marmot trap, attaching a piece of canvas to a metal frame. The bait, which I recall him saying was goat's flesh, is placed on the canvas when the trap is set. Two children, a beautiful, dark-complexioned girl wearing a dress—their three-year old daughter—and an older boy, Davaadorj's young brother, came in. The infant in the bed was the couple's two-month old son. Tending the girl was my host's younger sister, who was probably in her late teens.

I was served milk tea and slices of bread with creamy yellow congealed khailmag, the cream and flour mix. Davaadorj and I covered the standard topics of conversation. Then the illustration representing the silver fountain at Karakorum on the carpet covering the wall behind the baby's bed led to the subject of my visit to Mönkh Khan's palace site nearby. I had seen the same illustration on a wall carpet in the ger Boldsaikhan and I stayed in at Bum in Govi-Altai. The little girl, hugging a large pot filled with the same yellow khailmag and covered with thin blocks of dried cheese or aaruul or both, staggered toward me. I took a smaller one of the squares. Otgoo offered me a glass of homemade vodka but I declined. Before taking my leave, I gave her a new pencil and two fifty-tögrög bills and her daughter three pieces of candy. I also left some candy for Davaadorj's brother, who had gone outside. I had decided in Mörön that giving candy to children would be one way to show a new, friendlier self to the world; the stay in town had also restored my sociability.

"Sain yavaarai!"
"Sain suuj baigaarai!" ("Stay well!")

The road climbed steadily. After discontinuing in the afternoon of the first day out of Tsagaan Uul, the telephone-pole escort that had been provided during most of the hike was reinstated. Apart from a brief frolic here and there, the poles would stand by me, assuring me that I was on the right road, as far as Khatgal on the southern edge of Lake Khövsgöl, then turn up again at Khankh at the northern, just in time to share in the glory of the final stretch. Among the wildflowers I would encounter on today's hike was the prostrate gentian with its dark-blue bell-shaped flowers at the tip of a leafless stem.[3]

Later that morning, a Russian minivan passed me and stopped. A man emerged, grinning, from the right side of the vehicle and advanced towards me. "No thank you; I'm walking"—the rote explanation was on my lips when, wonder of wonders, I recognized my friend Fr. Joseph, the Salesian priest from Czechoslovakia whom I went to for Confession at my parish in Ulaanbaatar! In fact, a request of his, that I offer up whatever difficulties I faced on the hike for the success of a summer youth camp, and some spiritual advice from my last visit to the Sacrament had helped sustain me these past six weeks. A second van stopped.

Suddenly, the alien wilderness is transformed into the familiar lounge at Sts. Peter and Paul. Gathered around me and Fr. Joseph are Fr. Andrew, newly ordained, from Vietnam; Fr. Simon from Korea; and two or three Mongolian men and several boys. The Salesians are taking a group from their Don Bosco Center in Ulaanbaatar for an outing on Lake Khövsgöl.

My pack becomes an object of general remark as it is hoisted up to test its weight. Fr. Joseph and I exchange news—the ordination Mass, presided over by a cardinal and three bishops, at the Ulaanbaatar Hotel in early July and some of the highlights from my trip. My water bottle is filled after I drink from it. Cameras flash in several group shots and in a parting one of me walking with my pack on and then the caravan is gone, pulling up the long grade toward Khujirtiin (Salt Marsh's) Davaa. I plod onward, suddenly reconciled by this brief respite to the solitude and travail of my journey.

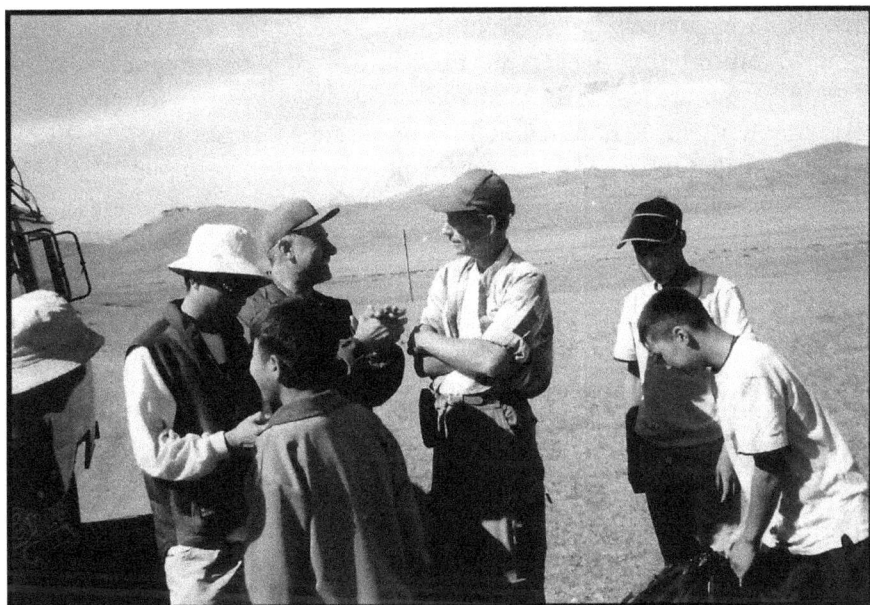

47 - Roadside encounter

Shortly before the road finally crested at the pass that afternoon, I saw my first hare of the trip—a tolai bounding away from the roadside just after I walked past without seeing it. There is no more vegetation here than at other places I have seen, for "That must be a poor country indeed that does not support a hare."[4]

A vista of distant blue mountains offers from the top of the pass. Somewhere in the valley I am about to cross, a kettle dating from the Bronze Age was unearthed in 1985. The date given with the exhibit of the artifact in the Zanabazar Museum of Fine Arts in Ulaanbaatar is 2,000 B.C. I was now entering Alag Erdene (Multicolored Jewel) Sum. Descending steeply after the usual circumambulations at the ovoo and a brief halt, I noticed a subtle catch in my right knee; I had twisted it slightly at the ovoo. It seemed ironic that it should have happened while performing a ritual designed to ensure good fortune and safety to travelers.

I meet a young Moscovite pushing his bicycle up the grade. His companion is further down the hill. The two men left Irkutsk, the Siberian city near the southwest shore of Lake Baikal, on July 22nd and are bound for Beijing, where they will take the Trans-Siberian Railroad back. We are at opposite ends—they a week into, I about a week from the end of, a grand summer adventure. I had met another pair of formidable bicyclists, an American man and German woman, one day at the internet facility in the telecommunications building in Mörön. They had been three years making their way around the globe and, out of money, were about to return home. Cheers for these and all of the young people who, undaunted by terrorist escapades such as 9/11 the year before and, this very summer, the Patt Junction Bus bombing in Jerusalem and Nagar Massacre in Jamu, India, plunge into the turbulent world and take their dream trips abroad anyway. It is partly their exuberance for adventure, courage before the unknown, and defiance of media-fed hysteria and suspicion that keeps communication between nations from breaking down altogether.

When I had entered the valley, another passing Russian minivan stopped. This time it was a Mongolian woman, probably in her late twenties, who walked around from the passenger's side of the cab toward me. "Guillaume?" she asked, and my friend and former colleague Dolgorlkham stood before me! She taught Beginning French at the International College in the spring of 1999. It was turning out to be Roadside Reunion Day on my trip. She introduced me to an elderly gentleman who had also gotten out of the van. He was one of two tourists—the other, a young man, emerged soon after—from Orleans whom she would be showing around the lake for a few days. They are soon gone. But the trip feels so different, is now so much more enjoyable and rewarding, that I hardly recognize it as the same trip where I lost the way out of Altai or walked with blistered feet for two weeks in the Gobi.

Frozen patches of cirrus-cloud cover and, more recently, a breeze had kept the day from getting too hot. Moreover, my water bottle was full again. Nevertheless, when I sighted salt lake Erkhel Nuur and the adjacent ger camp that I was told on the jeep trip would be opening its doors soon, I restrained myself from pushing on to the next water stop. Judging from the sensation in my knee, I might have already walked too far that day. Approaching the rows of quaint yellow-and-black gers enclosed by a low fence of neatly stacked stones, I found little evidence of occupation and, inquiring at a ger next door, learned that the camp was scheduled to open next month. I decided to pitch my tent beside the salt lake after collecting water from the local well. The family at the ger spared me the trouble of walking back two or three kilometers south to the well by offering to fill my bottle and container from their barrel.

Thunderclouds with lightning bolts were maneuvering on the other side of the large lake as I walked west toward it. Partly because I was hurrying to beat the rain and worried about carrying such a heavy load with my knee acting up, the lake seemed to get no nearer, if not to actually retreat before me. I had estimated only a twenty-minute walk. The level steppe was playing the enchanter with me, as it did on the evening's walk to Khaliun in the Gobi. When, after about forty-five minutes, I finally did reach the lake, I saw seven swans—neither more nor less—embark from the nearer stretch of shore and, spaced well apart, like a fleet of battle cruisers maintaining their own separate wakes, sail leisurely, imperturbably off. These "seven swans a-swimming" were the first sighted on my hike. They were no doubt whooper swans, virtually the only species of swans in Mongolia encountered in the Khövsgöl Nuur area.[5] Far to the right, just before the shoreline bent to the west, there was a great squabbling amid a large congregation of white birds that looked rather like swans but sounded like ducks. They were probably bar-headed geese, listed in the *Red Book* of endangered species in Mongolia. Across the lake, white mountains shading into green and reddish brown added yet another memorable aspect to the scene.

Racing against the weather, I stake out my funnel-shaped tent, the smaller rear end to the wind, on the slight incline of the sandy beach. The ground is perversely hard beneath the thin layer of sand, and there are no rocks to hammer stakes with. After screwing and treading the stakes in, I notice the rising breakers on the lake shifting direction. The tent will have to be reoriented to prevent the wind from catching the wide front and sending it like a balloon, possibly a manned one, careening across the steppe. Pop! The wind strikes the tent structure while I am holding onto it and annihilates it like a bubble. Before I have staked the tent a second time, the wind shifts again, so I re-reorient. It is beginning to feel like the proverbial politicians' polka.

After re-staking, I dive into the tent, partly to hold it down. Immediately, the rainstorm hits. The wind blows fiercely and I am afraid my little tent,

> . . . the fragile ship of courage, the ark of faith
> with its store of food and little cooking pans
> and change of clothes [,] (VII)[6]

won't hold up. After thirty or forty minutes of buffeting and drenching from the elements, though, my tent emerges intact in the subsiding storm. There is only a little puddle in the right, rear corner of the floor, probably caused by a sag in the flysheet. I get out in the lingering daylight and cook a pot of instant noodles. It has been a rare day's voyage. Besides the friends, flowers, and first hare and swans, I have encountered traces of a new self.

Have you built your ship of death, O have you? (II)[7]

I was packed and ready to depart at dawn. Birds were honking on the lake. A herd of horses that galloped up as I followed the irregular shoreline north escorted me as far as a small marshy watering spot. Reaching the point where the noisy convocation of bar-headed geese was assembled the night before, I saw a small flock of birds take to the water. Light gray in color, smaller than swans and in shape reminding me of guinea hens, they were probably herring gulls.[8] There were also a lot of small dark waterfowl that appeared to be common coots, as well as some ruddy shelducks, swimming on the lake. Several black-and-white birds that looked and sounded like geese and were probably tufted ducks[9] took flight.

The morning was overcast and cool and a breeze blew against me. Chastened by a little soreness in my right knee, I took more frequent stops. The road ascended to an upland valley. Khatgal and the lake were now about fifty kilometers away. As the road began to descend, I could see the valley of the Egiin Gol, the river that flows out of the lake, up ahead. Khövsgöl, here I come!

The road climbed to a pass of the Khavirgiin (Rib's) Uul. In addition to the ovoo, there were two metal signs in Mongolian: one with "Welcome" on its south side and "Have a good journey" on its north, another announcing Alag Erdene, the center of the sum by that name, which I had entered the day before. The town was situated on the Egiin beyond the slope of the hill on my right.

Across the road from the signs, a large traveling party with a Zil 130 stood talking or passing a volleyball. I went over to the truck and sat down. I exchanged a few words with one or two young men who had approached me at the signs. Then the group shoved off, leaving me, still sitting, to my once-coveted privacy. I remembered my treatment of the party with the volleyball on the banks of the Delger-Mörön. One of the difficulties with conversion is the payback that Nemesis immediately starts demanding. I consoled myself with the memory of my rest stop here with Enkhjargal and Mary on the trip to the lake.

The view of Alag Erdene from the foot of the mountain was exceptionally picturesque: at the base of steep slopes heavily wooded with larch, an aggregate of buildings, including a long white one, another beside it of several stories, and a third, smaller one, each with a pistachio-green roof. From this distance the town looked rather like an exclusive ski lodge.

At another sign, where the road branched sharply toward town, two men in deels, the first with a girl beside him, sat at two blueberry stands. Another opportunity to be sociable today, with the promise of greater dividends. The first man, who smoked a cigarette rolled with printed paper, did not have a bag or glass, so I proceeded to the second, much older man's stand. He piled the ners (blueberries) from his metal canister high in a small glass and I ate the luscious, slightly tart fruit with my spoon, seated by the stand. The berries had been picked on the mountain which the vendor pointed to behind us. I asked about the buildings with the pistachio-colored roofs in the townscape and was told they were "surguuli," meaning a primary or secondary school—or both, and "tsetserleg," a day care. When I ordered another half-glass, the man filled it three-quarters full. My total was three-hundred tögrögs, about $2.75. I gave Davaasüren, the girl, who had accompanied me with her father to the second vendor, some candy before setting out.

That afternoon, as I was crossing a series of stony dry channels of a riverbed, I encountered the Salesians' caravan returning from the lake. Fr. Joseph got out and we talked briefly. Before we parted, I asked him to pray for my physical and mental health. I did not think it necessary to add, with regard to the second half of my request, that I had not slept well the night before due to worry about an interpersonal conflict from the past year in Ulaanbaatar. The obsession about my fellow parishioner had begun to afflict me again. It was as if, in finally approaching the border, my diabolical mind was trying to sabotage the trip by keeping me from resting at night. Before this, the obsessive thought, if it appeared, had not posed a threat; the other mental impediment I was crusading against, the urge to quickly get somewhere, had seemed to supplant it. I did not stop to think that the two might be connected and that I was struggling with an imp sprung from my lingering excessive attachment to the journey's goal.

By six o'clock I was ascending a hill, a black kite circling overhead, about thirty kilometers out of Khatgal. The slight catch in my right knee was gone. The rain clouds that developed during the day had not yielded more than a few scattered drops, though the cool breeze still blew. After reaching another hilltop, I saw patches of water that I assumed were the Egiin Gol in the valley below. A herder boy whom I hailed after descending seemed to confirm this, but when I entered the plain, steering left of some gers, I found only a few freshwater ponds. I pushed on between two hills to another ger to ask directions to water.

At a corral in the yard a grandmother, casually cooing the infant in her arms, offered me water from their supply and accompanied me to the ger. The river now appeared a little further on. I could have told her I would go and collect water there instead, but, as I learned yesterday, my friendlier self could embrace a less self-reliant one as well. I set a comfortable limit, though, by declining all but about ten of the heap of aaruul briquettes that another woman held out to me with both hands. The water was stored in a large black metal barrel with a square cut in the wall and placed lengthwise on a cart. There was a beautiful month-old brown colt outside the ger—a much petted creature also petted by me.

I returned to the largest of the ponds and pitched my tent, annoying a pair of ruddy shelducks and several smaller ducks, possibly their brood. At the foot of the nearby hill on the other side of me from the pond were stone posts or upright slabs—more ancient burial markers? In a museum in Ulaanbaatar much later,[10] I would see Iron-Age Hun artifacts from an area of the Egiin Gol valley much further downstream. They included bronze and clay pots, pieces of a horse's bridle and harness, a pair of bone chopsticks, the birch bark lid of a container with decorative designs etched on it, and leaf-shaped metal decorations adorning a tomb. Some scholars have argued that the Huns were descendants of the Xiongnu, the people credited with the image of the two standing figures I saw on the Tsagaan Gol canyon wall.

Two boys from the ger I visited showed up before I started preparing dinner. One of them held his hand out to me with several greasy looking shagai, or sheep ankle bones, in it. I assumed, or pretended to think, that he meant I should merely look at them in his hand. About the size of a knuckle bone, they are used as dice, marbles, or counters in a variety of games in Mongolia. I gave the boys the last of my candy and, failing to get across my wish to be alone now, descended to the deception of withdrawing into my tent as if I were turning in for the night. I emerged only when they were a long way off. No conversion is without its occasional setbacks.

Eating some of the aaruul wedges, which were surprisingly sweet and soft, with my pot of noodles, I deeply regretted not accepting the whole pile in spite of the additional weight. The wind had gotten very bad, but it subsided a bit after I lay down in the tent again. For the second night in a row my sleep was disturbed by the same obsessive, worrisome thought, the one I'd decided to try breaking the OCD cycle with on this quest for inner freedom.

The sky cleared during the night, even if my mind did not, and by the light of the half-moon, I was able to pack and break camp by dawn. It was one of the coldest mornings I'd encountered this summer, and I made most of the long walk back to the road with one or both hands stuffed into my trousers' front pockets. Edelweiss were scattered with great prodigality in the usual stunted or closely cropped grass. While following an abandoned parallel road, I passed a sign showing what must have been the mileage from Mörön to some point north. It affected me a little like the eerie ghost town of Ögöömör in Zavkhan. An even more interesting obsolete sign, though, appeared after I had crossed the next hill. Resting by the roadside, I noticed faded lettering tricked out with stones on the slope of the hill opposite me. I could make out several of the letters of the two or three short words, which were set in two lines, but the meaning of the sign eluded me.

When I pointed out my discovery to the driver bringing me from Khatgal to Mörön after my hike, he and the Mongolian family traveling with me would decipher the words as "Manlai Nam," or "The Best Party." The sign was a bit of local promotion for the Mongolian People's Revolutionary Party. This communist party—recast along more democratic lines—maintained political control after the 1990 democratic revolution until 1996 and had returned to power in 2000. Zayabaatar, the man I interviewed in Khaliun, was the party chairman for his sum.

In a few hours I am standing at what will prove to be the last ovoo at a pass until the one above Khankh on the northeast shore of the lake, in turn the last one of my hike. Off the road's right edge, the hill descends to the deep-green bottomland of the Egiin Gol, its several channels blue and glittering under the blue sky. The upper portion of the long slope bordering the valley is draped with a long solid strip of larch growth.

I rest, first, beneath a large metal sign bearing the words "Manai Khotod. Tavtai Moril!" ("Welcome to Our City!") in dim letters at the top. A bleached painting shows a woman wearing a crown and proffering the long blue khadag with both hands, the blue folds of her dress fading into the lake she is standing in. There are mountains and clouds in the background and fish swim in the transparent water. The traditional icon of hospitality that I first saw in the hotel lobby in Tsagaan Uul has been localized into a personification of Lake Khövsgöl as well. The adaptation reflects the epithet "Mother" that I would later learn is applied to the lake. Beside the welcome sign another sign spells K-h-a-t-g-a-l in a building-block stack of metal squares, with "12 kilometers" written on the square at the base of the stack.

I climb the low steep hill above the road and rest a second time, drinking orange Metamucil and snacking amid the larches. Descending to the entrance to Lake Khövsgöl National Park, I register at a cost of one-thousand tögrögs, $9.10, per day for a visit of ten days. That's my estimate of the maximum time it will take me to reach the Siberian border on foot and return here by vehicle.

The park office was still in view behind me on the straight, level road when a stomachache began and, quickly increasing in intensity, forced me to lie down in the field. Had the pain started while I was resting on the hill before the park boundary, my indisposition would have seemed less ominous. Was this a warning of some danger awaiting me in the park? Hugging the earth to keep it from spinning away, I wondered what could have brought the sickness on. The aaruul? Warm Metamucil on an empty stomach? The ache had evolved from hunger pains.

I soon discovered the pain was less if I lay in a certain position. An hour or so later I was on my feet again, grateful the fit had passed so quickly. Just before Khatgal, the Egiin broadened in one enormous deep channel, announcing that its source, Lake Khövsgöl, was near. From where I rested on the bluff, I could see the former wool-washing plant, a long white building with a green roof and smokestack, farther upstream on the bluff at a bend in the river.[11]

A domestic MIAT plane flew over my head to the Khatgal landing field as I was sitting on the bluff. I imagined a fresh batch of foreign tourists from Ulaanbaatar descending on the guesthouse where I planned to stay and filling all of the vacancies. Thyme 3 was the base camp for Nature's Door, the agency handling the trip to the lake that I made with Enkhjargal and Mary. On that trip I had looked over Thyme 3 and spoken to Ben, a British man who, with his father, had set up the agency and guesthouse in collaboration with a local Mongolian woman.

Reaching the main street in town, I passed a ger camp and the government-owned Blue Pearl Hotel, among other lodgings. I was famished and almost as eager to get to a delgüür as I was to Thyme 3. When I finally reached one in a row of several on the main street, I downed some emergency high-energy rations in the form of a Snickers bar as soon as I had stepped down from the door with my purchase. The guesthouse was about as far as possible from the point where I entered the town. Its rail-fenced enclosure and white plastered bungalow abutted the hill at the north edge of town. The building was converted from a garage for trucks that, during the era of the thriving trade with Russia, transported goods unloaded at the nearby dock to Mörön and other destination points in Mongolia. Plans were underway to convert the ruined garage to the right of the main building into another dormitory and a bakery.

48 - Egün Gol at Lake Khövsgöl

The guesthouse had three large bedrooms, each with four bunkbeds, a lounge and dining area with fireplace, and kitchen and shower room with solar-heated water. Overnight accommodations in one of the rooms and in one of five gers set up on the grounds in front cost 4,000 tögrögs, or about $3.50. Guests could also camp on the grounds for 2,000 tögrögs.

I had long been anticipating the glow of admiration in Ben's eyes when he beheld me, having completed as promised the hundred-kilometer stage from Mörön to Khatgal and now in a fair way of accomplishing my trans-Mongolian trek. Instead, it was a replay of the bathetic moment of the arrival back at Boldsaikhan's cousin's ger in Altai.

Ben was in Ulaanbaatar at present, one of the staff informed me. Another valuable lesson in humility for the egotistical traveler.

After securing a bed, I discussed the west shoreline of the lake with Andrew, a British youth who organized excursions for Nature's Door and was now preparing to leave with a group on a fishing safari. I had been told a bridle-hiking trail disappeared halfway up the lake's western side. Instead of continuing north along the shoreline, as I had planned, he suggested taking the trail as it swung west at Jiglegiin Am gap toward Renchinlkhümbe Sum, then turning off on an exploratory north by northeast march along streams and over a pass back to the lake, where the walking would have gotten easier again. Although my map showed above Jiglegiin Am a narrow strip of level green between the dense red topographical lines and the blue space of the lake, his did not. The shore might be a mountain wall. If I were to explore his proposed route and find it practical, he could recommend it to other backpackers and to horseback riders who came to Thyme 3. The Daniel Boone in me was roused.

I ate a delicious tuna salad sandwich and bowl of vegetable soup from the list of Western dishes chalked on the menu board. It was now 6:00 pm and the Visitor's Center in Khatgal closed at 7:00. Dismissing the idea of resting and taking advantage of the amenities at Thyme 3 for a day, I stored my pack in the locker under my bed and walked at record speed to the Center at the other end of town. I arrived in enough time to finish collecting the notes on the exhibits that I had started during my visit at the Center on the jeep trip.

On the way back I visited the row of delgüürs just before closing and stocked up for my hike to Khankh, which I estimated would take about five days. At Thyme 3, I found a lot more guests out on the plank veranda in front and in the lounge. I took a cold shower and ordered a tuna pizza and two dried fish, along with a cup of hot water for emptying two of my envelopes of hot chocolate into. Sitting at the table at the far end of the dining area with my dinner and the copy of *Jane Eyre* I'd found in a short row of books on a windowsill, I felt my dormant passion for reading reawaken. How fresh and inviting the words on the page—no, the whole world of books—appeared after my summer of strenuous backpacking. I could take just as much, if not more, fulfillment and pleasure from reading at Thyme 3, it seemed, as I could in walking along scenic Lake Khövsgöl. Or maybe, like C. S. Lewis's boyhood friend Arthur, in just poring over the novel's opening sentence. I did not realize at the time how much my present mood owed to this particular novel's opening.[12] "There was no possibility of taking a walk that day," Jane begins. They "had been wandering" outdoors that morning, but the weather had turned so bad "that further out-door exercise was now out of the question."[13] For a weary foot traveler like myself, an announcement about the end of walking sounded heavenly.

The table next to mine was occupied, first, by a young French couple, then, by an older American one. On the sofa and armchairs before the fireplace sat several young men from Holland, some of whom had just returned from a long horseback trip halfway up the west side of the lake—no doubt the jaunt to Renchinlkhümbe. At the first dining table from the entrance foyer were three youths, an American and Canadian man and a Mongolian woman.

The polyglot talk was calming; I was now a foreigner among foreigners. "Everybody who has made the trip has talked about how fantastic it is," someone said in English. Contentment and repose mingled with anticipation and excitement in the room, producing a fertile social atmosphere. After the meal I continued reading—a starved book lover with his engrossing novel—on the deck until dusk, then joined for a short while the American and Canadian, now sitting alone.

"What an incredible adventure!" one of them exclaimed after hearing about my foot journey. "It must give you a great sense of accomplishment." I had also mentioned my proposed writing project and when they asked whether the travel book was to have a theme, I replied candidly that "mother" would be prominent. They wanted to know whether I was the one who had the police permit to approach the border—I had referred to it once or twice in conversation earlier that day—and, then, how I obtained it. They were planning to ride horses up the west shore to Khankh and then to climb Mönkh Saridag Uul (Eternal Mountain Covered with Snow and Ice) in the Dornod Sayanii Range north of the lake on the border. They may have read the words of warning in the Lonely Planet guide: "Don't stray too far from Khankh; nearby is the Russian border, where smugglers may be arrested or shot."[14] I retired to my room, which I had all to myself, refreshed by my association with my own kind at the guesthouse this evening.

ᠵ ᠵ ᠵ

Chapter 9
Beside Mother Lake: Khövsgöl Aimag
from Khatgal to Jiglegiin Am

And what if behind me to westward the wall of the woods stands high?
The world lies east: how ample, the marsh and the sea and the sky! (55-56)[1]

It is still dark when I rise the next morning, August 1ˢᵗ. I have slept well for the first time in three nights. The threat posed to my enterprise by obsessive thinking seems to have passed. If so, I have triumphed in one part of my two-fold crusade, breaking the OCD cycle of obsessing and confronting about little things in others' behavior. And now I wouldn't have to fix a worry before taking a trip; I could turn the other cheek and it would pass.

Quickly packing, I emerge from the sleeping house when there is just enough light to see the trail by and make my way up the hill to a saddlebow that Andrew advised me to take to the lake. I cross it in the growing light and there, at the bottom of the hill, with a mildly colorful sunrise over it, lies the mythical lake. For the next six and a half days, I would walk beside it and for yet another day sail back down its length.

Khövsgöl—the Turkic word means "rich lake"[2]—is one of the world's largest and oldest freshwater lakes. One hundred and thirty-six kilometers in length and averaging twenty in width and 138 meters in depth, the lake ranks fourteenth, by volume, among the world's freshwater lakes and contains over one percent of the world's fresh water. A part of the Baikal Rift System, which includes the even larger and older Lake Baikal in Russia, the lake formed two to three million years ago[3] when tectonic fracturing caused by the ongoing collision of India with the Asian Continent left a long north-south graben, or rift valley, that subsequently filled with water.[4] To quote Thoreau's lines from Milton applied to Walden Pond,

> So high as heaved the tumid hills, so low
> Down sunk a hollow bottom, broad, and deep,
> Capacious bed of waters----.[5]

The "tumid hills" in this case are the Khoridol Saridag and Bayaniii (Wealth) Nuruu, horsts, or upward-tilted fault blocks, bordering the lake on the west.

I am sitting at a lookout point atop a high rock ledge on the Shoreline Trail, the lovely gray lake below me. It is probably about 8:30 am. What appears to be a wooded island not far across the water is actually a rounded peninsula on the opposite shore of the lake's southern inlet. A pier at the southern extent of the watery prospect is presumably part of the Khatgal docks. The morning is gloomy, but the cloud cover that brought a very brief shower soon after I reached the lakeshore is now thin and tattered. Two gulls, probably the "black-headed" species I first saw in the Jarantain Gol valley the day I left Sogoot, wing by. Hammering from building construction or repair work on the shore nearby invades the stillness around. Someone starts up the hymn "How Great Thou Art" on a wind instrument. A missionary Protestant church group building a private camp?

Not long after I have returned to the trail, the sun comes out. Until now, except for brief intervals, I have been following major roadways on the hike. What I've been missing walking treeless dusty roads! Threading the thick larch woods on the black path marked by patches of green paint on trees, I am once again on the Appalachian Trail in New England, a twenty-year old making his way to Georgia. I will return! I will take up that old unrealized dream again and finish the hike just as I am finishing this one.

But the lake beside me is even more beautiful than I expected and the lesson about the reverence due the journey in the present moment also comes to mind. Stopping, I take in the picturesque scene with its Claudian elements of foregrounded tree limbs and hazy Hesperidean vanishing point. Behind the boughs of a larch at the edge of the bluff I'm on, the ruffled lake's multiple shades of blue fading into light gray stretch days and days away to a horizon of infinitesimal cumulous clouds—beads strung on a long string. There are no motorboats or yachts. Only a large north-bound boat, the passenger ferry for a ger camp at Toilogt Point, passes before the rounded peninsula on the opposite side. A few meters offshore the water is tinted light green in patches. The pellucid waves gurgle and thump as they wash a beach of gray rocks and pebbles neatly arranged in increasingly larger sizes up the gradient. Two pieces of driftwood, former larches, encumber the shore. A large clump of tall-stemmed fireweed, a member of the evening primrose family, displays its purple blossoms in front of a boulder.[6]

After so many days overshadowed by the uncertainty and trouble of finding good water, I luxuriate in the change. Like the clear streams of Maine and New Hampshire on my Appalachian Trail hike in the 70s, the pristine lake is a ready-to-hand source of cold drinking water, which also means I no longer have to carry it. Getting a drink at the next halt, I start a large white bird from its perch far up the shoreline. It soars close to the water's surface a short distance, then returns to its perch. Soon after, it floats off shore and I notice it bob the upper half of its body up and down, like a pump handle, several times.

At mid-morning I passed coming the other way a lone backpacker, a young man who did not stop and barely returned my greeting. More retributive justice. With Khatgal practically at my back, I was no doubt a mere weekend trekker to him. Karma was kinder when, at noon, I encountered a party of four young hikers, an Israeli man and woman and two American men. We eagerly traded information on our traversed sections of the park, an unequal exchange, since they had been walking for at least three days after being taxied up the lake by the motorboat at Thyme 3. The reindeer-herding Tsaatan family I'd arranged to visit by horse was in the hills above Toilogt Point on the lake, they said, so I decided to dispense with the horseback ride.

Shortly after this meeting I saw my first of many brown squirrels and, just after, a small white-breasted gray one. Checking guide and reference books after my return to Ulaanbaatar, I discovered I had seen the rarely sighted flying squirrel. Had I known this at the time, I might have stopped to watch it take off from its tree. Later I did watch a mother northern pochard, a duck with a dark head and light-gray body, rush out from the shore into the lake, driving her small brood before her. I was just beginning to sample the fabulously "rich" assortment of wildlife around the lake.[7]

By the time the ten-kilometer Shoreline Trail joined the overland road that runs between Khatgal and Jankhai Davaa, I had also seen numerous wildflowers. Many of them, including the shrubby cinquefoil and flowers resembling star of Bethlehem and Queen Anne's lace, were recognizable from earlier stages of the hike.[8] Among the plants seen for the first time this morning were fireweed, mentioned above; purple gentian; and what appeared to be milkweed and spiderwort.

The day has become as clear and luminous as yesterday, and the lake's sparkling extent is a deep rich blue, in keeping with its reputation as the "dark-blue pearl of Mongolia." The low bluffs of Tsagaan Ereg (White Coast) at Jankhai where Enkhjargal, Mary, and I ate a picnic lunch of smoked fish, bread, and cheese have been in my view for some time. As I finally draw near, I decide to pretend it is the moment when my girlfriend and I sat side by side on the shingle. In this way I might steal from the setting that refreshment for my lonely, fearful heart that I could not get from her actual presence.

Following the top of the bluff, I encounter, within a hundred meters of so of the cherished spot, my first edelweiss of the day: The flowers signifying eternal love have sprung from my heart. There she is! My beloved! I take my old seat on the beach beside her and once again we talk, looking out on the waves. But the setting is both comforting and, precisely because it contains everything from that previous visit except her, more desolating than other places. How forlorn, the sound of the waves washing the shore.

> Forlorn! the very word is like a bell
> To toll me back from thee to my sole self!
> Adieu! the fancy cannot cheat so well
> As she is famed to do, deceiving elf!
> Adieu! adieu! (71-75)[9]

Before leaving Jankhai I stopped by Thyme 1 camp, where I had made tentative arrangements with Otgon, the woman who had co-founded Nature's Door with Ben and his father, for the bridle trip to the Tsaatan family. I wanted to inform her about my change of plans. Since my visit she had given birth to a daughter, who was now sleeping, but she invited me into her ger, with instructions to speak quietly. A personable, intelligent woman of middle age with an exceptionally good command of spoken English, she shared her innovative ideas for expanding the camp's program for tourists. Too often visitors complained of boredom; after the lakeside tour and, possibly, some fishing, there was not much to do here. She wanted to offer an orientation, scheduled over several days, to traditional Mongolian culture. One day could feature games, such as khorol, which is played with carved wooden counters, and those played with shagai, the sheep ankle bones. The local craftsmen who make sets of khorol games would also benefit. On another day a mini Naadam, with the tourists' voluntary participation in the archery and wrestling competitions, might be held. Exhibitions of ethnic costumes, food, and dance could be staged on other days. Otgon mentioned that Nature's Door had, in fact, already hosted one or more performances of Tsaatan, Darkhad, and Buryat tribal dances by a children's ensemble. As she talked, it was clear that Thyme 1, which she helped start, was an object of great personal interest and pride, like her newborn daughter. In proposing the orientation program, she was not out to make a lot of money.

"I want to make the camp different," she explained.

As I continued on my way, the wide blue lake with its cresting waves looked indeed like the Mongolian "dalai," or "ocean," as it was referred to in a large graphic sign I'd seen at the park's entrance. I passed some yaks with a calf grazing between the road and the water. "Yaks by the seashore," I tagged the unusual scene. A few gers appeared, for the traditional pastoral lifestyle is still pursued within the park's boundaries. A woman gave me the location of the ger where I'd been told Enkhtuya, the shaman in the Tsaatan family I planned to visit, was currently staying. She specified a ger that I would come to near the Toilogt tourist camp. Two small girls came up and I gave them each some candy.

I passed two teenage boys sitting beside the road. When they overtook me a short time later, asking "Are you having a good vacation?" and then seemed bent on accompanying me, I became uneasy and, turning off the road without a word, sat down to wait until they had a good lead on me. My feeling of shame at my paranoia and lack of courtesy was reserved for the return of solitude and assurance of safety afterwards.

Soon I reach an unoccupied split-log picnic table. Since it is now early evening, I decide to eat dinner here, then look for a spot to pitch my tent away from the road. Collecting water with difficulty on account of the strong waves, I begin cooking the macaroni bought in Khatgal, marveling at the serviceableness of the flat raised surface with attached bench. It is the first wooden picnic table—I sat at an iron one on Zagastain Davaa after Uliastai—of my entire hike.

A beautiful young girl arrives and begins sidling up to me on the bench. Pushing her gently away, with sharp words and frowns added, I manage to discourage her from staying. Just after the pot is cooked, however, she returns with her little brother. I greet her with a "Sain baina uu?" but won't allow her to sit down at the table. I inwardly curse my luck in receiving this timely dinner-hour call. Coaxed out by the incident with the two teenage boys, my old, reclusive, misanthropic self has reemerged in full armor.

I consider the tactics at my disposal. I could play the grandfatherly host, ask them their names and give them pieces of candy and bits of chocolate in the hope that they won't abuse my hospitality and outstay their welcome. No, that is expecting too much of human nature, and I have no tent to retreat into the way I did during the visit from the two boys in the Egiin Gol valley. I would be sure to buy their company for the rest of the evening if I did that. Or, I could try to chase them away with angry shouts, abrupt sweeping arm motions, sticks and pebbles. No, that would entitle them to remain as a just punishment and may create unhoped for diversion for two fun-starved kids. Here I light on a brilliant strategem. It is the same one that preserves the sloth in the Costa Rican rainforest and the fringe-toed lizard in the Southwestern desert from predators: freeze.

And so, as the two stand there looking at me and, later, sit a short distance away calling out, I gaze, right elbow on the table and chin supported by my hand, straight ahead across the meadow at a pair of demoiselle cranes performing their airy courtship dance near the shore. The Thinker himself could hardly have shown more resolve. At last, my unbidden guests rise, drift off toward the slope of a hill that I can see out of the corner of my right eye—I dare not move until I am outside their range of vision—and disappear. Thus,

> Where love or hatred fail,
> Boredom will prevail.

Repacking after eating my dinner, I climbed the steep slope beside the road and erected my tent where the gently inclined crest met the forest. From my camp, I could see a broad section of the lake, gray and ribbed with rushing waves. If my behavior toward the children called for any remorse or retribution, I didn't experience it that night.

It was "baikhgüi" the next morning at the ger near the Toilogt tourist camp where Enkhtuya supposedly was. I was told I would have to visit her by motorbike back in the hills, taking with me as translator and guide one Gantsetseg (Steel Flower). I found this woman at the split-log picnic table, of all places, standing beside a large party of Americans seated cheek by jowl around it. The tourists had camped overnight at the site. Some saddled camels with their drivers from the Toilogt camp were waiting in the wings.

Gantsetseg, an attractive woman in her mid to late thirties, agreed to meet me at half past eleven at the shops near the ger I had just walked from. Her brother could take us to Enkhtuya's place on his motorbike. Returning along the lakeside, I ordered three khuushuur—flat, hand-sized, fried rolls filled with chopped meat and onions—at a ger guanz. I was invited in to wait, but the sight of the fresh hide spread on the floor with the skin-side up, a pile of internal organs slopped on it, and the cluttered, bloody cutting board on a table dissuaded me. I was served the khuushuur in the ger of the couple who owned the guanz. Fresh from the basin of boiling oil on the stove, these Mongolian burgers with their crisp crackly envelope of dough were the best I'd ever eaten. The total cost was 450 tögrögs, less than fifty cents.

Gantsetseg and her brother arrived as scheduled. As we ascended the wooded foothills of 2,961-meter Ikh (Big) Uul, she and I talked above the motorcycle's whirr. Like me, she was an English language teacher whose academic training was in literature. One of her colleagues at the school in Khatgal where she taught fifth to tenth graders was a U.S. Peace Corps volunteer.

A Russian minivan loaded with tourists returning from Enkhtuya's camp passed us on the road. When the route dwindled to a steep path, we left her brother and continued on foot. The long stiff climb up the scenic gorge took us beneath the face of a sublimely rugged white and gray spur of Ikh Uul. It might have come straight out of the Gobi, this barren block of the Khoridol Saridag Nuruu. The arid ridges and upper slopes that I would often see in this range were evidence of limestone and dolomite.[10]

We stopped frequently to rest or take note of some tree or flower that I asked her to identify in Mongolian. She found two kinds of willow shrubs. What she called the "white" willow had a larger and more elongated leaf than the "black" one. A plant resembling a locust tree sprout but having a very hairy stem was called "temeen süül" ("camel tail"). Many years ago, she said, its leaves were smoked by the elderly as a treatment for high blood pressure. I have since been able to identify it as a cut-leaf schizonepeta, a member of the mint family. It produces spikes of light blue-violet blossoms.[11]

Emerging from the larch forest, we could see behind us a band of the blue lake at the end of the long cradle formed by the gorge. Much more of the lake was visible by the time the path finally entered upon an upland meadow enclosed by steep mountain walls at its farther end. In the meadow stood a single white wigwam. A small herd of grazing reindeer, that mainstay of the Tsaatans' existence, roamed about.

As we were ascending the gentle slope, a man on horseback approached on the path. "A tourist," I thought, until he exchanged a few words in Mongolian with Gantsetseg. Something in his facial features, combined with baldness, uncommon among Mongolian men of middle age like himself, had suggested an occidental type. He was Enkhtuya's husband. The Tsaatans are of Turkic origin.[12]

The wall of the wigwam was of cotton canvas rather than the reindeer hide I had seen in the Visitor's Center in Khatgal. A stove pipe projected from the top with the stick poles, the bark still attached. There was a small party of American tourists seated inside with the family, but they left soon afterwards. Enkhtuya sat on the right side of the room near the back smoking a cigarette, a red scarf banded around her head. She was a pleasant-featured woman of slightly above average weight. Her ten-year old daughter sat on her right and, beside the daughter, on the left side of the room, her husband.

49 - View to east with gorge and Khövsgöl Nuur

A reindeer-skin bag was suspended from one of the hook-like prongs of an antler section attached to a roof pole. A rug of the same material was spread on the floor near where Gantsetseg and I sat before the wall on the right side. It was the only time I remember sitting on this side of a family tent in Mongolia, so ger protocol does not seem to apply to teepees. Lying on the floor at the back of the tent was at least one leather bridle, ornamented with silver or silver-plated rings and embossed work, as well as a plain leather one.

We were served milk tea; boortsog, the fried cookies; and aaruul, including the granular khorkhoi, or insect, variety I had seen given to wrestlers at the Tsagaan Uul Naadam. The shaman woman's face was composed in a serene kindly expression that I wanted to attribute to an inner light. During our meeting and the ensuing interview, her manner was easygoing and cordial. She was born in Tsagaan Nuur (White Lake) Sum, as were her parents, fifty-one years ago. She and her family lived in the village during the winter and had been coming to the lake area for the past six summers. My impression from Gantsetseg's translation was that they wanted to be more accessible to tourists, who seldom visited them in Tsagaan Nuur. They had occupied this spot for five days.

To my question whether life for the Tsaatan people is more difficult now than before democracy, Enkhtuya answered that life was very difficult before. I understood her to say their only income then was from the sale of wild berries, game, and the meat or products of domesticated reindeer to Russians living in the area. Weddings were celebrated "in this kind of tent. We build a tent for our son and daughter-in-law. When we go to get the daughter-in-law, we must ride a white reindeer. When she is brought here, we kill a reindeer and boil its back. We cook food and celebrate for three days."

"How do you get information?"

"'The eyes are blind, the ears are deaf,'" she replied, quoting a popular Mongolian saying. "We don't have access to any newspapers, have no radios or TVs. We don't know what is happening around the world. We live in remote mountainous regions and spend our days and nights looking after reindeer."

"What do you think of tourists?"

"The tourists are good people. We Tsaatans are happy when a lot of tourists come because our life is difficult. We are able to make money showing our reindeer."

"Can you get medical care when you need it?"

"We treat ourselves with the plants that grow here. We are able to recognize them when we see them. We gather the plants, dry them, and keep them for use when needed. If we have a serious problem, we go to the hospital." Later she also mentioned how blood from the reindeer's antler was very useful for treating problems such as "low blood volume or blood pressure."

She told a brief folktale about the origin of the Tuvans, reindeer-herding relatives of the Tsaatans, whose republic lies to the northwest. "The reindeer fawn is called a 'yanzaga.' An old woman found a wild female yanzaga in the khangai [a well-watered and forested mountain region]. When it grew up, it gave birth to a male yanzaga. From this only female yanzaga, the number of reindeer increased. From these reindeer, the Tuvans arose."

"Do you want your children to carry on the same lifestyle or get an education in order to live in the modern way?"

"I have six children, the oldest, twenty-nine years old, then twenty-seven, twenty-five, twenty, eighteen. The youngest, ten years old, is attending second grade in elementary school. I want them to find jobs and earn money."

The Tsaatan people are clearly a vanishing breed. According to one source, the village of Tsagaan Nuur, Enkhtuya's winter residence, was home to only about 150 Tsaatans in 2000. The 2000 census of those calling themselves "Tsaatan" was 269.[13] Sereenendorj reported during the tour of the museum in Mörön that their livestock count was down to one thousand in 1980 and was currently half of that. Hostile soviet policies, which drove them into housing projects at Ulaan Uul, and, more recently, the disruptive impact of tourism are among the factors responsible for the low numbers. At least some of Enkhtuya's six children are likely to abandon the traditional way of life.

When I asked her how the Tsaatans' lifestyle is different from other Mongolians', she replied, "Our life is much more difficult than theirs. It is a hard life. We spend two or three days traveling to reach food supplies. Some of us can't get the food."

Behind her, suspended vertically from the tent wall, was a khadag, the blue silk banner, with four tassels formed of strips of colored cloth attached at the bottom. Affixed to another tassel in the middle of the banner were two crossed feathers, one, if not both, blue trimmed with brown. A small bronze or brass disk was also displayed on the banner: the shaman's mirror.[14]

"I have three students who live on Indian reservations in the U.S. This was given by one of them," she said, referring to the two crossed feathers. "This kind of thing is used by the people who are shamans like me. It closes the door through which bad things come." The gift reflects both the universality and aboriginal nature of shamanism.

I had come to see Enkhtuya as much in her capacity of udgan, or female shaman,[15] as of Tsaatan and requested a demonstration of the ritual. She would not be able to perform it today on account of the many groups of tourists calling, she said, but she agreed to describe it.

"First, we don special boots, then a deel, then a hat. Next, we take up a drum, by which we will establish a connection with Burkhan Tenger [the sky god]. Beating the drum, a process known as 'murav,' we call upon the sky god. In this way, we can remove people's sadness, sickness, or misfortune. The ritual closes the door of their bad sign.

"The colors of the khangai-earth and the four seasons, of the water, sky, god, and lus [the god of land and water]—all of these are parts of an ancestral spirit." This statement was apparently made with reference to the khadag, which is blue like the sky,[16] and the five tassels of colored cloth strips pinned to it. She went on to say that in making the shaman's journey the day before she had found that all of the ancestral spirits were accessible. The word she used was either "teleetei," which may be translated "immanent" or "accessible," or "chölöötei," meaning "free" or "available."

"People must keep their valuable things in the khoimor [the place of honor at the back of the tent]. That's why I keep this bridle and whip in this area next to my ancestral spirit-Tenger's talisman." The bridle was apparently the ornamented one noted earlier in the back of the tent. It seems, then, to have been used when making her spiritual excursions. The talisman was, of course, the khadag with the attached cloth tassels.

"You might think I have access to only a few ancestor spirits, but I can make contact with thirty-five.

"The shaman has three duties: fortune-telling, averting misfortune, and healing the sick. I help people in these three ways."

When asked about her training, Enkhtuya replied that she had been instructed in the shaman's craft at the age of seventeen, when she began practicing. She also said that she had a teacher at the present time. Her response to my last question, whether it was difficult to practice shamanism during the soviet era, was, "No, it was OK. I used to close it [the door through which the opponents of shamanism might enter] and go ahead with my job."

A large group of tourists was now arriving. Enkhtuya asked if I would be coming to visit her again.

"Maybe. If I marry a Mongolian woman"—and my manner conveyed that I was considering it—"I am likely to return." Before departing I handed her what remained of my gifts for rewarding hospitality: a black pin-striped canvas bag and, inside it, a ballpoint pen with an American-flag logo on it, a tiny sampler-sized bottle of perfume, two spools of thread, and candy that I had bought in Khatgal expressly for this visit. I also included more than five-thousand tögrögs, about $4.50, partly to cover the charge for several photos I had taken. She bent her head and touched the bag to her brow in thanks, a convention that I witnessed several times while in the aimag. In giving her far more than I had other hosts in proportion to the hospitality received, I detected an impulse of cringing superstitious obeisance in myself. Enkhjargal had told me it was dangerous to get on the wrong side of shamans and I wasn't going to take any chances, it seemed.

A young American man had come with the latest batch of tourists, and, as we talked briefly outside the tent, it fell out that we had passed each other on the road to Khatgal four days before. I remembered him calling out from a minivan on the plain before Erkhel Nuur to ask if I wanted a ride. Earlier in the summer he had bought a horse in Arkhangai Aimag to the southeast and toured the countryside on it.

On our way back down the gorge, Gantsetseg stopped to pick the leaf of a rhubarb plant growing beside the path. She ate the stem, which is used in Mongolia, as in other parts of the world, to make jam.[17] She had told me her husband was a woodcarver who specialized in traditional games for sale to tourists. When we got back to the ger of the couple who owned the guanz, she showed me a sample of her husband's handiwork. The carved pine khorol game box with domino-sized pieces was embellished with symbols and figures of animals in the cyclical twelve-year Buddhist calendar. As in Monopoly, the object of the game is to acquire the most property, though the tangible assets in this case are humbler—gers rather than houses and hotels on Park Place.

I purchased a few more items, including candy for the neighborhood children, at one of the delgüürs. Then Gantsetseg and her brother and I ate khuushuur in the tidied-up guanz-ger. A bulging sack of gauze cloth suspended from the wall near the entrance dripped into a partially filled basin: aaruul in the making. Suddenly, the girl and boy I had played possum with at the picnic table came in. I learned that the girl had a mental disability. I recalled her silence and uninhibited, trusting behavior in approaching and leaning against me, as well as my stern rebuff, on her first visit to the picnic table. At last the frozen springs of fellow feeling for the little pair began to thaw and the ache of remorse awakened. When I found them again later and gave them some candy, I tried to make it clear it was meant as a gesture of apology.

I was leaving the neighborhood after parting from Gantsetseg when an elderly woman standing near the road beckoned me to her ger. I politely declined the invitation since it was already afternoon. Were a few kilometers worth missing the acquaintance of this hospitable local?

I passed the tourist camp at Toilogt Point, the last one in operation that I would see on the lake's western shore. Mountains of the Khoridol Saridag, both round and glaciated into sharp jagged ridges, soon began to appear on the left. They were probably spurs of Ikh Uul. Now a wide meadow lay between the mountains and the lake. A few hundred meters ahead, forest replaced the meadow. Beyond that? The view seemed to show mountains descending steeply to the water. The Khoridol Saridag Nuruu stretches ninety kilometers along the western shore. When I reached the slopes ahead, some intervening level ground disclosed itself, however.

On one stretch of open shoreline that afternoon, I noticed, dimly sketched on the far northern horizon of the lake, some other mountains. "Hallelujah!" I shouted and, waving my ball cap, addressed them: "Sain baina uu?" The Dornod Sayanii Nuruu, going back sixty-five million years, around the time of the Gobi dinosaurs' extinction and long before the lake was formed,[18] lies on the northern border of Mongolia. My destination was finally in view.

Once in the early evening, passing a large meadow, I started two demoiselle cranes and then a gray heron.[19] Entering the meadow for a better look at them, I found a toono, the wooden circular centerpiece of the ger roof, lying on the sod. It was painted red and pieces cut from soda cans were used to improvise some of the small metal plates nailed at regular intervals along the rim. The lost or discarded toono was a rare and rather unsettling sight, for losing personal items, especially essential parts of one's house, is considered bad luck in Mongolia. I have since learned that it may have been left with the intention of using it again when the family returned to the spot in its annual migrations, a fairly widespread practice.[20]

Soon afterward I saw my first chipmunk of the hike, darting from the side of the road to a sawed-off tree trunk. Chipmunks would turn up fairly often in the woods bordering the lake. In the evening I also saw a common sandpiper, jolting its head like a chicken and bobbing its tail as it walked on the shingle of the wooded shore. Its insistent squeaking wail, occasionally breaking into two or three short plaintive notes, sounded to my lonely susceptible mind like a warning. I'd better restrain myself and camp here tonight, I decided.

Before cooking dinner, I tried repeatedly to build a fire on the shore to keep the insects away, but the tinder of paper from my pack and twigs and bark from the underbrush refused to ignite. It was like witchcraft— the tinder seemed dry—and as the evening advanced I had to force myself, like a losing gambler, not to make just one more attempt. The paper must have been treated and the wood ever so slightly damp from yesterday morning's rain or a rarified spray from the surf. By then it had turned too cool for bugs anyway. After my usual pot of noodles, I slept soundly, my little tent like a safely landed boat pulled into the trees offshore.

Departing at dawn, I passed an encampment of several tents with hitched horses standing nearby. The sun came up over the lake, blue under an all but cloudless blue sky. Two croaking demoiselle cranes flew across the scene, silhouetted in the horizon's golden blush and, phoenix-like, were consumed by, before emerging from, the flaming sun.

50 - The sunrise on Khövsgöl Nuur

At a fork in the road just after, one of the green-paint trail markers I'd seen along most of the lakeshore route since Khatgal flattened itself to a leftward-pointing arrow. I dutifully turned away from the lake and for the next three hours, at least, followed the green blotches up a steep mountain road. Once, in the climb up the gorge the day before, I momentarily lost my footing and the sudden jarring movement in regaining my balance left a little sensitivity in my left ankle. I guarded my legs jealously now against over-exertion, resting whenever an ache developed. In the meantime, a stupendous view of mountains and lake was arranging itself around me.

I had passed the timberline and was nearing the top when a fork in the road danced off down the slope to the west, taking the perfidious green blotches with it. I could see what must have been the same road farther off climbing in a straight, graded stretch a flat-topped mountain to the southwest. I took the other fork, more from a desire to see the view than from any hope that it would descend northeast to the lake. The road soon dissipated itself over the rock. It must have been designed for servicing a small radio tower, a square reflector panel mounted on a pole. I was standing on top of Chüchee Uul.[21] The altitude reading on my GPS at the tower was 2,416 meters, slightly lower than Zagastain Davaa north of Uliastai, though the greater contrast with the surrounding country made it seem much higher.

Clutching at a gossamer of hope, I was led a little further on to an ovoo, its blue khadag badly shredded by the wind. No, nothing but a bouncing drop down to the lake from here. I have gained my most spectacular prospect of the trip, though: a panoramic view of the blue lake with the island Dalain Modnii Khüis (Sea's Wooded Navel) far to the northeast and the Dornod Sayanii Nuruu, dwarfed by distance, running along the northern shore; much nearer on the left, the craggy top and cliffs of a light-gray mountain daubed here and there with light red; behind me, eerie, whitish-gray peaks, like the ghosts of mountins, cascading to a chasm. The stupendous scenery, with my increased regard for the process of the journey since Mörön, softened the sting of losing my way this morning.

51 - Looking north from the summit of Chüchee Uul

Playing for a fine dramatic moment in my adventure in the mountains, I sat down near the lookout ovoo to catch up on my diary. I was on my feet again almost at once. This windy spot, "close to the sun in lonely lands" with "the wrinkled sea beneath," $(2, 4)^{22}$ might be all right for eagles but is too oppressively alien and solitary for the heart of social animals like human beings. The elemental mountainous landscape and lake existed long before we did. I hastened back to the road.

Now on my right, the light-gray and reddish mountain appeared to be linked to the peak I was on by a sagging ridge. Noticing a steep track on the slope of this mountain and imagining it was human-made, I quickly banished a demonic whisper to take it on the chance of discovering a way down to the lake.

> What if it tempt you toward the flood, . . .
> Or to the dreadful summit of the cliff
> That beetles o'er his base into the sea. . . ? (1.4.50-52)[23]

The voice was another unexpected manifestation of my old goal-centered self, jealous of any time or energy not devoted to reaching the border. When I got back to the west slope, seeing the sheer whitish-gray peaks rising out of the chasm beyond it and realizing I had strayed north, I cut a sharp left until, with some relief, I recovered the road.

The flat-topped mountain that the fork in the road led to was 2,792-meter Uran Dösh (Skillful Anvil), familiar to me from an oil landscape by the front desk of the Delger-Mörön Hotel. It and the island Dalain Modnii Khüis that I had seen from the mountaintop are featured in a local folktale about the origins of the name "Mother Lake."

At one time Lake Khövsgöl had no water after an ogre drank all of it. An old woman and thumb-sized boy passing through the dry lakebed uncovered a spring by moving a large rock, and, digging a well there and making a home, used the rock to cover the well. One day when they failed to put the rock back on the well and water filled the lake, another ogre drank all of the water. The boy, who had grown to normal size, killed the ogre and used the top of a mountain to cover him up. As water continued to pour out of the well and the lake threatened to overflow, the old woman dived underwater and reset the rock on the well. Not having the strength to swim back to shore, she drowned. The lake was given the name "Mother" in her honor. Today the top of Mount Uran Dösh used to cover the ogre is the island Dalain Modnii Khüis.[24] The epithet "Mother," though unknown to me at the time, was yet another expression of a predominant theme of my trip. Eej Khairkhan, the "Sacred Mother" mountain in the Gobi near the start of my hike, and, now, "Mother Lake" provided a fitting frame for a journey taken in honor of my deceased mother.

When the long road had finished unwinding itself down, it was about noon. I scarcely hoped to see the campers where I had passed at dawn, but there they were! I could get directions about the way. Walking up to the group of about five young men and women seated near a fire with a cooking cauldron, I found myself suddenly greeted familiarly by a young blond fellow I had seen at the internet room in Mörön. I now also recognized a tall slim youth with glasses and whiskers who had rescued me from a technical difficulty or two at the computer.

"You were very helpful," I told him. I may have humorously added that I'd come seeking his help again, this time with finding the road.

Like my two uninvited guests the day before yesterday, I have shown up just in time for dinner, but I meet with a much kinder reception. The tasty rice dish in the cauldron, of which the tall youth is the chief chef, has been prepared with mushrooms and a piquant red sauce. Chopped green onions in a jar can be added for seasoning. A large bag contains what appear to be briquettes of cheese or dried milk curds, or both. Sharing in this delicious and nourishing meal which they devoted the morning to preparing, I envy the youths' far more developed capacity to enjoy the experience of the journey.

They are university students from Slovenia. I manage to conceal my American's ignorance of world geography by asking where they are from in Slovenia, rather than where Slovenia is. In or around the capital, Ljubljana, they tell me. I also recognize the young Mongolian woman serving as their English-speaking guide; she had briefly sounded me out at the internet office as a prospective client. She asks me now where I am headed.

"Khankh," I tell her.
"Oh, that's a long way."

Her words and the doleful look that accompanied them would come to mind often during the next few days. She informs me that the area around Renchinlkhümbe is much more scenic than what I will find around Khankh. When I mention my visit with Enkhtuya and her family, she remarks flatly, "They're not real Tsaatans." She confirms that I should have taken the right-hand fork instead of following the green arrow.

The group will depart shortly to continue riding north along the lake, so it is with the prospect of seeing each other again that we say "goodbye" and I set out.

"Maybe we will read your book!" one of the women calls out to me as an afterthought.

Following the lake once more, I finally get past the high, rounded, predominantly gray mountain I spent the morning on. Somewhere along the lakefront this day, I will pass, probably between five and ten kilometers offshore, the deepest point in the lake, an astonishing 262 meters down. In the late afternoon all of the Slovenians overtake me except a couple who have decided to walk, leading their horses. Then two tall crash-helmeted travelers on mountain bikes pull up beside me. More acquaintances from the Mörön internet room, the couple who are bicycling around the world.

Our exchange on the footing of a prior meeting and on the actual road of adventure is much more animated and genial this time. He is from Seattle, my birthplace, and she, Germany, my paternal ancestors'. They have found the trail tolerable going and, like the Slovenian party, will take it west from Jiglegiin Am to Renchinlkhümbe before circling back to Khatgal on another route. Referring sardonically to his skills as a fisherman—there is clearly a history of bantering on this subject between them—he invites me to join him at the lakeside tonight and, should we land any fish, to dine with them at their camp. He is probably in his late thirties, she, somewhat younger. Her bicycle has a spare tire looped over the frame in back.

In the early evening the clouds that had gathered in the afternoon boded rain, canceling any dinner invitations I might have thought of accepting. I found a passable camping spot in a patch of sward in a wooded area beside the lake. I remained lying in the tent after a brief thundershower. Since it was now too wet to make a fire, I would wait for the cooler night air to come and drive off the mosquitoes. After a spell of heavier, blustery rainfall achieved the same purpose, I prepared a supper of noodles and hot chocolate. I preferred solitude and self-sufficiency tonight, I told myself, forgetting the desolation that drove me off the mountaintop earlier that day.

禿禿禿

Chapter 10
On the Road to Shambala: Khövsgöl Aimag from Jiglegiin Am to the Russian Border

I can tell my sister by the flowers in her eyes
On the road to Shambala
I can tell my brother by the flowers in his eyes
On the road to Shambala[1]

Roused at dawn by light raindrops pattering on my tent, I got up and packed. Rain fell steadily as I made my way to Khar Us (Black Water),[2] where I found the tents of both the Slovenians and American and German couple pitched on the meadow. No one was stirring. I stand at a loss on the stream bank. Wading the many swift channels will be next to impossible. Then I notice upstream short rows of slender tree trunks laid down end to end. Walking to this bridge takes me near the two small tents and covered bikes of the cyclists. I am a belated and unsuspected visitor to their camp. Silently wishing them a good journey ahead, I doubt that we will meet again on this or any other trail. So far we have not. On the other side, I find an encampment of several tents, probably that of the twelve Russians I'd heard yesterday were riding south on the trail. I was now abreast of Dalain Modnii Khüis, the island featured in the folktale, about fifteen kilometers offshore.

The rain had stopped and the gray cloud cover broken up into white and light-gray clouds when, soon after Khar Us, I came to Jiglegiin Am. I had reached the halfway point on the western shore.[3] As I crossed the gap, I saw a hoopoe bird for the second time on the trip. Curiously, both appeared at the critical moment when I was confronted with two alternative courses: the first bird, seen at my camp near Tosontsengel while I considered hitching a ride into town instead of continuing on my way, the second, while I debated proceeding along the lakeshore or, as Andrew at Thyme 3 suggested, scouting a way around the mountains. Inquiring of a few local herdsmen that I happened upon, I was surprised to hear that there was a lakeside road or trail north. I decided on the first route, less persuaded by their report than dissuaded from the second one by my limited food supply, enough for only three or four days. Yes, the role of pioneer scout and trail blazer wasn't one that offered every day, particularly in the 21st century, but my eating and sleeping habits weren't conducive to the mental clarity needed for charting courses in the wilderness. If the mountain route should elude me, I might not have enough food to both backtrack and complete the march northward.

In crossing the wide meadow to a bare mountain sloping down to the water, I was relinquishing any chance of a further meeting with my friends the bicyclists and horseback riders. In fact, the herders I had just met proved to be the last people I would see until late on the following day. Walking up the lakeside along the slope, I could find no road or path; only intermittent tracks appeared in the gravel down on the shore. Resting above a cliff that dropped to the blue water, glittering in the sun, I was inclined to turn back to the Renchinlkhümbe route. Without a trail on these slopes, it would be a tough job getting to Khankh in three or four days. I decided to press on for a while and see,

> Yet knowing how way leads on to way,
> I doubted if I should ever come back. (14-15)[4]

Then—God be praised! —I stumble onto a narrow bridle path, lanced into the mountainside and half hidden by grass in places. I congratulate myself on my bold disregard of the opinions of outdoorsmen and guidebooks about the impracticality of travel along the northern half of the shore. Beyond the path's right edge, the mountain drops off a hundred meters or more to the lake. At one point the path is interrupted by a short abrupt step in the terrain, resetting itself a few meters higher, and I am suddenly climbing in a semi-squatting position, my left hand touching the ground—there is nothing to touch on the other side of the path. A half hour later the slope becomes less steep.

After descending the mountain, the path disappeared in one of those rich lakeside pastures that Renchinlkhümbe herdsmen bring their flocks to in the winter months. A wooden corral stood near the shore. The level area soon played out, and, after scrambling along a steep trackless mountainside for half an hour, I had to ascend in order to reach more level ground before the slope became a cliff.[5]

In some tall grass near the crest of the slope, I started several pigeon-sized birds with brown crested head, white neck, gray and dark-brown speckled breast, and brown back. They were probably northern lapwings. I found the path just after that but lost it again in tall grass after making another descent to a level area with a corral. Then, continuing level through woods, I found a faint vanishing track. I seemed to have passed the worst stretch of the mountainous lakefront, and I rested on the shore, snacking on Cocoa Cola mix and cookies. The sky was mostly blue, the air pleasantly cool. At the north end of the lake, the Dornod Sayanii

Nuruu, the range marking the border of Mongolia, was much more distinct than when I spotted it just after Toilogt Point two days ago. Little by little, with one foot placed in front of the other, I was getting there.

I returned to the track and by keeping my eyes on a point several meters ahead, instead of immediately before me, found that I could detect more easily the occasional bent grass blade left by the last horseman. Later that afternoon, the sloping edge of a large luxuriant meadow that stretched before me afforded a delightful couch. I lay back and dozed while the grass and flowers swayed above my head in the breeze.

Passing through the meadow, I came upon a wondrously clear deep pool fed by a stream. The smooth rounded stones on the bottom roughly a meter beneath the surface shone with the distinctness of objects viewed through a pane of pale green glass. A lush growth of grasses, rhubarb, purple-blooming fireweed, willow shrub, and other vegetation crowded the verge. Skirting a small lagoon created by two strips of land jutting into the lake and linked by a sandbar, I saw a solitary whooper swan floating on the water. The swan saw a solitary human.

Soon after my next halt in the late afternoon or early evening, I received a rude shock when the path vanished altogether and the lake's margin rose like a wall. Suddenly, I was working my way up almost vertically, gripping the trunks of charred trees left by a forest fire on the mountain. I passed through thickets of the blackened remains of trees and saplings, ripping the bottoms and smudging the fronts of my khaki trouser legs.

Passing over the brow of the slope, I found acres and acres of low shrubs loaded with ripe purple fruit. Blueberries? I sampled one. Yes, they seemed to be. I should stop and eat, then gather as many as possible, I told myself. But the barest possibility of my being wrong and getting sick eating poisonous fruit so that I could not finish the hike held me back. Clearly, my fervor for reaching the border, stirred into flame by the sight of the Sayanii Nuruu across the lake, was compromising my enjoyment of the trip again.

Often a path would turn up among the blueberry shrubs, disappear for a while, and reappear further on. I was on an emotional rollercoaster as I followed the fitful track, elated and relieved at one moment, despondent and anxious the next. It was getting late. I had to watch against being pulled off on a tangent from the lake. The "trail" may have actually been many different fragmentary paths made by berry pickers or even foraging animals combing "Blueberry Hill," as I later christened the spot.

With great difficulty, I descended along a spring in a ravine, heavily wooded and strewn with fallen timber, that began on the north slope of the mountain. I struggled against the irrational fear that I wouldn't be able to get back to the lake. Once, when my way was blocked by the dense undergrowth, I deliberately paused to calmly consider the best route through in spite of a lurking sense of terror at being lost at night in a remote wilderness. In his *Travels with a Donkey*, Robert Louis Stevenson comments on his experience of losing his way in a wild remote region of the Pyrenees:

> Ulysses, left on Ithaca, and with a mind unsettled by the goddess, was not more pleasantly astray. I have been after an adventure all my life, a pure dispassionate adventure, such as befell early and heroic voyagers; and thus to be found by morning in a random woodside nook in Gévaudan—not knowing north from south, as strange to my surroundings as the first man upon the earth, an inland castaway—was to find a fraction of my day-dreams realized.[6]

Though not exactly "pleasantly astray," I was nonetheless conscious in my present extremity of finally gratifying a deep-seated romantic urge to experience danger and drama.

When I got to the small valley that ran east to the lake, I discovered its bottom was a bog. Stepping lightly on the spongy ground amid the stream channels, I am almost at the bare hill slope on the other side when I come to the main channel. It is a non-negotiable. I knew I should not have taken the lakeside route this morning. But wait. There is a tree fallen across it upstream. Making my way carefully over to it, I cross on the wobbly trunk to solid ground. A grassy knob attached to the slope will make an excellent camping spot. I am quite reconciled to my decision and surroundings now.

2

I departed at sunrise instead of the dawn hour I had gotten used to in order to have enough light to see the trail by, should there be one. The day broke clear and cold. A well-defined bridle path led along a terrace of the shore.[7]

Then both path and level ground ended, and I was forced to pick my way through fallen trees along a mountainside. I decided to try the shingle, which would at least provide a level grade. With enough food for only a few days, I am haunted by a statement that I seem to remember my biologist friend Lkhagvasüren once making in reference to his group hike around the lake: "It took us a month." What if today and tomorrow's hike are like yesterday's? Suddenly, haste has a different, justified aim.

For at least an hour and half I hurtle up the beach, frantically straddling, stepping onto, ducking under, and swinging out over the waves around gigantic slippery driftwood—the trunks, branches, and roots of former larches. Yesterday I was fearful of twisting a knee by turning the wrong way in nimbly working through stretches of fallen timber or of breaking an ankle by stepping into a streambed pothole hidden in tall grass. The slight aches and jabs that I had begun to notice in my legs seemed to warrant this fear. Today I was running much greater risks with far less concern in my anxiety to cover ground.

There were pitifully few stretches of shoreline uncluttered with driftwood. Once, in climbing the bank to avoid an especially bad area of wreckage, I noticed a bridle path on the terrace that now lay offshore. Hopeful, yet with a goodly measure of doubt held in reserve, I took the path. It led to a meadow and wide dry riverbed. Consulting my map, I discovered I was at the mouth of the gap I had planned to take northwest to the lake on the exploratory route through the mountains. The lakeside route had taken just one day. Didn't Andrew's suggestion that I try following this gap back to the lakeshore imply that it would be easier walking from here?

On the north side of the valley, a splendid landscape of the Bayanii Nuruu enhanced my growing sense of well-being: jagged peaks with steep bare slopes of white, green, and light-yellow cradling clouds in their lower folds. Beyond the gap a clearly defined bridle trail showing much use completed the restoration of my spirits since the desperate scramble along the beach. Since it was unlikely horseback riders returned north on the same path after riding to the gap, they might be supposed to travel to Renchinlkhümbe on at least part of the route I had considered exploring through the mountains. There may not have been much real exploring to do. At the next, smaller meadow, which contained a dry stream bed, the path duplicated itself in a parallel, though less worn, track, suggesting jeeps had also penetrated this far from the north.

An ache in my right leg had begun to worry me when I reached a beach of roundish golf-ball sized stones in the afternoon. To the left of the large wooded peninsula lying up ahead, white, rugged, 3,491-meter Mönkh Saridag Uul (Eternal Mountain Covered with Snow and Ice) of the Dornod Sayanii Nuruu rose in a grand muscular display. Now that the going was easier, I decided to stop and rest my leg. Maybe I'd better even wait out the day and camp. The image of Moses detained before reaching the Promised Land may have come to mind again. It seems I'd forgotten my mother's insight and my recent good intentions about savoring the pleasures of the journey; I would stop in this scenic place merely for the sake of attaining the goal.

I spread out my dew-drenched tent in the sun to dry and lay down in the shade of a tree. After a long rest, I stripped and went for a brief swim in the cold clear water. The waves were less active than they had been in the morning. The overarching sky was as beautiful and clear as the lake below it. Far out on the waves, one whooper swan floated, suggesting a canoe on the ocean. Once during my stop on the beach, a large black and gray bird passed by, flying several yards over the water in search of fish or carrion. I have since learned that it was probably the rare white-tailed, or sea, eagle.[8]

I shaved and washed some clothes on the shingle. Then I lunched on Metamucil, dried pineapple slices, and cookie crumbs while catching up on my log. One item of botanical interest to record was finding several small Scotch pines, as well as a large, badly leaning one, during my sprint along the beach. They were the only needle-leaved trees I had seen, or at least noticed, besides the far more common Siberian larches, all summer. The khorol game that Gantsetseg's husband crafted was apparently made from Scotch pine.

It was now several hours since I stopped. Of course, I decided to push on, while closely monitoring my leg. The peninsula, which I soon entered, consisted of a wooded mountain attached to the mainland by a sodden low-lying meadow. On my 1:500,000-meter topographical map, the white meadowland was scarcely distinguishable from the blue lake, so that the mountain looked like an island, which it no doubt was at one time. The trail eventually petered out. I slogged through stretches of standing water, keeping to the springy grass humps as much as possible. Occasionally, I recovered a line of horse-hoof prints only to lose it upon reaching higher dry ground. Reconnoitering up and down before proceeding didn't help. It was going to take a long time to cross this marshy lowland, which, according to my map, was almost twenty-five kilometers in extent. A couple of river crossings were also to be part of the fun. Without realizing it, though, I was already crossing the first river, the Khodon Gol, which flowed out of the Bayanii Nuruu to the west and formed a delta on the meadow.

I now remembered Andrew referring to this area with the substantive phrase "the-only-place-where-you-might-run-into-trouble" when we were discussing the western shore. I should have known better this morning than to expect a primrose path the rest of the way to Khankh. Far ahead, the plain did appear to lie at a slightly higher elevation, and I could see what might have been a ger next to a log building. It looked rather squarish, though, and I had not seen a ger in the three days since Toilogt Point. The few wooden structures I had passed so far on the upper half of the shore were empty. I doubted there would be anyone around.

I began to grow more uneasy. I now had food for about two days. Why hadn't I been more careful in Khatgal when preparing for the lakeside stage of my hike? As I lay resting on the top of a low brush-covered escarpment, the thought that I was going to die, that I would starve to death before reaching Khankh, struck me with unusual force. It seemed entirely possible, even probable. In that darkest of moments, I remember feeling more disturbed by the prospect of being found, a decayed and half-eaten corpse, than by death itself. "Jesus," I prayed, "if you exist, get me through this alive. . . ."

Shortly after continuing on my way, a stomachache like the one I had on entering the park developed. Lying in a stupor on the ground, I imagined what would become of me if the sickness proved more serious and persisted this time. It was, after the incident of getting caught in the rainstorm at Khujirt, the moment of gravest danger on the hike.

At or near this juncture I received an answer to my earlier petition from the unlikely quarter of a cow's throat, a sonorous "moo!" that suddenly reached me across the plain from the direction of the two buildings. Cattle meant, of course, people in the area. Then, my stomachache passed much more quickly than the previous one. Soon after proceeding, I could see a herd of cows near the buildings, one of which proved to be a ger after all, then two figures riding horseback, the first human beings I had set eyes on since early yesterday morning. There were also a few gers at the foot of the wooded mountain that rose to my right on the peninsula.

When I finally reached the log rail fence surrounding the homestead, I asked a boy where the gate was and he escorted me to the right past a corral where a woman sat milking a cow. She smiled openly and brightly as I walked by. The boy removed one end of the top three rails from the fencepost and directed me to the house. Suspended in a row on a line of rope or wire in the yard were several scythes, straight homemade poles with hooked blade at one end and two pairs of stubs, splayed like the legs of a miniature sawhorse, at the other. On a large piece of cloth spread out on the ground, cheese or aaruul chips and squares were drying in the sun. A wooden churn with the cream mounded high in it stood beside the entrance. I seemed to have come to the land of Canaan.

"Baina uu?" I called.

"Baina."

A handsome man in his early forties with swarthy skin and a trim physique sat smoking a cigarette on a bed in the far-right corner of the single room. He offered me a seat on the conventional short square stool across the room from him. After a few brief preliminary exchanges, I asked him about a road and the distance to Khankh. He pulled a stool up to a small table between us when I produced a map. A good road ran between a point immediately north of here to the town, eighty kilometers away, though I could expect a muddy stretch at the top of the lake, he said. There was a bridge over the Ikh Khoroo Gol in that region.

His wife, who wore a bright blue-patterned gown, had come in from her milking in the yard. A boy and a beautiful younger girl were also in the house. After our discussion about the route, the man returned to the bed, pulling himself back this time to lean against the wall. My spirit of proud independence having been chastened a bit by the harrowing adventure on the meadow, I indicated that there was something else I must ask them. I had only a little food for the rest of the way to Khankh; the walk from Khatgal was taking me longer than expected. Might I have dinner here, in addition to taking some food with me? I will pay them.

Their answer, of course, is an unhesitating "yes." In rural Mongolia, such a request is rather like asking a Gideonite for a Bible. The woman had already put wood in the stove to boil water for tea. Now she makes haste to prepare a meal. She works so quickly I feel obliged to tell her I am in no hurry—a claim that must have sounded a bit strange in my ears. Placing the little table before me, she hands me a bowl of milk tea and sets down a thermos, a small inverted vodka glass at the top serving as stopper. Then she puts slices of fresh light-brown bread; a bowl of öröm, or thick cream; and three pieces of mutton sausage on the table.

The house was furnished above the level of most of those I had visited on my trip. A section of the right wall appeared to form a second khoimor, or shrine area, besides the usual one against the short rear wall, or at the back in gers. Behind me before the long left wall was a sewing machine on a table. Strings of fresh meat and two or three more scythes, without blades, hung from an upper beam at the front end of the room. A tall metal cream-separator with long projecting spout stood before the wall to the left of the doorway as one enters. A carpet representing the silver fountain at Karakorum hung on the wall behind me. I had seen the same carpet in the ger at Bum and in Otgoo and Davaadorj's house outside of Mörön, but it was an especially suitable home decoration in this land flowing with milk and honey. Airag, made from mare's milk, and boal, from honey, were among the liquors dispensed by the original fountain.[9]

Thirty minutes after my request, I am served a bowl of delicious soup made of püntüüz, the clear rice noodles, mixed with fried mutton. In the meantime, the three of us talk.

> "Where were you born?" I ask them.
> "Khankh."
> "I was born in Seattle, Washington. It is on an ocean."
> "I was also born in a town on an ocean," she remarks, laughing.
> "Did you lose many animals in last winter's zud?"
> The woman lets off a short cynical "huh!" as if to say, "Did we lose many? Boy, did we ever!"
> "Many," the man replies. "Horses, cows. . . ."
> "*Sheep*," she interjects.

She informs me that in mid-July twelve Americans on horseback stopped at their home. The visitors played volleyball with the family and camped overnight. Chris and Mary were very good people. The Americans gave the children the volleyball and her a little cloth polar bear or snowman, which she points to hanging against the large mirror in the shrine area against the right wall. Earlier the man had mentioned that a Polish fellow, a lone hiker like myself, passed by recently.

I understand them to say that I am welcome to camp in their yard overnight, but I let them know I want to stop at the lake tonight. When I have eaten, the woman puts homemade butter between slices of bread and places them in a large plastic bag containing stringy borts, dried beef or mutton slices. I would make many a hearty sandwich out of this meat on the following day.

Before leaving, I gave my hostess money, anticipating her objections by saying that, while I understood we were friends and money wasn't expected, I had no more gifts and wanted to express my thanks in some way. She thanked me in the customary manner, bowing her head and touching the bills to her brow. The boy accompanied me a short way to a small running stream.

As I walked on, refreshed by the friendly society and timely aid of this hospitable couple, I realized all of a sudden that I had forgotten to get their names. When I intercepted a young mounted herder on his way to a log house, I asked him for them, but he didn't seem to understand my question. Thus, the husband and wife who were among my chief benefactors on the hike and contributed about as much to its success as Pürevsüren, my hostess on the night of the rainstorm, or Gunaabazar, my guide out of Sogoot, must remain anonymous in this account. May their reward in heaven be all the greater.

The youth did inform me that the road was about one kilometer to the left, where a line of trees could be seen. I asked him if I would eventually meet the road by continuing straight and he said, "Yes." I had proceeded a little way when he and a woman began shouting and signaling to me from the log house. The sun was close to setting. "They want to offer me lodging for the night," I thought, and, pointing ahead and waving, I walked on. Shortly after this, I heard several shouting voices and turned to see the same pair with another man. He called out and signaled to go left. Waving my thanks, I turned off and, before long, reached the road. I had made it through the wilderness.

In a while it became clear that I would not have intersected the road had I continued going straight and that I had saved a lot of walking by bearing left when I did. I was deeply moved by the generosity of the party who had pointed out the way. They could easily have left me to my own devices when I failed to understand the first time. I began to realize how strong a spirit of social mindedness and fraternal benevolence existed in this hidden valley of northern Mongolia. It was comparable to that in Sogoot, where the locals had also gone out of their way in both hospitality and giving directions. Moreover, the couple I had just visited appeared to be thriving, the zud notwithstanding. And no wonder, with plenty of green pasturage, extensive forests, and Khövsgöl, or "rich lake," in the area. Here, amid a scenic wonderland of evergreen forests, lush meadowland, and clear Mediterranean-blue lake with towering Mönkh Saridag and lesser peaks in the background, a gentle kind-hearted folk enjoyed a tranquil, prosperous, pastoral existence. Wasn't this as close to an earthly paradise as one could hope to find anywhere?

With my mind turning on thoughts like these, I pounded down the road at dusk in high spirits, repeatedly singing the one-line refrain "On the road to Shambala" from the old hit recording by Three Dog Night. I'd heard of Shambala, a kind of utopia in Buddhist apocalyptic lore, from my reading of Jasper Becker's *The Lost Country: Mongolia Revealed.* He refers to stories which locate the kingdom of Shambala in the former Gorno-Altai Autonomous Soviet Socialist Republic, now Altai Republic, next to the Republic of Tuva and at the northern extent of the Altain Nuruu. He points specifically to the valley below 4,783-meter Gora Belukha, in

Russian, White Mountain. The valley lies almost due west roughly a thousand kilometers from the point I had reached on the lake. According to one of Becker's sources, Shambala is "a model society without want or fear where people lived for a hundred years, rich, strong and beautiful until their death." A quote that he includes from Solzhenitsyn's *Gulag Archipelago* portrays the great fecundity of the region: "Rivers of honey flowing between banks of wheat. The steppe and mountains. Herds of sheep, flocks of wildfowl, shoals of fish. . . ."[10]

In terms of both location and physical and social description, the area I was now passing through seemed not so very far removed from this fabled land. Recalling Becker's argument that the Shangri-La of James Hilton's *Lost Horizon* was based on Shambala,[11] I imagined myself telling the world, "I have found Shangri-La in a valley of the upper Lake Khövsgöl region in Northern Mongolia!"

> Wash away my troubles, wash away my pain
> With the rain in Shambala
> Wash away my sorrow, wash away my shame
> With the rain in Shambala
>
> Everyone is helpful, everyone is kind
> On the road to Shambala
> Everyone is lucky, everyone is so kind
> On the road to Shambala[12]

Darkness was falling when I made the last of the day's fortunate discoveries: a small stream in one of the channel beds of a river, presumably the Mungarag, the second shown in the valley-bottomland on my map. It meant both drinking water that night and an easy crossing in the morning. Finding a spot upstream, I hurriedly pitched my tent in the last lingering light and was soon snug in my sleeping bag.

I rose with the sun but set out much later than usual after updating my diary and breakfasting on mutton-and-butter sandwiches, the bounty of my recent hosts. Tuesday, August 6th, was an autumnal day, overcast and cool. Just before regaining the lakeshore, I saw a park ranger amble over from a log structure to a point on the road ahead of me and stop. He was a short man and smoked a cigarette rolled with printed paper. My remarking on the weather as I stood before him with my pack off, digging out the visitor's permit, was not designed to distract or mollify him, as his response, dead silence, suggested he thought. My permit was good until the 9th.

The shore, when I finally recovered it, was sandy beach, the first I had seen on the lake. A boy in a yak-drawn cart loaded with several wooden saddles and what appeared to be saddle blankets passed coming the other way. Like the picturesque scene of the migrating camel herder and his wife on the first day of the hike, and many a scene of rural Mongolia since, this picture was substantially unchanged from centuries ago. I would not encounter a second wheeled vehicle, of any kind, on the road that day.

A sharp pain beginning in my right knee, I got off the road immediately, spread out to dry my sleeping bag and tent, wet with dew, and lay down near a tree. Nothing can stop me now, I tell myself. If waiting out the ache doesn't work, I will stow my gear on this wooded hill slope, walk to Khankh, then hitch a ride back to retrieve it. A little later, eating another of my mutton sandwiches on a bank by the waves, I made out a white dot on the hillside far across the water: the town itself, namesake of the border post that is my destination!

After a long halt, I proceed slowly, anxiously interpreting each minute sensation in my legs. Is that a hitch developing in one knee? Could this slight throb be the ankle pain returning? I enter another vast lowland meadow, stopping at a homestead on its margin for a few minutes to confirm the way. At my feet are prostrate gentians and black larkspurs, known as the "sad braid flower,"[13] among other flowers.

Ahead against the sky is the majestic Dornod Sayanii Nuruu, a long row of steep slopes, jagged in outline, dark gray striated with numerous lighter gray lines. On the right side of the range, Mönkh Saridag, highest peak in Khövsgöl Aimag,[14] has a wedge of snow on it. Two white bands undulate down the right side of the mountain at different angles: rivers.

Picking my way across the huge meadowland, I eventually reached a log cabin where a middle-aged couple, the wife wearing a wide-brimmed hat, worked with scythes in the tall grass in their yard. I have forgotten why I stopped here. It was probably a combination of the man's extraordinarily hearty "Sain baina uu?" as I was passing and my present disposition to rest at every opportunity to save my legs. He wanted to serve me tea in the house, but I declined and we talked, lying in the grass, through the log rail fence while his wife continued mowing.

My abstemiousness paid off, for, after several minutes, he suddenly caught sight of something on the lake's horizon facing him and pointed.

"*Sükhbaatar!*"

"*Sükhbaatar?*" The ferry that I was told in Khatgal no longer made runs to Khankh?

I had heard in Ulaanbaatar prior to the hike that it was possible to ride the famous boat, frequently depicted in paintings of Lake Khövsgöl, back down the lake on one of the regular commercial runs between the two towns. I imagined myself aboard it on a celebrative return journey from the Russian border. In my visit to Khatgal with Enkhjargal and Mary, however, I learned there were no boats operating commercially, that is, for the transport of merchandise or raw materials, at this time. It was another consequence of Mongolia's independence from Russia; the once flourishing trade between the two countries, which had been the raison d'etre for the two port towns and the boat, had dried up. I had not yet learned that the *Sükhbaatar* was purchased in 1997 by the Tas corporation based in Ulaanbaatar,[15] and converted into a charter boat for private cruises.

The man directed my gaze to a tiny black vertical stub between two trees. When I look back on the incident, I can't see the black mark; I may have only willed it there. He said the boat would arrive in Khankh tonight and depart tomorrow morning. Yes, it was possible to book a seat on it. Tickets were 3,500 tögrögs, a little over $3.00. After what I considered a decent interval of more talk, I got on my feet, reshouldered my pack, and bid the couple farewell.

Casting all anxiety about my legs to the winds, I set out at three times the speed I had been walking before the halt. It was just possible that I could get to Khankh, now about thirty kilometers away, by nightfall. I was not troubled by leg pains again for the rest of the hike. Spurred by the thought of making the *Sükhbaatar*'s port of call in time, I flew along the road the rest of that day, rarely stopping, while I marveled at the mind's effect on the physical organism. I was willing a surprising degree of stamina and fitness to my body.

Losing my way at the entrance to a region of low, rounded, treeless hills, I signaled to a mounted herdsman. While he was escorting me to the road hidden by the terrain, we came to a large stream, so I clambered up behind him and we rode across. He accepted the five-hundred tögrögs or so that I gave him with the customary gesture of thanks. As I raced up and down the hillocks and mounds of closely cropped grass, an alpinesque view danced before my half-believing eyes: the towering snow-capped pinnacle of the Dornod Sayanii with evergreen woods dotting its lower slopes and a hamlet of log dwellings nestled at its base.

> High stately mountains of Khentei, Khangai, and Soyon [Sayanii],
> Forests and thick-wooded ridges—the beauty of the North, . . .
>> This, this is my native land,
>> The lovely country—my Mongolia. (1-2, 5-6)[16]

I finally stopped again when I reached the hamlet at the confines of the scene, confirming its reality. Khoroo is situated on the Ikh Khoroo (Big Enclosure) Gol, which rises on the slopes of Züün Soyon Uul and flows fifty kilometers to the lake.[17] Sitting down on the green bank of the rushing river, I scooped up the cool snow-fed water with my bottle and drank.

A woman had come to collect water just before me. Two boys ran down to the river a little upstream. One was steering a small inflated rubber wheel with a hooked metal stick, a modern version of the hoop and stick game popular in ancient Greece and Rome.[18] The boys approached cautiously, then fled like startled birds when I greeted them. Soon I was on my way once more. I did not appreciate until much later how I had participated in a great immemorial tradition of the natural world by resting here; the mouth of this river is a major stopping place during the annual bird migrations.[19]

Continuing my flight north, I crossed the new log bridge that my anonymous host and hostess of the day before had told me about. It was constructed like the two broken-backed bridges I crossed the Shireegiin Gol on the day before reaching Uliastai, having post supports set in wooden boxes filled with rocks. The railroad beam reinforcing the log flooring along both outer edges was an added feature. Ascending the bluff, I saw, perched on the top of a hillock, what I at first took to be two black goats but then recognized as vultures.[20]

This sighting set the mood for my tour of the lake's end, a low-lying Cimmerian zone seen to good effect under a lowering sky near the close of day. While I was on the slope above it, a herdsman rode up just in time to point out a shorter route down a right-hand fork. After the descent, following the fork north away from the lake, I saw an abandoned homestead up ahead, the grass inside the large enclosure depressingly high. A dog, coming from its direction, passed me on the road without comment. Then, more details suggested an explanation to my romantic imagination. Inverted and stuck onto one of the fenceposts was an empty vodka bottle. The house suddenly appeared when I passed a bump in the terrain; the lake, then, could not be seen from the house. Without the beauty of Khövsgöl to feed his spirit and inculcate morality, the former owner had turned to alcohol and his fortunes declined in consequence. It was one of my finest Wordsworthian moments on the hike.

Rounding the top of the lake with its several ingressive streams, flocks of honking ruddy shelducks, and one small fledgling tourist's camp, I encountered the formidable channels of the Bayan (Rich) Gol. This was no doubt the muddy stretch that the couple told me about yesterday. I leapt over one stream, accidentally walked through another, and stepped on stones over the rest. Gers began to turn up again, and, in passing one with some youths out in front, I was invited to stop in. Being back in my habitual stride, I did not. Though reaching Khankh by nightfall was now out of the question, I might be able to get there before the boat departed in the morning.

The road steered away from the shore to follow solider ground at the foot of the auspiciously named Bayasgalan (Joy) Uul. Shortly before nightfall, a small dry ravine that offered shelter from the wind, which had begun to rise, abutted on the road. I found a level and fairly smooth patch of ground and set down my pack for the day. It was lucky I did, for it began to rain while I was setting up my tent and this later proved to be the last sheltered spot in a long stretch of road. I slept rather well that night despite going supperless to bed and feeling a little dampness from leaking rainwater. Thus ended another day under Providence.

2

The rain, which had stopped for some time when I began striking camp at early dawn, started again before I had finished. It would fall, the fine drizzle sometimes condensing into a light shower, all that morning and most of the afternoon. I didn't mind much, though, for today, with its promise of reaching the border and possibility of catching the *Sükhbaatar*, all was bright and warm within.

The road along the base of Bayasgalan Uul soon converged on and began following the lakeshore. Seen at dawn in the rain, wooden houses down on the meadow near the waves looked unspeakably remote and solitary, like lighthouses on an Arctic coast. A motorcycle or two passed, headlights flaring. The air was redolent with the same herbal scent that first invigorated me on the upper slopes before Gants Davaa near Uliastai.

Once, in looking up from the road, I saw a small brown animal resembling a doe's fawn advancing slowly in the same direction several meters ahead of me. The ears were darker than the rest of the body. It hobbled, muzzle to the earth, into the field that sloped down to the road and lake. Where was its mother?

Thinking a motherless fawn an anomaly in nature, I initially concluded from my later researches in Ulaanbaatar that the animal belonged to one of the small deer species, either the Siberian roe or the musk deer. Of the two, the first was more likely, since the musk had been hunted for its commercially valuable gland to the brink of extinction in the area. Then, Professor Kh. Terbish at Mongolian National University gave me several reasons why it was probably the fawn of a red deer, another rare species in the park, though less so than the musk. First, fawns tend to sleep longer than their mothers and therefore might be seen unaccompanied at this hour. Second, a grown deer would not have moved so slowly at a human's approach. Third, at that time of year, a red deer fawn could have been a week or ten days old, and thus not yet grown strong and wary enough to flee. Fourth, the animal I saw was smaller than a musk deer and, though about the size of a roe fawn, it lacked its spots.[21]

Following a left fork up onto a saddlebow, I was impressed by the depth and obscurity of the larch forest around me. The word "taiga" or "forest" used with reference to one of Mongolia's natural zones was no misnomer, I thought. As on my first morning beside the lake seven days ago, I was reminded of the Appalachian Trail, specifically the Maine wilderness. I marveled that this was the same Mongolia I had spent walking through desert and steppe in. In deciding to walk longitudinally across a country where Central Asia's natural zones converge,[22] I had inadvertently staged a great ecological tour for myself. I reached a large ovoo of dry tree trunks and branches stacked upright into a pyramid. Beyond, the road descended to open fields. This was my last ovoo on the hike. Today one of my standard three petitions made to the spirit of the pass as I circled three times would be answered.

As I entered Khankh through the residential area on a slope above the lake, I was reminded of the Russian villages I had seen on my recent trip on the Trans-Siberian Railroad: a collection of log houses, some painted or with painted window frames and shutters, partitioned off by rail fences. The two pleasant-featured women who appeared at the window of one house where I stopped to ask directions to a guanz seemed to be of Slavic or part-Slavic extraction. It may have been the context, a Siberian window frame, in which they were seen, but in fact Khankh is largely a Buryat town.[23]

The women pointed to an adjacent hill with more houses. I ascended the steep slope and singled out a large dwelling with blue-painted, jigsaw-cut porch palings and blue saw-tooth trim along the gable. Potted geraniums were visible in a window.

Seeing a man beside the army-green Russian minivan parked next to the house, I called out, "Is this a guanz?" He seemed to confer with someone in the yard or on the porch for a moment, then invited me to enter, indicating the gate. In one of Providence's finest, most whimsical strokes of the trip, I suddenly found myself on entering the yard standing face to face and exchanging stupefied looks with a man I knew from the Wednesday night Alcoholics Anonymous meeting at my church in Ulaanbaatar. He had apparently recognized me when I called out. He was a regular at the meeting, which I had set up with my pastor a few years before to help address the widespread abuse of alcohol, particularly vodka, in the community. At the time there was only one other AA meeting throughout Mongolia. I understood him to say that two fellow AA members in Ulaanbaatar were now in Mörön giving a seminar on the program and that he had assisted at it before coming to Khankh. He and his wife had been visiting her sister and were getting ready to depart for home. A half hour later and I would have missed him.

I was invited into the house and offered a seat at the dining table before a window in the kitchen. Baasanbat (Strong Friday), my friend's sister-in-law, served me milk tea, slender sticks of pastry, bread with cheese, mutton with macaroni soup, and blueberries, which I could sprinkle with sugar. I have made another breathtakingly fast half-circuit on Lady Fortune's wheel, and I blink doubtfully for a moment at the loaded board before me and the sputtering wood stove across the room. I am still seeing dripping trees and mist.

The house interior was divided by walls into kitchen, living room, and bedroom, which requires another visual adjustment after months of single room houses and gers. Also new were the tall cabinets for dishes and books, wallpaper, and ceilings closing off the rafters. A stag's head hunting trophy was mounted high on a wall of the kitchen. Pots, pans, and lids and a small piece of drying meat hung from a rack on another wall. Affixed to the space over the door behind me was a talisman in the form of a small clay replica of a mask from the Buddhist tsam, a colorful and dramatic dance that was brought to Mongolia from India and Tibet in the 1600s. Spectators of the dance are supposedly purified of harmful thoughts and emotions.[24] Amid all this novelty, one overly familiar item did not fail to make an appearance: a specimen of the ubiquitous laminated photo-poster showing yet another idealized table setting. Thanks to Baasanbat's hospitality, the contrast with reality wasn't nearly as stark this time as in the guest lodgings in Tseel or the guanz after

Zagastain Davaa. In the living room off of the kitchen, her young son sat playing a game on the computer. Its proximity to a power station in the Republic of Buryatia in Russia gave Khankh, unlike Khatgal, continual access to electricity. Kerosene lamps were used at Thyme 3.

52 - Baasanbat's house, Khankh

I had asked for news about the *Sükhbaatar* soon after entering the house and was told that it had not arrived yet. The family not having a phone, a call was obligingly made from a neighbor's to inquire about a ticket for the return trip; there was no answer. Soon my friend and his wife and Baasanbat's husband departed. I arranged a ride back to Khankh from the border with her neighbor, a small, mustachioed gentleman. He would meet me in his jeep at the border patrol post at 5:00 pm. If I set out from here at 11:30, that would give me ample time to cover the twenty-three kilometers. I would pay him 10,000 tögrögs, about $9.00, for driving alone out to the post and bringing me back.

The rain had stopped temporarily when I set out for the final stretch. With my hostess' leave, I had stored or hung up to dry most of my things at the house and was now carrying only valuables—money and documents—and a few essentials such as my water bottle and maps. I entered a larch wood on a path that she had said led to the border road. A young, slim woman wearing jeans and carrying a small metal canister in one hand came onto the path from a fork just ahead of me. Her straight hair was brownish or brownish-red, identifying her as a Buryat. I called out to ask about the way to the road. She stopped and turned around a meter or so away from me and—yikes!—I almost jumped back in shock. I was looking at a face without lips. There were places apparently touched up by plastic surgery. Fortunately, I was able to control my automatic reaction and, when she asked me if I wanted to buy some berries, to reply "No thanks" in a casual manner before walking on.

As we neared the edge of the wood soon after, a poor elderly couple bearing loads of folded cardboard on their backs came up the path from the opposite direction and stopped to talk with her. Then, where the neighborhood of picturesque cottages began, I encountered two young blond-headed children, a girl and boy or two girls, sitting together putting picked daisies into a glass or jar as a vase. Their faces wore the most engagingly innocent expression as they looked up at me in silent response to my greeting. The rapid sequence of vivid, archetypal images imparted a fairy tale or dream like atmosphere to this wood. It was the enchanted forest the knight must pass through before the end of his quest.

The dirt-and-gravel road to the border post was by far the widest and best-graded road I had walked this summer. Moreover, instead of a single-file escort of electricity poles, I was now accompanied by poles on both right and left. This border road, which turns east toward Lake Baikal after entering Russia, is the preferred route of Mongolians traveling between this region and Ulaanbaatar. The Khatgal-Khankh road on the east side of the lake was notoriously bad.

I passed a lone larch tree tied with a blue silk khadag. "Have a good journey!" it seemed to say. An immense meadow stretched to distant mountains.

Clusters of round hay bales were scattered over the area closer to the road and beside one of these stood a white tent, a stove pipe projecting through the hipped roof. Such tents seemed to have largely replaced the ger in this region, presumably because the steep roof facilitated run-off of the frequent snow and rain. The teepees of the Tsaatans were no doubt a similar adaptation. On the left side of the road, the meadow soon terminated at a larch forest.

I rested where two men, one an elderly Buryat, were constructing a large wooden bridge over the road. They had been working for a month, they said; a ger was set up next to the bridge. The road ascended a low hill and swung left before passing a few log homes. It was probably on this stretch that I realized I should have allowed for a walk of thirty instead of twenty-three kilometers when I arranged to meet my driver. He and Baasanbat had mentioned a first, outlying border post seven kilometers in from the one on the actual border, but it did not occur to me until now that he would not be able to proceed beyond it and that it was here they had understood I was to meet him. I would have to double back seven kilometers to this point from the border—and in double time.

53 - View across meadow near Khankh

I received, and turned down, my last offer of a ride from a passing vehicle. It had started to rain again by the time the wooden building and lookout tower of the first station came into view on a rise. As I made the gradual ascent, I prepared a short speech to accompany my documents: U.S. passport, Mongolian work permit, and the authorization to approach the border that I had used at the Burgastai port. When I was told by the officer at Burgastai to begin my hike two kilometers back from the station, I had reconciled myself to what seemed a negligible distance. Seven kilometers, though, was a bit too wide for the fuzzy band I saw when I thought of "the border." I would push for the second post, even offering to leave my pack at the station as surety, if necessary.

A youth in camouflaged combat uniform stood facing me before the roadblock when I reached the station office and watchtower. We shook hands.

"I am walking from the Chinese to the Russian border. My driver will come here at 5:00 pm," I began, documents in hand. Soon several officers had gathered and were asking me questions. One, an older man with a don't-give-me-any-of-your-nonsense look, examined my permit.

"Why do you want to walk to the border?" I understood him to ask.

"I am writing a book."

"Where is your watch?" I had said I would be back at five but wasn't wearing a wristwatch.

"That's too heavy. My clock is inside this," I said, producing the GPS from its canvas sheath at my belt. The device was probably as useful now as a credential as it had been as a compass. He gave the OK and I walked around the lowered barrier pole, pack and all.

It was now about three o'clock. Striving for a seven-kilometer-an-hour pace, I bolted up the straight level road. Light rain continued to fall. Two small metal-box constructions posted on a block on either side of the road bore, welded to their front, the insignia of the two bordering nations, hammer and sickle on the right, soyombo, a neat composite of geometrical symbols of prosperity and perpetuation,[25] on the left. I passed two people mowing hay with scythes. Near them stood a colored camping tent, the only human habitation of any kind I saw in this no-man's land between the two border stations. Finally, far away on the crest of a hill, some low buildings with a tower could be distinguished.

"Sain baina uu? Zdravstvuite!" I call out, waving my cap. Feeling a little disappointed, I put myself back in the Gobi in June to bring home the actuality, and fully experience the glory, of this moment. Even then it isn't quite what I expected. I had anticipated and envisioned to death the excitement of reaching the border. It was a last-minute opportunity en route for learning the first lesson I had set out, as if on a quest, to learn: Don't be in a rush to arrive; slow down and be in the journey. I had left Mörön enlightened enough but in the past few days slipped back into my habit of hurrying past people and places to a goal. And I was certainly in that space now. My basic lesson in progress, namely, that making headway on a journey is a matter of the breadth and depth of one's experience rather than kilometers, was indeed in-progress: one not yet fully learned. Judging from my pace for the past three days, I had also forgotten the other, practical lesson clearly taught by my two-week convalescence in Mörön, that, even if you did measure progress in kilometers, hurrying could slow you down "in the long run."

As I deliberately took in the long, variegated perspective of landscapes and events of the past two months and considered what the trip had taught or tried to teach me, I did briefly review my other aim of self-conquest: letting go of the compulsion to confront others about small hurts from the past. Encouraged by the way I had completed my trek despite the compulsion, I renewed a resolve from a previous long-distance hike not to worry about little things. I had been able to leave the incident with the fellow parishioner behind me and no longer needed to fix an obsession of this kind before taking a long trip. Having courageously ventured onto unfamiliar ground of the spirit and broken the obsessive-compulsive cycle, I could also expect to enjoy more inner freedom on a day-to-day basis.

Among the lessons that I focused on in my overview of the summer was Enkhjargal's value and importance in my life. I had found myself, unexpectedly at first, continually turning to thoughts of her to sustain me in the tedium, loneliness, and anxieties of the journey. It seemed unlikely I would have stayed with the enterprise without her image and the prospect of calling or seeing her at the next aimag capital to lighten my steps. In a similar way, I now had a greater appreciation for other dear friends, especially those of auld lang syne in the U.S. The wilderness acted as a strong stimulus on my memory of our happy times together. Another incentive may have been the example of rural Mongolians' sociability.[26] How often had I encountered family members and friends enjoying each others' company at home or on the road and received invitations to tea or offers of rides. I'd had ample evidence that very day as a guest in Baasanbat's home.

My interview questions about comparing life before and after democracy bear reconsideration in light of this phenomenon. They seem rather misplaced if, for many rural Mongolians, quality of life is measured largely by relationships and social interactions. What did a higher or lower standard of living signify as long as they had each other? Life was neither better nor worse provided their family members and friends were around. The mixed responses I got to those interview questions may support this premise.[27] Was I hoping to gauge Mongolia's progress economically and socially since the coming of democracy? Maybe a nation's progress and well-being are to be understood not in economic or political terms but at the level of the citizens' everyday interconnectedness. And since socializing and being in the present moment often go hand in hand, we might add of the citizens' capacity to enjoy life in the here and now. Mongolians have the saying "Margaashiin makhnaas önöödriin uushig." ("Today's lung is better than tomorrow's meat.") Of course, developing appreciation for others and for the present was largely my intended program during the hike, and I was fortunate in being surrounded by examples—when I chose to notice them, that is.

Another realization, that I can trust God and His Son more, emerged as I recalled instances of prayers answered in a crisis, such as when, unsure of the road to Mörön on the first day out of Tsagaan Uul, I met the family in the jeep or, running out of food on Lake Khövsgöl, I came to the couple's homestead. My occasional misgivings, especially early on, that the Heavens were opposed to the hike, had been unfounded. Even with the many difficulties and mishaps, there was a general sense of having been watched over and provided for. The weather, with a few exceptions, had been cooperative. There was sufficient drinking water—at least one stop per day at a spring, well, ger, or delgüür before the unfailing, giant cistern of Lake Khövsgöl. My ankle had healed and my stove been fixed. No wild animals or thieves attacked. The influence of a certain new addition to the community of saints in heaven, I was convinced, was partly responsible for this operation of Providence. How could I interpret the motif of "mother" woven by songs and place names through the summer in any other way? Whether I had been preserved on the hike for the sake of getting to the border, or of learning the lessons of trust in God and appreciation for others and the journey, was a question I didn't bother to consider.

Climbing the hill to the border post, I counted down the last nine in the line of telephone poles on my right. At about 3:50 pm, I passed through the open gate at the entrance to the post. The concrete pavement branched to the right and ran through a red barn apparently designed for storage of government-owned emergency fodder. A uniformed young

54 - View of Khankh on Khövsgöl Nuur

man came out of the single-story wooden building past this fork and stood in the middle of the road facing me. A little further on was an unopened gate and, on the other side of it, more buildings, a watchtower, and Russia. I drew up to the youth.

"This is where I stop," I announce reassuringly, pointing down at the pavement. I had arrived, after forty-one days of walking and just under two months from the day of setting out with Boldsaikan from Burgastai.

There remained one task to perform, though, before my journey would be complete. After I returned to Baasanbat's in her neighbor's jeep that afternoon, descending the hill, I worked my way down lanes and around buildings to the lake.

I had identified from a pocket of my pack a certain plastic zip bag containing a grain or two of rock and a little desiccated plant tissue as the one I had used to store the ceremonial pinch of soil from Burgastai. When, leaning over the waves, I shook the bag out, the grit, flung back by the wind blowing to shore, managed to hit the water just shy of the land. I had, in essence anyway, fulfilled my pledge.

ቶቶቶ

Epilogue.
Returns

All this was a long time ago, I remember,
And I would do it again, but set down
This set down
This; were we led all that way for
Birth or Death? There was a birth, certainly,
We had evidence and no doubt. I had seen birth and death,
But had thought they were different; this Birth was
Hard and bitter agony for us, like Death, our death.
We returned to our places, these Kingdoms,
But no longer at ease here. . . . (32-41)[1]

That same evening after reaching the border I am sitting on the bed in the captain's cabin on the *Sükhbaatar* catching up on my log. The room communicates with a larger lounge-dining room to the left and is also furnished with two metal chairs with vinyl-covered cushions and a refrigerator. On the wall behind me hangs a framed collage of several photos of people and a lakeside view. A high piping whistle sounds from somewhere. Through the windows on the right and front walls, I can see the smooth dusky lake surface, the adjoining dark wooded hills, and a fading blue patch of sky in the clouds. We have started to move, swinging out toward the middle of the lake. I'm on my way home—and, in the process, making a good comic-adventure episode for my book.

Hearing from the driver who brought me back to Khankh from the outlying border post that I could get passage from the ship's captain, a friend of his, I packed my things and he drove me down to the concrete dock. A man in cap and uniform came up and introduced himself as the ship's mechanic, as well as a friend of my driver's. He was of slightly below average height and above average girth and had a brisk manner of speaking and moving. His breath was spiced with the bouquet of vodka. He told me to wait, then left with a group that had apparently just disembarked. Also seeking a berth were several young Russian men. It seems they had planned to ride horses down the lakeshore but had run into a difficulty: the local herdsmen weren't willing to farm out their horses as the animals had to be fed the newly cut hay. The group had decided to tour the Gobi instead.

I was standing by myself at the edge of the dock when the mechanic returned to discuss terms. Was I alone? Was a fare of 2,500 tögrögs—

the figure I heard him quote—acceptable? Indeed, I was delighted by the prospect of saving about $50 by taking the boat instead of my driver's jeep. But now he was saying something in a subdued, confidential tone, indicating the Japanese tourists in life jackets who had gathered at the opposite end of the dock just offshore. The finger held to the lips was clear enough, but what should I be quiet about? The cost of the ticket, I assumed; the group of Japanese must have paid quite a bit more per head than the almost complimentary-ticket price I would pay. The *Sükhbaatar*'s transformation from commercial ferry to charter boat was beginning to dawn on me.

I balked at the suggestion of my best self that I raise objections, ask for clarification, maybe even cancel. I had looked forward to the boat ride for so long—from early in the planning stage through most of the hike— and had held myself to such a furious pace for the last day and a half that I managed to find room in my conscience, even if it sagged a little, for silent compliance.

He motioned me to follow him down the dock. We and a Mongolian couple got into a motorboat and he sped us over to the ship. When we were on the deck, he quickly ushered me into the first room in the hallway. It was cluttered and appeared to serve as a combined dining and storage room for the crew.

"Please sit down," he said. "Don't leave this room. The Japanese are coming. . . ." He closed the door.

So, I was to keep quiet about my very presence on board! Not long afterwards, the first orange life jackets began to file past the porthole. Some of the stream of tourists stopped to lean over the railing and gaze across the harbor at the town. An attractive young woman and a man stood talking, their backs a meter or two away. It was turning out to be an episode in the best comic-picaresque tradition—an American foot-traveler spirited aboard the famous *Sükhbaatar* by a Mongolian crewman in spirits, hidden scarcely an arm's length away from the jealous rightful passengers, the band of Japanese tourists cavorting all unsuspecting on the deck.

Soon after this, another seaman, somewhat older than the mechanic, opened the door and, speaking hurriedly and in a slightly hushed voice, bid me take up my pack at once and follow him. We passed quickly back up the corridor. Before I could enter the stairwell after him, however, an elderly Japanese gentleman, who happened to be sitting at the crowded dining room table where he could see through the open door down the hall, met my eyes with a tired deadpan expression. We entered a cabin at the head of the second-floor corridor off the stairs. The seaman, who proved to be the ship's captain, bid me sit down on the bed.

"Stay here! Don't go downstairs!" he ordered, with clarifying emphasis. Then he left.

२

It is the following afternoon. We have tied up at Khar Us, site of the medicinal springs where I left behind my friends, the American and German couple and the Slovenians, sleeping out the rain in their tents. The Japanese, some with fishing rods, have disembarked for a turn on the shore. Despite the sunny and warm weather, I am sulking on the long, cushioned bench and table before a pair of windows in the lounge-dining room adjacent to the captain's cabin. There is a glass cabinet with diplomas, paintings, binoculars case, and navigational compass in one corner and metal locker in another. On the floor next to the bench are two empty bottles and an empty carton of Rémy Martin Neapolitan Extra Old.

I have been in a wretched mood since early morning, my unavoidable recompense for tinkering with the moral law yesterday—as well as for more serious violations of it earlier. Mother Nature eventually intervening in our otherwise watertight plot against the Japanese last night, I was met in the corridor downstairs on the way back from the bathroom by a young woman who asked me in broken English to step inside the dining room at the head of the hall. My two partners in crime, the mechanic and captain, stood in the room and I took my place between them. Then a tall middle-aged man opened the hearing, asking in good English,

"Who let you on board this ship?"

"He did," I replied, pointing to the mechanic on my right.

"Why?"

"I don't know. I suppose to oblige the friend who asked him to take me on."

He said this was a chartered boat and that they had refused four men who wanted to board in Khankh. These were no doubt the hapless Russian youths I met on the dock.

"Our security cannot be guaranteed, you understand, if we admit other passengers. Are you alone? Obviously, we cannot kick you off now. We would ask, though, that you not intrude upon our activities but keep to yourself as much as possible during the voyage."

I assured him that my presence on board in no way constituted a threat to their security. I had been hiking all summer, I said, having just walked across Mongolia from the border with China. I was planning to write a travel book and wanted to include an account of a ride aboard the *Sükhbaatar* in it.

"Yes, but you understand our side of the picture. . . ."

We parted courteously, shaking hands and bidding each other "good night." Moments after I had returned to my hideout upstairs, the captain appeared and, clasping my hand and grinning, gave it an impassioned wring. Evidently, the parley had gone well and everything been smoothed over. There was a little alcohol on his breath.

My humiliations as a passenger on the *Sükhbaatar* weren't over yet, though. After turning in, I heard the boat scrape bottom, grating on gravel, in two brief swipes. The captain, who had said I would be sleeping in the cabin bedroom, reappeared and told me to move to the adjacent room. I was settled for the night on the cushioned bench when he and the mechanic and two or three other men sat down around the table to eat dinner. For the next hour, at least, they dined, drank, and socialized, while the backs of the two sitting on my bench pressed up against me. They showed about as much solicitude for my comfort as the Mongols who, after winning the battle of the Kalka River in 1224, dined with their royal captives suffocating under the boards beneath their feet.[2] The pair on my bench even lingered for some after-dinner conversation when the others had left.

Early this morning, after we'd weighed anchor and cleared the mountain at the head of the peninsula, the captain began demanding the money for the fare and, when I handed him 5,500 tögrögs expecting change, told me the cost was 20,000! I would not pay anything more until I had spoken to the ship's mechanic, I said. In the sequel of our conversation, he more than once insisted that I was a "bad man" for making the Japanese passengers angry at him. When the mechanic finally emerged from his berth around noon, he claimed he'd said 25,000, not 2,500. After a brief show of anger, I gave in to be done with the matter, paying another 14,500.

So, the mood of hilarity that I embarked in has turned sour; the joke, it seems, is on me. I will remain in this upstairs room, as if that will hasten our departure from Khar Us and bring the trip to an end all the sooner. I vindictively reflect on how wealth—for only the wealthy, I concluded, could afford a private excursion on Lake Khövsgöl—breeds anxiety about the security of one's property and a taste for the sort of exclusive diversions that confirm one's superiority over the masses. It was a thoroughly gratifying assessment of the situation.

Had my reflections been carried a bit further, I might have realized I was only getting back what I earned in not respecting the Japanese passengers—and, if I included the last few months, a lot of other people as well. I might have detected the remarkable resemblance between my fellow passengers' attitude and behavior and my own during much of the summer. Hadn't I also wanted to have the grand adventure, the scenic views and memorable episodes, all to myself? Wasn't the threat to my self-image as the solitary explorer of remote regions at the root of my wish for privacy and impatience with visitors at rest stops and campsites? Small wonder that my Japanese interrogator had deferred to my understanding of their position. I understood it only too well! How could the interview have gone otherwise than in the harmonious manner it did?

My trials aboard *The Sükhbaatar* the day after the completion of my hike, then, can be explained as the inexorable operation of retributive justice,

> for the measure you give will be the measure you get back.
> (Luke 6.38)[3]

Even with my progress in overcoming self-centeredness, when, for example, I behaved in a friendlier way after visiting the monastery in Uliastai and recuperating in Mörön, a debt remained. I wasn't the only one who had suffered when, preoccupied with my physical progress across Mongolia, I stiff-armed others like a running back to get to the goal. I was undergoing the same desolation of the spurned outsider that I'd inflicted upon so many: Enkhjargal shortly before my departure, the visitors who called on Boldsaikhan and me at our lodgings in Tseel and Khaliun, family and government officials who came to our campsite near Khaliun, children and youths who accompanied me into Uliastai, boy that I angered on the plain before Telmen, party of jeep travelers with the volleyball on the Delger-Mörön, boy and girl who showed up at the picnic table on Lake Khövsgöl, and so on. Had an unspoken wish to hike alone infected my interactions with my guide, as in the decisive "Babbling Springs" incident?

To the extent that I was learning, in spite of myself, from my unhappy charter boat ride, it was a voyage on The Ship of Death—to use

D. H. Lawrence's phrase—and a continuation of the journey I'd been on all summer,

> the longest journey, to oblivion[,]

> . . . the long and painful death
> that lies between the old self and the new. (V)[4]

Later during the stop at Khar Us, I managed to overcome my resentment enough to escape from my cell for a while, watching the fish darting in the clear blue-green water off the ship's stern.

When we were about to enter Khatgal in the early evening, I stood before the railing outside the forecastle taking in the scene of the approaching inlet and port. At that moment, I felt like a soldier aboard a battleship arriving home from a war in which his country was victorious. I had completed, despite numerous difficulties and privations, the trek I set out from Ulaanbaatar to make two months before. Yet the real war, the one for self-conquest where the death of self was victory, was far from over. The lesson from the hike about the nature of true progress, namely, being able to slow down and appreciate the unfolding journey, especially the people encountered along the way, was still one in-progress, rather than already learned. And, partly for this reason, even the physical, foot conquest of the land would prove illusory.

2

Around 9:00 pm on June 14th of the following year, 2003, I sit on a low sand dune writing in my log. Through some trees to the east I can see the same squat, turreted, yellow castle of the Burgastai border post where my permit was inspected and my hike began a year ago almost to the day. This time I am viewing the post from the other side, though. For the past day and a half, I've been walking east through bleak, grit-blanketed desert from the actual, physical border with China. With her genius for irony, Nemesis arranged that all the time I'd had my sights on Russia last summer, gloating in a completely solid transecting curve marking my route—and making my mark—on the map of Mongolia, there was a major fault in the picture, a glaring gap where the line should have begun. While working on this book after returning to Ulaanbaatar, I discovered a slight error on the map I'd used: Burgastai was not on the boundary with China as it showed but about sixty kilometers east of it!

Looking into the matter, I was told that the map's positioning of Burgastai anticipated an upcoming reconfiguration of the boundary between the two countries. I'd walked across Mongolia, yes, but a bit ahead of schedule, completely bisecting the country in, say, 2004 or 2006.

Instead of good-humoredly recognizing another reproof for misunderstanding the nature of true progress on my walk, I felt embarrassed. I was like a man who has just marched in a magnificent costume in a holiday parade and then found a gaping hole in the seat of his pants. I had to go back and do that sixty kilometers. Yes, the grand lesson from my summer adventure about the tyranny of destinations and importance of enjoying the journey had left me, to use both pun and oxymoron, a chronic borderline addict who had a lot of progress to make after all. So I went again to the Headquarters of Border Troops in Ulaanbaatar and obtained a permit to get within range of the rifles at the pillbox-like post building and tower on the Chinese border. Boldbaatar (Steel Hero), my foot escort from Border Troops at Altai village station, had to warn me at least twice yesterday to steer to the left away from the line about two-hundred meters from us. It looked rather like I was being escorted off the premises after being picked up by the Mongolian patrol. We sipped warm milk tea from his canteen in stages as we trudged in maybe thirty-seven degrees Celsius heat under a cloudless sky. He used his walkie talkie often to report our progress.

The landscape, desolate enough as we crossed salt flats at the start of our walk, was even more barren after he left me later that afternoon and I continued on a dirt road. The flats had yielded three gazelles and, besides large saxaul shrubs, low cane shoots; sukhai navch (dead leaf), prickly plants with leaves resembling the sage's; and beautiful pink flowers shaped like bluebells. Here only scattered saxaul sprang from the pebbly, grayish-brown desert floor, where a white moth appeared now and then. Some low hills on my right gradually interrupted the ocean-like, geometrically level horizon.

That night I camped beside an almost eroded away knoll with lovely desert scenery all around. Rocks provided natural tables and chairs and sandy earth under brown pebbles made a soft carpet. The few horseflies and gnats that showed up didn't stay long. At nightfall a mouse also paid me a brief visit, stopping by my granola-bearing pack. After the orange disk of the sun slipped from view, the moon rose almost full. It was a fine campsite, one of the best of my entire Mongolian trek, yet what a contrast between this solitude and the intensely social life I'd been leading a few days before in Ulaanbaatar.

The landscape became a bit less stark and monotonous during today's hike. Shortly after I set out at dawn, the dim silhouette of Aj Bogdiin, the mountain range that Boldsaikhan and I crossed to reach Bum on day three, June 14th last year, came into focus on the left. The ground was less bare, having more abundant saxaul growth, as well as crawling beetles, ants, and lizards. The level plain broke into low inclines and was variegated with swamp cottonwood-bearing dunes and round hills of what looked like brown basalt. I would often pass clumps of sheep's wool and collections of empty green and brown beer bottles left lying in the sand off the road by merchants. Like yesterday afternoon, Boldbaatar and my driver, Gazar, occasionally showed up in the jeep supplied with a water drum.

In the early evening, when I was within two kilometers of Burgastai, a lark singing nearby invited me to stop and camp on this dune fringed with swamp cottonwood, short spears of cane, tall feathergrass, Bassia dasyphylla—small plants with olive-green leaves—sprouting saxaul, and large thorny shrubs with white rose-like flowers, among other plants. With the border station finally in view, I am less isolated here. That is, compared to last night's camp. I'm nowhere and miles from anyone if I think of my situation last week.

ꗬ

"I am now on my last kilometer of the walk across Mongolia," my log begins for the following day. Reaching the station earlier in the morning, I was shocked to find nobody around. It was a bit eerie, walking the other way past the silent yellow, turreted, main building in the compound where my minivan was blocked from advancing and I showed my documents the summer before. So I'd been more alone last night than I thought. Yet another return for all of the times I'd kept others at a distance that previous hike? Or what about a more recent example, my decision to come out here again this summer when I did?

But I'm not thinking of these things now. I'm too busy trying to walk and write at the same time. "The sun is shining through a hazy sky. It is about 9:00 am. Ahead on [the] mountain to [my] right a guard stands, leaning on a pole-like instrument, now looking at me through it." Too intent on keeping my appointment with Gazar parked at the gate where Boldsaikhan and I began walking that evening one year ago to think about how I left Enkhjargal, my bride of only five days, at our apartment in

Ulaanbaatar for this rendezvous with the Chinese border! "There he is! A song by Bolormaa on his cassette player."

So, you might say I ended up where I began in more ways than one: not only physically, but also psychologically, at Burgastai. Coming out here alone within less than a week of our marriage on June 7th to pursue my cross-country obsession was a measure of just how much the lesson about the journey being more important than the goal and people being an important part of the journey was a lesson-in-progress. If I couldn't stay by the side of my newly wedded wife in my haste to complete a border-to-border epic walk, how capable was I of being with the people encountered on it?

To call it a lesson-in-progress, though, implies there was some progress. The turning away from self toward others, evident by fits and starts on the earlier hike, can also be seen by comparing the two Burgastai visits. When I came the first time, I had just told Enkhjargal to regard me merely as her friend while I was away. By the time of the second visit, instead of setting our love relationship by to be picked up if and when I chose, I had committed myself to it by marrying her. That's some progress.

This had not come without a struggle. The rival claims of my old self preoccupied with personal achievement and new, more outward-facing one that began to emerge last summer had clashed almost the moment I got back to Ulaanbaatar. Arriving by minivan on August 11th, the day after predicted in Enkhjargal's dream, I went straight to her apartment, but finding—on a rare chance—no one at home, I checked into a hotel. Having given up my apartment prior to leaving Ulaanbaatar in June, I moved into another flat without notifying her. I considered dropping out of the picture now that I didn't need her for completing the hike. I could keep my independence while devoting myself to the book, then have more adventures and write more books.

To the new self I'd been in sporadic pursuit of across Mongolia, though, such a mercenary approach to relationships was repugnant. Besides, hadn't my experiences on the hike and boat trip shown me there were consequences for myself also in snubbing others? These considerations weighing with my love for Enkhjargal, I decided to remain in. Over the next year I shared my journey of writing the manuscript of this book with her. I proposed that October, giving her the flower of eternal love, the edelweiss I'd picked on Gants Davaa above Uliastai. Married the following June at my parish, Sts. Peter and Paul in Ulaanbaatar, we've been enjoying our life's shared journey now for eighteen years. Only occasionally does she remind me of how I left her less than a week after our exchange of vows to tramp in the desert. And as far as the nature of progress, the circumstances of my return to Burgastai point to a final lesson from the hike: It doesn't occur in a

55 - Enkhjargal and author, December 2002

straight line but a spiral, involving in the general climb upwards a certain amount of circling back and returning.

Notes

Prologue
[1] *The HarperCollins Study Bible*
[2] Thoreau, "Walking" 592-593

Chapter 1
[1] Tsendyn
[2] At the time, there were only about three-hundred wild Bactrian camels left in the world and that number was decreasing (Finch 23).
[3] Cable and French 183, 185
[4] "Govi-Altai Aimagiin ONS Muzyei"
[5] *Mongolian Statistical Yearbook 2001*, 23
[6] *Mongolian Statistical Yearbook 2001*, 131-136, 142-144.
[7] Keats, "Ode to a Nightingale"
[8] Personal interview. Date unknown.
[9] 12,000-7,000 B.C. (The National Museum of Mongolia)
[10] G. Menes and Ts. Ochirkhuyag. Personal interview. 9 July 2003.
[11] D. Erdenebaatar. Personal interview. Date unknown.
[12] Brooks, "My Brief Guide"
[13] "Ger"
[14] "Ger"
[15] Finch 27
[16] J. Tomorsukh et al. 27
[17] *The Mongol Mission* 176
[18] Finch 36
[19] Shakespeare, "Hamlet"
[20] G. Menes and Ts. Ochirkhuyag. Personal interview. 9 July 2003.
[21] "Govi-Altai Aimagiin ONS Muzyei"
[22] D. Bolortuya. Personal interview. Date unknown.
[23] Tsend. Personal interview. 26 June 2002.
[24] Peter, Paul, and Mary
[25] Dovdoin Bayar. Personal interview. Date unknown.
[26] Personal interview. Date unknown. Damdinsürengiin Tseveendorj's 2000 article "The Weapons of Genghis Khan's Soldiers" includes an illustration of five types of arrowheads, two of them designed for hunting and three for warfare, which were first used during the Iron Age in Mongolia. These or similar arrowheads seem to have been used at least until the time of Genghis Khan. Two of the points used in warfare in the illustration resemble in shape and size the one I found, though having, like some of those on display at the Altai museum, straight instead of curved blade edges. The article also mentions that locals consider it good luck to find one of these so-called "bullets from the sky" and they keep them among their valuables (129-130).
[27] "Passeriformes: Alaudidae"
[28] Plummer and McGeary 217
[29] Bazar. Personal interview. 15 June 2003.

244

[30] Finch 14; Brooks, "Mongolia's Sacred Ovoos"; Enkhjargal Engels. Personal interview. 15 March 2018.
[31] D. Bazargür and D. Enkhbayar 37-39

Chapter 2
[1] Sormuunishyn
[2] Enkhjargal Engels. Personal interview. Date unknown.
[3] D. Myagmarsuren, ed., "Network of Special Protected Areas"
[4] Hardy 166
[5] Ts. Dorjsüren 17
[6] Source unknown
[7] Morgan 45; Fitzhugh 183
[8] Ts. Dorjsüren 22
[9] "Tsagaan Goliin Khadnii Zurag" 61
[10] Source unknown
[11] One interesting illustration of this comment I have since discovered is the experiments that have been carried out in cross-breeding argali, or wild sheep, and ibex, wild goat (Sermier 270).
[12] Kh. Terbish. Personal interview. 30 June 2003.
[13] D. Bazargür and D. Enkhbayar 30-31
[14] *The Secret History of the Mongols* 60, 62
[15] "Strigiformes: Strigidae"
[16] Shakespeare, "Love's Labour's Lost"
[17] Sharaviin 135
[18] The National Museum of Mongolia
[19] Sharaviin 36

Chapter 3
[1] Cavafy
[2] The Merkits were a warlike tribe who lived between the Selenge Gol basin and lands occupied by the forest-dwelling tribes to the north. In the period before Temüüjin's conquest of the country, they possessed a powerful army (Shirendyb et al. 99).
[3] The powerful Naiman tribe inhabited the region between the Altain and Khangain Nuruu and as far east as the Orkhon Gol at the future site of Karakorum, first capital of the Mongol Empire. The relative superiority of their culture is seen, for example, in the employment of Uighur scribes by some of the Naiman nobles (Shirendyb et al. 99).
[4] D. Bazargür and D. Enkhbayar 36-37
[5] "Willem Van Ruysbroeck"
[6] Dawson xxi-xxii
[7] *The Mongol Mission* 148, 156, 177
[8] Plummer and McGeary 123-124
[9] Sharaviin 32
[10] *The Travels of Marco Polo* 73
[11] Plummer and McGeary 123-124

[12] This species of raptor is dark brown, with a somewhat paler head, and has a wing span reaching about one and a half meters. It uses its long, slightly notched tail as a rudder in flight, which is typically a serene glide far different from the dogfight maneuvering I was now witnessing (J. Tomorsukh et al. 35; "Black Kite").

[13] Ts. Boldchimeg. Personal interview. 14 August 2003.

[14] Sharaviin 136

[15] The tarvagan shiir, whose Latin name is Thermopsis dahurica Crefr., belongs, in fact, to the pea family ("Thermopsis dahurica Crefr.," *The Plant List*). Mongolians use it as a home remedy for lung diseases, fever, and coughs ("Thermopsis dahurica Crefr.," Gonchigiin).

[16] Sharaviin 13

Chapter 4

[1] Browning

[2] Finch 5

[3] Finch [Front jacket flap]

[4] "Panzeria lanata" 189

[5] J. Oyumaa 6

[6] G. Menes. Personal interview. 9 July 2003.

[7] Shirendyb et al. 221-222

[8] "Khangai"

[9] Buryats are members of a Mongolian tribe native to the Lake Baikal region in Siberia ("Buriad Yastan").

[10] A Kalmuk Mongolian born on the Volga in Russia in 1860, Dambiijantsan appeared in the somewhat dubious guise of a wandering lama in western Mongolia in 1902. Within ten years he had assembled an army of two thousand, which, with the three-thousand troops under the commanders sent by the Bogd Khan, the theocratic monarch of Mongolia, captured the fort in Khovd, the last foothold of the Manchus, in August of 1912. Ja Lama was awarded the title Nomunkhan by the Bogd Khan. Capitalizing on this name and his role as protector of the local population against bandit Kazaks, who were being egged on by the Manchus, he established himself as the ruthless and half-crazed tyrant of a fledgling independent kingdom in western Mongolia. His brutal policies led to his arrest by Cossacks and deportation to Russia in 1914, where he remained until the Bolshevik Revolution. Back in Mongolia in 1918, he persuaded some five-hundred families to accompany him to a remote area near the western border with China, where he began construction of a stone palace funded by looting raids on the trade route between Mongolia and Tibet. Suspected of having designs to create an independent state, he was shot by agents of the new socialist government a few years later. To convince the people, who regarded him as a magician impervious to bullets, of his death, his head was hung up on display in Uliastai. Brought to Ulaanbaatar in 1925, the head was stolen by a student and taken to St. Petersburg, where it is preserved today (Bat-Erdeniin 139-141, 174-175, 232-233).

[11] In his *Travels in Northern Mongolia*, first published in 2001, Don Croner mentions that, a few years before he was writing, a movie about Dambiijantsan was shown throughout Mongolia (18). It is possible, then, that the herdsman's apprehension owed something to the movie industry's revival of Ja Lama's story.

[12] Personal interview. 8 November 2002.

[13] Personal interview. Date unknown.

[14] Begzyn

[15] E. Ganbold. Personal interview. 20 November 2002; "The Edelweiss Flower"

[16] Kh. Terbish. Personal interview. 19 June 2003.

[17] Sermier 275

[18] Located near the border between the region occupied by the Khalkha tribe of Mongols, that is, virtually all of Mongolia to the east, and the unsubjugated Oirat tribe, who occupied the western region, the town began as a Manchu defense fortress against the Oirats in 1733. A Maimaicheng, or Chinese trade district, grew up in the area around the garrison (Croner 9, 13). By the time Russian traveler Aleskei Pozdneyev visited in the late 19th century, Uliastai was the chief administrative center of Mongolia and the second largest city, after Urga, or Ulaanbaatar, in terms of size, area, and population (Pozdneyev 157). At the beginning of the 20th century, there were eighty-six Chinese stores, shops, and offices in Uliastai, the second-largest number after Urga (Shirendyb et al. 207).

[19] Sermier 274

[20] Pozdneyev 172

[21] Pozdneyev 178

[22] D. Erdenebaatar. Personal interview. 1 August 2003.

[23] Sterne 28

[24] Pozdneyev 177

[25] "Bogdiin Gol"; "Zavkhan Gol"; "Otgon Tenger"

[26] Dovdoin Bayar notes in *The Turkic Stone Statues of Central Mongolia* that the sculptured pair in these complexes, believed to represent husband and wife, sit cross-legged, a position denoting authority and dominance in the household. The servants or attendants stand or kneel (71-72).

[27] Dovdoin Bayar. Personal interview. Date unknown.

Chapter 5

[1] *The HarperCollins Study Bible*

[2] Sermier 275

[3] "Sutra"

[4] D. Erdenebaatar. Personal interview. Date unknown.

[5] Dovdoin Bayar, *The Turkic Stone Statues* 71. Crossing the Mongol Altain Nuruu from the west in the 4th century A.D. (Sharaviin 40), the Turkic people were employed in metalworking by the ruling Zhuzhans. Seizing power from them in the mid-6th century, they established an empire that extended from the Gulf of Korea to the eastern border of present-day Kazakstan and Khirgistan, and from Lake Baikal in Siberia to the Great Wall of China (Shirendyb et al. 82-84).

[6] N. Ser-Odjav 69

[7] Dovdoin Bayar, "Unpublished Report"

[8] N. Ser-Odjav 69

[9] N. Ser-Odjav says "squinting" (69).

[10] N. Ser-Odjav 69; Dovdoin Bayar, "Unpublished Report"

[11] N. Ser-Odjav 107, 69

[12] N. Ser-Odjav 69

[13] Based on his research at Urt Bulagyn, one of the largest of many khirigsüürs in the Khanuy Valley about six-hundred kilometers west of Ulaanbaatar, Dr. Francis Allard speculates in a 2002 article that the central mound at khirigsüür complexes is the burial site of a religious figure who was regarded, if not as a god, as an intermediary of the gods (13-14). A few years later Allard and D. Erdenebaatar jointly published a scholarly report on their researches in "Khirigsuurs, ritual and mobility in the Bronze Age of Mongolia," *Antiquity*, vol. 79, no. 305, pp. 547-563.

[14] *Beowulf*

[15] Gray

[16] Wordsworth, "She Dwelt among the Untrodden Ways"

[17] Croner 20

[18] Ossendowski 127-128

[19] Croner 19

[20] Ossendowski 128-129; Sermier 275

[21] In case my view of wolves seems too cavalier, here is a passage from the chapter "Delusions about Mongolia" in *More about the Mongols,* a book compiled from the diaries and letters of the 19th-century Scottish missionary James Gilmour:

> It is sometimes supposed that people in Mongolia are in danger from wild beasts. It is not so. Wolves are the only dangerous animals, and they are dangerous to cattle only, not to men. Either the Mongol wolf is a different and less formidable species than the Russian or Chinese wolf, or for some other reason it deports itself differently. It may be that the . . . ease with which at all times, summer and winter, day and night, it can supply its wants, keeps it from banding together in packs and developing ferocious tendencies. (232)

[22] Croner recounts the legend of the boy who, in his parents' ger one day, miraculously separated out the water that he had poured in fun into a bucketful of milk. Considered a wonder worker, the "Separator Lama" lived as a respected and influential lama at the monastery until the soviets' destruction of the complex and his disappearance in the late 1930s (27-28).

[23] Croner 5-6

[24] Like man stones, a bugan chuluu (deer stone) was a focus of ancestral worship but at least a thousand years before during the Bronze and early Iron Ages. In the early shamanistic cult practiced in Mongolia, the deer or reindeer was worshipped as a sacred ancestor ("Böö Udgan").

[25] Dovdoin Bayar. Personal interview. 30 September 2002.

[26] Volkov 180, 50

[27] Allard 13

[28] Although khirigsüürs and deer stones are both products of the Bronze Age, D. Erdenebaatar informed me that the association of the two features at one site occurs maybe five or six times at most in Mongolia. I would later visit a site in Khövsgöl Aimag containing several khirigsüürs and deer stones. In his 2002 study on ancient slab tombs and burial mounds in Mongolia, he postulates a separate origin for khirigsüürs and deer stones and gives the 3rd millennium B.C. as the earliest period of contact between the tribes producing the two types of monuments. Slab-burial construction, which was used in the tomb I had noted in the Tömört Gol valley, was practiced by yet another tribal group, one indigenous

to the Khangain Nuruu region of central Mongolia. The co-mingling of the tribes of different ethnic backgrounds constructing khirigsüürs, slab tombs, and deer stones, he states, "created the cultural foundation for the development of the regional Xiongnu nomadic state" (D. Erdenebaatar 150).

[29] Croner 27

[30] J. Tomorsukh et al. 39

[31] Wordsworth, "Michael, a Pastoral Poem"

[32] Sermier 205; S. Badamkhatan and Ch. Banzragch 7

Chapter 6

[1] Shelley

[2] Sharaviin 161

[3] Sharaviin 162

[4] "Khotgoid Duu"; "Khotgoid Yastan"

[5] Emerson

[6] Aaruul, typically eaten with yogurt at breakfast and as a snack by children (J. Tomorsukh et al. 26), is routinely offered to guests in Mongolia. It is made by boiling yoghurt mixed with airag, the fermented mare's milk, then straining out the yellowish, watery liquid and allowing the residual paste, which is divided into briquettes, to dry in the sun. Marco Polo reports that Mongolian soldiers each carried about four and a half kilograms (ten pounds) of aaruul on campaigns. In the morning a small quantity was placed in a leather bottle containing water. By evening the agitation of the contents through a day's hard riding yielded a thin porridge for the soldier's supper (*The Travels of Marco Polo* 94-95).

[7] Michie 186

[8] Gilmour 12

[9] J. Oyumaa 7-8

[10] J. Oyumaa 8

[11] Sharaviin 13

[12] J. Tomorsukh et al. 33

[13] O. Batsükh. Personal interview. 25 May 2003.

[14] "Mongolian Wrestling"

[15] "Mongolian Wrestling"; Enkhjargal Engels. Personal interview. 26 April 2018.

[16] O. Batsükh. Personal interview. 25 May 2003.

[17] Dashdorjyn

[18] Croner 6

[19] Sermier 207

[20] An article on Erchüü in a Mongolian study on the country's historical sites claims that Friar William first met the khan and resided here ("Mönkh Khaanii Erchüü Khotiin Tuir" 181). The friar's account does mention that Karakorum is a ten-day's journey away (*The Mongol Mission* 170), which is apparently the time it would have taken to travel there by cart from Altan Gadas ("Mönkh Khaanii Erchüü Khotiin Tuir" 181). Also, his reference to the "Onankerule" region, which is south and southeast of Lake Baikal and in the vicinity of the Orkhon and Kerulen Rivers (*The Journey of William of Rubruck* 116), as a "ten-day's journey due east" does not, looking at the map, seem to rule out Altan Gadas as the starting point. However,

the friar also writes that after his arrival at the royal "orda" (camp), the khan "only moved camp in a southerly direction twice; after that he began to return northwards, that is, towards Caracorum" (*The Mongol Mission* 170). The khan would have had to travel a great distance, roughly half of Mongolia's breadth, and over part of the Khanghai Nuruu—in winter—to be in the position to move north to Karakorum. In addition, why would the khan have chosen a point so far north for his winter palace site? Whether Friar William's mission took him to the particular palace of Mönkh Khan's at Altan Gadas, then, is uncertain.

[21] "Mongol Bakh"

Chapter 7

[1] Whitman

[2] A more exact dating based on recent radiocarbon analyses from the site would be from 3,200 to 2,800 years ago (Kovalev et al. 83).

[3] American archeologist William Fitzhugh believes the expression shows someone, possibly a shaman, singing or chanting (Fitzhugh 188).

[4] Volkov 65-66, 194

[5] D. Erdenebaatar, 221; D. Erdenebaatar. Personal interview. 1 August 2003.

[6] Kovalev et al. 87-89, 91

[7] "Mönkh Khaanii Erchüü Khotiin Tuir" 180-181

[8] "Mönkh Khaanii Erchüü Khotiin Tuir" 180-181; "Mönkh Khaanii Ordnii Tuuri"

[9] Sereenendorj. Personal interview. 18 July 2002.

[10] "Mönkh Khaanii Gerelt Khöshöö"

[11] "Mönkh Khaanii Gerelt Khöshöö"

[12] Shirendyb et al. 118

[13] *The Travels of Marco Polo* 89

[14] Sereenendorj. Personal interview. 18 July 2002.

[15] Pursued by a large Manchu army, the leader fled with his force toward Shishged, where he hoped to muster more troops. When he reached Öliin Davaa, he dismissed all but one hundred of his men and began making his way with great difficulty toward Russia. He reached Jiyankhas in Khankh Sum with a company of fifty men. The Manchus, guided by two local members of the pro-Manchu nobility, overtook and besieged the rebels' outpost on a hill. While trying to break through to freedom early in the morning on November 28, 1756, Chingüünjav was captured. He was taken to Beijing and executed the following year ("B. Chingüünjav 1710-1757"; "Chingüünjav"; Bat-Erdeniin 92). Khankh is the last town I would pass en route to the border.

[16] B. Khaltar et al. 35

[17] "Khövsgöl-Khüns"

[18] A woman in the office informed us that the mill had been dismantled and the new one was still under construction, so there was nothing to tour at present. My suspicion that the report was at least partly fabricated in order to keep us out seemed confirmed one evening later that week. As I was walking past the mill toward the hotel, I heard the slow chug chugging of machinery coming from a small wooden building on the other side of the board palisade along the road. The aroma of a large yellow pile of fresh sawdust, which loomed above the level of the palisade, was in the air. Then, after my return to Ulaanbaatar I discovered it was

apparently here that, in 1997, an American operating a sawmill in Mörön shot and killed a Mongolian employee, allegedly in self-defense during an argument (Sermier 206). The American had been released from jail and permitted to leave the country by the following year, when I arrived in Mongolia and saw coverage of the incident in the local English press. Small wonder, then, if the woman in the office was wary of an American stranger who showed up asking for a tour!

Chapter 8

[1] Dendevyn

[2] Whitman

[3] Most varieties of gentians found in Mongolia have been traditionally used to treat coughs and liver ailments ("Prostrate Gentian").

[4] Thoreau, "Walden" 524; Of the three species of hares found in Mongolia ("Lagomorpha: Leporidae"), the tolai and mountain hare, or chandaga, are common ("Lagomorpha").

[5] J. Tomorsukh et al. 33

[6] Lawrence

[7] Lawrence

[8] Kh. Terbish. Personal interview. 20 June 2003.

[9] Kh. Terbish. Personal interview. 20 June 2003.

[10] Probably the Zanabazar Museum of Fine Arts

[11] The factory was built in 1932-33 under soviet patronage and by 1985 some 1,742 tons of wool were being washed per year ("Noos Ugaakh Üildver").

[12] Lewis writes of him, "He could get endless enjoyment out of the opening sentence of *Jane Eyre . . .*" (Lewis 152).

[13] Brontë 7

[14] Mayhew 210

Chapter 9

[1] Lanier

[2] Becker 289

[3] Finch 34; Visitor's Center, Khatgal

[4] J. Tomorsukh et al. 11; Sharaviin 31; Finch 34

[5] Thoreau, "Walden" 529

[6] The name "fireweed" is apparently derived from one of its habitats—burned out areas. It is also called "mountain tea" because of the brew made from the plant after the stem and leaves dry out and turn brown. Mountain tea brewing has been widespread in the area during times of economic stress ("Fireweed, Rosebay Willowherb").

[7] The lake's riparian ecosystem and surrounding area host 244 species of birds and sixty-eight of mammals (Finch 34).

[8] The woody stems of the cinquefoil, a small bush studded with five-petalled yellow flowers, were traditionally made into scrub brushes and brooms. It is also brewed as a medicinal tea ("Shrubby Cinquefoil"). More than 150 of the eight-hundred recorded species of vascular plants in the lake region serve as medicines, either alone or in compounds (J. Oyumaa 14).

[9] Keats, "Ode to a Nightingale"

[10] J. Tomorsukh et al. 12

[11] A variety of other local uses is listed in *Wildflowers of Northern Mongolia*:: pipe tobacco, mouthwash for alleviating toothache, and cockroach repellent ("Cut-Leaf Schizonepeta").

[12] Tsaatans, whose name means "shepherds of the Tsaa," or reindeer, are believed to have settled in the Khövsgöl Lake region from the area of the present-day Tuva Republic of Russia. The Tuvan language derives from a Uighur branch of the Turkic. The Tsaatans speak Uighur ("Tsaatan"; "Tuva Khel").

[13] "Tsaatan"

[14] "Böögiin Toli"

[15] "Böö Udgan"

[16] The khadag was referred to as a symbol of the blue sky in Chapter 1.

[17] Rhubarb is also used by locals to treat indigestion, fevers, tumors, and burns, among other ailments. In the account of his visit at Mönkh Khan's winter court, Friar William records how an Armenian monk used a mixture of shredded rhubarb root and holy water to successfully treat the khan's chief wife, Cotota Caten (U. Ligaa 323; *The Mongol Mission* 167-168).

[18] Visitor's Center, Khatgal; J. Tomorsukh et al. 11

[19] Kh. Terbish. Personal interview. 19 June 2003.

[20] Sh. Gansükh. Personal interview. 28 February 2003.

[21] Brooks, "Mongolia's Sacred Ovoos." Chüchee Uul and the mountains adjoining it are part of the Khoridol Saridag Nuruu Strictly Protected Area, which was created partly as a refuge for the endangered argali, or wild mountain sheep (D. Myagmarsuren, ed., *Special Protected Areas* 42). According to the report I'd seen at the Visitor's Center in Khatgal, only twenty-seven argali were counted in 1997. The snow leopard, another endangered species in Mongolia, is no longer seen in the Khoridol Saridag Nuruu.

[22] Tennyson

[23] Shakespeare, "Hamlet"

[24] J. Tomorsukh et al. 10

Chapter 10

[1] Three Dog Night, Tennessee Symphony Orchestra

[2] Khar Us is a nationally famous spring due to the curative powers of both its water and fish. The so-called Balius fish, said to possess extraordinary medicinal virtues, attracts a host of Mongolians here every June (J. Tomorsukh et al. 16).

[3] This gap is used by herding families in Renchinlkhümbe Sum in their annual migration of about 150 kilometers across the Khoridol Saridag to the lake and back. The sum is located in the Darkhad Depression, a bastion of shamanism in Mongolia and home of the reindeer-herding Darkhad people (J. Tomorsukh et al. 21-22; Sharaviin 154).

[4] Frost

[5] The steep slopes in the area north of Jiglegiin Am, the southern end of the Bayanii Nuruu, are ample evidence of the glaciation that has occurred throughout the history of the lake. The predominantly sedimentary rock that I had encountered in the Khoridol Saridag Nuruu was also being replaced by a mixture of older,

Proterozoic-era igneous, sedimentary, and metamorphic rocks. Later, these, in turn, would give way to a preponderance of igneous formations (J. Tomorsukh et al. 12).

[6] Stevenson 56

[7] The one, three, and nine-meter terraces along the western lakeshore may be evidence that the Khoridol Saridag and Bayanii Nuruu, fault blocks from the creation of the lake's original rift valley, are still rising (J. Tomorsukh et al. 12; Sharaviin 31).

[8] Kh. Terbish. Personal interview. 19 June 2003.

[9] *The Mongol Mission* 176

[10] Becker 127, 307-308; "Map of Mongolia"

[11] Becker 308

[12] Three Dog Night, Tennessee Symphony Orchestra

[13] Because of its dark color and alleged usefulness in making hair grow when washed in its leaves and flowers ("Black Larkspur").

[14] J. Oyumaa 6

[15] "Sükhbaatar Khölög Ongots"

[16] Dashdorjyn

[17] "Ikh Khoroo"

[18] "Greco-Roman Hoop Rolling"

[19] Sermier 210

[20] The meter-tall black vulture occurs throughout Lake Khövsgöl National Park (J. Tomorsukh et al. 35).

[21] Personal interview. 18 June 2003.

[22] Finch 4-5

[23] The Buryat people, who live mainly in Khankh and Tsagaan Nuur Sums, are famous in Mongolia for their delicious breads, jams, and cream, as well as the wooden houses I was now viewing ("Buriad Yastan").

[24] "Tsam"

[25] "Soyombo"

[26] In *Mongols* by Baabar (Bat-Erdeniin Batbayar) and R. Enkhbat, the caption for a photo of a large gathering of rural folk identifies Mongolians' distinctive "ability to maintain their sense of community in the vast wilderness of Central Asian steppes. . . ." (69).

[27] Of ten locals interviewed, five said or suggested that life was better before democracy and five that life was either worse then or the same.

Epilogue

[1] Eliot

[2] *The Chronicle of Novgorod 1016-1471* 63-66

[3] *The HarperCollins Study Bible*

[4] Lawrence

Works Cited

Allard, Francis. "Sacred Bones, Fields of Stones." *Earthwatch Journal.* October 2002: 12-15.

"B. Chingüünjav 1710-1757." Minjigiin Nyamaa. *Hövsgöl Aimgiin Lavlakh Toli [Khövsgöl Aimag Encyclopedia].* Interpress, 2001.

B. Khaltar et al., eds. *Khövsgöl Aimag Mörön Khot [Khövsgöl Aimag City of Mörön].* Khövsgöl Moment, n.d.

Baabar (Bat-Erdeniin Batbayar) and R. Enkhbat. *Mongols.* English Edition. Monsudar Publishing, 2002.

Bat-Erdeniin Batbayar. *History of Mongolia.* Ed. Christopher Kaplonski. Trans. D. Suhjargalmaa et al. Monsudar, 1999.

Becker, Jasper. *The Lost Country: Mongolia Revealed.* Hodder and Stoughton, 1992.

Begzyn Yavuukhulan. "To Love Only You. . . ." *Modern Mongolian Poetry (1921-1986).* Ed. Dojoogyn Tsedev. Trans. D. Altangerel. State Publishing House, 1989. 172.

Beowulf. Trans. Kevin Crossley-Holland. Oxford World's Classics. Oxford UP, 1999.

"Black Kite, Milvus migrans-Birds-NatureGate-Luonto Portti." n.d. *NatureGate.* 12 August 2017. <www.luontoportti.com/suomi/en/linnut/black-kite>.

"Black Larkspur." J. Oyumaa. *Wildflowers of Northern Mongolia.* Lake Hovsgol Protected Area, 2001. 21.

"Bogdiin Gol." *Mongoliin Nevterkhii Toli [Encyclopedia of Mongolia].* Gen. Ed. B. Chadraa. Mongol Ulsiin Shinjlekh Ukhaanii Akadyemi [Mongolian Science Academy], 2000.

"Böö Udgan [Shaman]." Minjigiin Nyamaa. *Khövsgöl Aimgiin Lavlakh Toli. [Khövsgöl Aimag Encyclopedia].* Interpress, 2001.

"Böögiin Toli [Shaman's Mirror]." *Mongoliin Nevterkhii Toli [Encyclopedia of Mongolia].* Gen. Ed. B. Chadraa. Mongol Ulsiin Shinjlekh Ukhaanii Akadyemi [National Science Academy], 2000.

Brontë, Charlotte. *Jane Eyre.* Oxford English Novels. Gen. Ed. James Kinsley. Oxford UP, 1973.

Brooks, Jessica. "Mongolia's Sacred Ovoos." 15 March 2013. *Eternal Landscapes Mongolia.* 15 March 2018. <www.eternal-landscapes.blogspot.com/2013/03/stones-sticks-and-scarves-mongolias.html>.

—. "My Brief Guide to Traditions and Etiquette When Visiting a Mongolian Ger." 9 June 2011. *Eternal Landscapes Mongolia.* 9 March 2018. <www.eternal-landscapes.co.uk/the-mongolian-ger-the-cultural-traditions-of-the-ger>.

Browning, Robert. "Two in the Campagna." *The Norton Anthology of Poetry.* Eds. Margaret Furgeson et al. Shorter 5th. W. W. Norton, 2005. 664-666.

"Buriad Yastan [Buriad Nationality]." Minjigiin Nyamaa. *Khövsgöl Aimgiin Lavlakh Toli [Khövsgöl Aimag Encyclopedia]*. Interpress, 2001.

Cable, Mildred and Francesca French. *The Gobi Desert*. Macmillan, 1945.

Cavafy, Constantine. "Ithaka." *Songs for the Open Road: Poems of Travel and Adventure*. Ed. The American Poetry and Literacy Project. Dover Thrift Editions. Dover, 1999. 3-4.

"Chingüünjav." *Mongoliin Nevterkhii Toli [Encyclopedia of Mongolia]*. Gen. Ed. B. Chadraa. Mongol Ulsiin Shinjlekh Ukhaanii Akadyemi [Mongolian Science Academy], 2000.

Croner, Don. *Travels in Northern Mongolia*. Polar Star, 2001.

"Cut-Leaf Schizonepeta." J. Oyumaa. *Wildflowers of Northern Mongolia*. Lake Hovsgol Protected Area, 2001. 35.

D. Bazargür and D. Enkhbayar. *Chinggis Khaan (Činggis Qayan) Historic-Geographic Atlas*. 1997.

D. Erdenebaatar. *Mongol Nutgiin Dörvöljin Bulsh, Khirigsüüriin Soyol [The Culture of Mongolian Slab Tombs and Burial Mounds]*. Uls Shinjlekh Ukhaanii Akadyemi Tüükhiin Khüreelen [Academy of Sciences Historical Institute], Ikh Surguuli Arkhyeologi-Ugsaatan Züin Tenkhim [Ulaanbaatar University, Archeology-Ethnography Department], 2002.

D. Myagmarsuren, ed. "Network of Special Protected Areas of Mongolia." *Special Protected Areas of Mongolia*. Environmental Protection Agency, Mongolia, 2000. [inside back cover].

---, ed. *Special Protected Areas of Mongolia*. Environmental Protection Agency, Mongolia, 2000.

Damdinsürengiin Tseveendorj. "The Weapons of Genghis Khan's Soldiers." 2000.

Dashdorjyn Natsagdorj. "My Native Land." *Modern Mongolian Poetry (1921-1986)*. Ed. Dojoogyn Tsedev. Trans. D. Altangerel. State Publishing House, 1989. 13-15.

Dawson, Christopher. "Introduction." *The Mongol Mission: Narratives and Letters of the Franciscan Missionaries in Mongolia and China in the Thirteenth and Fourteenth Centuries*. Ed. Christopher Dawson. Trans. A Nun of Stanbrook Abbey. The Makers of Christendom. Gen. Ed. Christopher Dawson. Sheed and Ward, 1955. vi-xxxv.

Dendevyn Purevdorj. "Tracks." *Modern Mongolian Poetry (1921-1986)*. Ed. Dojoogyn Tsedev. Trans. D. Altangerel. State Publishing House, 1989. 227-229.

Dovdoin Bayar. *The Turkic Stone Statues of Central Mongolia*. Ed. D. Tseveendorj. Mongolian Academy of Sciences Institute of History, 1997.

---. "Unpublished Report on an Archeological Expedition to Zavkhan Aimag." n.d.

Eliot, T. S. "Journey of the Magi." n.d. *The Poetry Archive*. 20 October 2018. <www.poetryarchive.org/poem/journey-magi>.

Emerson, Ralph Waldo. "Ralph Waldo Emerson: Essays, First Series. 2. Self-Reliance." n.d. *The Literature Page.* 13 June 2018. <www.literaturepage.com/read/emersonessays1-29.html.>.

Finch, C. *Mongolia's Wild Heritage: Biological Diversity, Protected Areas, and Conservation in the Land of Chingis Khaan.* Avery, 1999.

"Fireweed, Rosebay Willowherb." J. Oyumaa. *Wildflowers of Northern Mongolia.* Lake Hovsgol Protected Area, 2001. 30.

Fitzhugh, William W. "The Mongolian Deer Stone-Khirigsuur Complex: Dating and Organization of a Late Bronze Age Menagerie." n.d. *Semantic Scholar.* 7 June 2018. <https://pdfs.semanticscholar.org/9700/cacce888e9aa8cd54bf83255 092f28119e29.pdf>.

Frost, Robert. "The Road Not Taken." *The Norton Anthology of Poetry.* Eds. Margaret Ferguson et al. . Shorter 5th. W. W. Norton, 2005. 801.

"Ger, Traditional Mongolian Dwelling." n.d. *Discover Mongolia.* 9 March 2018. <www.discovermongolia.mn/mongolian-traditional-dwelling>.

Gilmour, James. *More about the Mongols, Selected and Arranged from the Diaries and Papers of James Gilmour by Richard Lovett.* Religious Tract Society, 1893.

"Govi-Altai Aimagiin ONS Muzyei [Govi-Altai Aimag Local Research Museum]," n. d.

Gray, Thomas. "Elegy Written in a Country Churchyard." *The Norton Anthology of Poetry.* Eds. Margaret Furgeson et al. Shorter 5th. W. W. Norton, 2005. 410-413.

"Greco-Roman Hoop Rolling." n.d. *Health and Fitness History.* 14 May 2018. <www.healthandfitnesshistory.com/ancient-sports/greco-roman-hoop-rolling >.

Hardy, Thomas. *Far from the Madding Crowd.* The Works of Thomas Hardy in Prose and Verse. Vol. Prose. 2. AMS, 1984.

"Ikh Khoroo." *Mongoliin Nevterkhii Toli [Encyclopedia of Mongolia].* Gen. Ed. B. Chadraa. Mongol Ulsiin Shinjlekh Ukhaanii Akadyemi [National Science Academy], 2000.

J. Oyumaa. "Introduction." *Wildflowers of Northern Mongolia.* Lake Hovsgol Protected Area, 2001. 4-16.

J. Tomorsukh et al. *Lake Hovsgol National Park: A Visitor's Guide.* Discovery Initiatives, n.d.

Keats, John. "Ode to a Nightingale." *The Norton Anthology of Poetry.* Eds. Margaret Ferguson et al. Shorter 5th. W. W. Norton, 2005. 582-584.

"Khangai." *A Modern Mongolian-English Dictionary.* Compiled by Altangerel Damdinsuren. Interpress, 1998.

"Khotgoid Duu [Khotgoid Song]." Minjigiin Nyamaa. *Hövsgöl Aimgiin Lavlakh Toli [Khövsgöl Aimag Encyclopedia].* Interpress, 2001.

"Khotgoid Yastan [Khotgoid Nationality]." Minjigiin Nyamaa. *Khövsgöl Aimgiin Lavlakh Toli [Khövsgöl Aimag Encyclopedia].* Interpress, 2001.

"Khövsgöl-Khüns ["Khövsgöl-Foods]." Minjigiin Nyamaa. *Khövsgöl Aimgiin Lavlakh Toli [Khövsgöl Aimag Encyclopedia]*. Interpress, 2001.

Kovalev, A. A. et al. "A Ritual Complex with Deer Stones at Uushigiin Uvur, Mongolia: Composition and Construction Stages." *Archeology, Ethnography, and Anthropology of Central Eurasia* 44.1 (2016): 82-92.

"Lagomorpha." *Lake Hovsgol Protected Area Wildlife Checklist*. Lake Hovsgol Protected Area, 2001.

"Lagomorpha: Leporidae." *Dictionary of the Vertebrate Species of Mongolia*. Eds. Richard P. Reading et al. Mongolia Biodiversity Project, 1994. 47-48.

Lanier, Sidney. "The Marshes of Glynn." *The Norton Anthology of Poetry*. Eds. Margaret Furgeson et al. Shorter 5th. W. W. Norton, 2005. 752-754.

Lawrence, D. H. "The Ship of Death." *The Complete Poems of D. H. Lawrence*. Eds. Vivian de Sola Pinto and Warren Roberts. Viking, 1971. 716-720.

Lewis, C. S. *Surprised by Joy: The Shape of My Early Life*. Harcourt, Brace, and World, 1955.

Mayhew, Bradley. *Mongolia*. 3rd. Lonely Planet, 2001.

Michie, Alexander. *Siberian Overland Route from Peking to Petersburg through the Deserts and Steppes of Mongolia, Tartary, etc.* London: John Murray, 1864.

"Mongol Bakh [Mongol Toad]." Kh. Munkhbayar et al. *Mongol Ornii Khoyor Nutagtan, Mölkhögchdiig Todorkhoilokh Bichig [A Descriptive Record of Mongolian Amphibians and Reptiles]*. Eastern Steppe Biodiversity Project, 2001. 9.

Mongolian Statistical Yearbook 2001. National Statistical Office of Mongolia, 2002.

"Mongolian Wrestling." n.d. *New World Encyclopedia*. 26 April 2018. <www.newworldencyclopedia.org/entry/Mongolian_wrestling>.

"Mönkh Khaanii Erchüü Khotiin Tuir [The Ruins of Mönkh Khan's City of Erchüü]." *Mongol Nutag Dakh Tüükh Soyoliin Dursgal [Historical and Cultural Relics of Mongolia]*. Mongoliin Khümüünlegiin Niigemleg [Mongolian Humanities Society], 1999. 180-181.

"Mönkh Khaanii Gerelt Khöshöö [Mönkh Khan's Monument]." Minjigiin Nyamaa. *Khövsgöl Aimgiin Lavlakh Toli [Khövsgöl Aimag Encyclopedia]*. Interpress, 2001.

"Mönkh Khaanii Ordnii Tuuri [The Ruins of Mönkh Khan's Palace]." Minjigiin Nyamaa. *Khövsgöl Aimgiin Lavlakh Toli [Khövsgöl Aimag Encyclopedia]*. Interpress, 2001.

Morgan, David. *The Mongols*. Blackwell, 1994.

N. Ser-Odjav. *Ertnii Türegüüd (VI-VIII zuun) [The Ancient Turks (6th-8th centuries)]*. Ed. Ch. Natsagdorj. Vol. 5. Studia Archaeologica Instituti Historiae Academiae Scientiarum Reipublicae Populi Mongolici, 1970.

"Noos Ugaakh Üildver [Wool Washing Factory]." Minjigiin Nyamaa. *Khövsgöl Aimgiin Lavlakdh Toli [Khövsgöl Aimag Encyclopedia]*. Interpress, 2001.

Ossendowski, Ferdinand. *Beasts, Men, and Gods*. E. P. Dutton, 1922.

"Otgon Tenger." *Mongoliin Nevterkhii Toli [Encyclopedia of Mongolia]*. Gen. Ed. B. Chadraa. Mongol Ulsiin Shinjlekh Ukhaanii Akadyemi [Mongolian Science Academy], 2000.

"Panzeria lanata." Gonchigiin Tserenbaljid. *Mongol Ornii khöl gazriin urgamliin öngöt tsomog [Colour Atlas of Antropophilus Plants of Mongolia]*. Mongol Uls Shinjlekh Ukhaanii Akadyemi Botanikiin Khüreelen [Mongolian Academy of Sciences Botanical Institute], 2002. 189.

"Passeriformes: Alaudidae." *Dictionary of the Vertebrate Species of Mongolia*. Eds. Richard P. Reading et al. The Mongolia Biodiversity Project, 1994. 26-27.

Peter, Paul, and Mary. "500 Miles." *Peter, Paul, and Mary*. By Hedy West. Warner Bros., 1962.

Plummer, Charles C. and David McGeary. *Physical Geology*. 7th. Brown, 1996.

Podzneyev, Aleskie Matveyevic. *Mongolia and the Mongols*. Ed. John R. Kreuger. Trans. John Roger Shaw and Dale Plank. Uralic and Altaic Series, vol. 61. Vol. 1. Indiana University, 1971.

"Prostrate Gentian." J. Oyumaa. *Wildflowers of Northern Mongolia*. Lake Hovsgol Protected Area, 2001. 33.

S. Badamkhatan and Ch. Banzragch. *Khövsgöl Aimgiin Tovch Tüükh [A Short History of Khövsgöl Aimag]*. Erkh Chölöö, 1981.

Sermier, Claire and Juulchin Tourism Corporation of Mongolia. *Mongolia: Empire of the Steppes*. Trans. Helen Loveday. Odyssey, 2002.

Shakespeare, William. "Hamlet." *The Norton Shakespeare*. Gen. Ed. Stephen Greenblatt. Norton, 1997. 1659-1759.

---. "Love's Labour Lost." *The Norton Shakespeare*. Gen. Ed. Stephen Greenblatt. Norton, 1997. 733-802.

Sharaviin Shagdar. *Fifty Routes through Mongolia: A Guide for Tourists*. Trans. E. Tumurbaatar. Mongolian Business Development Agency, 1997.

Shelley, Percy Bysshe. "Alastor; or, The Spirit of Solitude." *Percy Bysshe Shelley*. Ed. Stephen C. Behrendt. Longman Cultural Edition. Longman, 2010. 5-25.

Shirendyb, B. et al. *History of the Mongolian People's Republic*. 2nd. Nauka, 1973.

"Shrubby Cinquefoil." J. Oyumaa. *Wildflowers of Northern Mongolia*. Lake Hovsgol Protected Area, 2001. 25.

Sormuunishyn Dashdoorov. "Rock Paintings!" *Modern Mongolian Poetry (1921-1986)*. Ed. Dojoogyn Tsedev. Trans. D. Altangerel. State Publishing House, 1989. 262-264.

"Soyombo." *Mongoliin Nevterkhii Toli [Encyclopedia of Mongolia]*. Gen. Ed. B. Chadraa. Mongol Ulsiin Shinjlekh Ukhaanii Akadyemi [National Science Academy], 2000.

Sterne, Laurence. *A Sentimental Journey through France and Italy by Mr. Yorick with The Journal to Eliza and A Poetical Romance*. Ed. Ian Jack. Oxford UP, 1998.

Stevenson, Robert Louis. *Travels with a Donkey in the Cevennes.* Charles Scribner's Sons, 1923.

"Strigiformes: Strigidae." *Dictionary of the Vertebrate Species of Mongolia.* Eds. Richard P. Reading et al. Mongolia Biodiversity Project, 1994. 24-25.

"Sükhbaatar Khölög Ongots [Sükhbaatar Ship]." Minjigiin Nyamaa. *Khövsgöl Aimgiin Lavlakdh Toli [Khövsgöl Aimag Encyclopedia].* Interpress, 2001.

"Sutra." n.d. *Merriam-Webster.* 24 August 2017. <www.merriam-webster.com/dictionary/sutra>.

Tennyson, Alfred Lord. "The Eagle." *The Norton Anthology of Poetry.* Eds. Margaret Ferguson et al. Shorter 5th. Norton, 2005. 639.

The Chronicle of Novgorod 1016-1471. Trans. Robert Mitchell and Nevill Forbes. Camden 3rd Series. Vol. 25. Royal Historical Society, 1914.

"The Edelweiss Flower: Its Meaning and Symbolism." 21 March 2017. *Flower Meaning.* 19 August 2017. <www.flowermeaning.com/edelweiss-flower-meaning>.

The HarperCollins Study Bible. New Revised Standard Version. Gen. Ed. Wayne A. Meeks. HarperCollins, 1993.

The Journey of William of Rubruck to the Eastern Parts of the World, 1253-55, As Narrated by Himself, with Two Accounts of the Earlier Journey of John of Pian De Carpine. Ed. and Trans. William Woodville Rockhill. The Hakluyt Society, 1900.

The Mongol Mission: Narratives and Letters of the Franciscan Missionaries in Mongolia and China in the Thirteenth and Fourteenth Centuries. Ed. Christopher Dawson. Trans. A Nun of Stanbrook Abbey. The Makers of Christendom. Gen. Ed. Christopher Dawson. Sheed and Ward, 1955.

The Secret History of the Mongols: The Life and Times of Chinggis Khan. Trans. Urgunge Onon. "Bolor sudar" Publishing, 2005.

The Travels of Marco Polo [The Venetian], Revised from Marsden's Translation and Edited with Introduction by Manuel Komroff. Horace Liveright, 1926.

"Thermopsis dahurica Crefr." Gonchigiin Tserenbaljid. *Mongol Ornii khöl gazriin urgamliin öngöt tsomog [Colour Atlas of Antropophilus Plants of Mongolia].* Mongol Uls Shinjlekh Ukhaanii Akadyemi Botanikiin Khüreelen [Mongolian Academy of Sciences Botanical Institute], 2002. 136-137.

"Thermopsis dahurica Crefr." n.d. *The Plant List: A Working List of All Plant Species.* 29 May 2018. <www.theplantlist.org/tpl1.1/record/ild-55424>.

Thoreau, Henry David. "Walden." *The Portable Thoreau.* Ed. Carl Bode. Revised Edition. Penguin Books, 1983. 258-572.

---. "Walking." *The Portable Thoreau.* Ed. Carl Bode. Revised Edition. Penguin Books, 1983. 592-630.

Three Dog Night, Tennessee Symphony Orchestra. "Shambala." *Cyan.* By Daniel Joseph Moore. Dunhill, 1973.

Ts. Dorjsüren. "Govi-Altai Tsagaan Goliin Khadnii Zurag [Rock Carvings of Govi-Altai's Tsagaan River]." *Ertnii Sudlal-Ugsaatnii Züin Büteel [Ancient Research-Ethnological Artifacts]*. Ed. N. Ser-Odjav. Vol. 2. Instituti Historiae Academiae Scientiarum Reipublicae Populi Mongoli, 1963. 16-26.

"Tsaatan." Minjigiin Nyamaa. *Khövsgöl Aimgiin Lavlakh Toli [Khövsgöl Aimag Encyclopedia]*. Interpress, 2001.

"Tsagaan Goliin Khadnii Zurag [Rock Carvings of the Tsagaan River]." *Mongol Nutag Dakh Tüükh Soyoliin Dursgal [Historical and Cultural Relics of Mongolia]*. Mongoliin Khümüünlegiin Niigemleg [Mongolian Humanities Society], 1999. 60-61.

"Tsam." *Mongoliin Nevterkhii Toli [Encyclopedia of Mongolia]*. Gen. Ed. B. Chadraa. Mongol Ulsiin Shinjlekh Ukhaanii Akadyemi [National Science Academy], 2000.

Tsendyn Damdinsuren. "Beautiful Flowers Are. . . ." *Modern Mongolian Poetry*. Ed. Dojoogyn Tsedev. Trans. D. Altangerel. State Publishing House, 1989. 79-80.

"Tuva Khel [Tuvan Language]." *Mongoliin Nevterkhii Toli [Encyclopedia of Mongolia]*. Gen. Ed. B. Chadraa. Mongol Ulsiin Shinjlekh Ukhaanii Akadyemi [National Science Academy], 2000.

U. Ligaa. *Medicinal Plants of Mongolia Used in Mongolian Traditional Medicine*. Printed privately by the author, 1994.

Volkov, V. V. *Olyenniiye Kamni Mongolii [Mongolian Deer Stones]*. 2nd. Nauka, 2002.

Whitman, Walt. "Song of the Open Road." *Leaves of Grass*. Eds. Harold W. Blodgett and Sculley Bradley. Comprehensive Reader's Edition. New York UP, 1965. 149-159.

"Willem Van Ruysbroeck." 20 July 1998. *Editors of Encyclopedia Britannica*. 23 March 2018.

Wordsworth, William. "Michael, A Pastoral Poem." *The Poetical Works of William Wordsworth*. Ed. Paul D. Sheats. Cambridge Edition. Houghton Mifflin, 1982. 238-244.

---. "She Dwelt among the Untrodden Ways." *The Norton Anthology of Poetry*. Eds. Margaret Ferguson et al. Shorter 5th. W. W. Norton, 2005. 471.

"Zavkhan Gol." *Mongoliin Nevterkhii Toli [Encyclopedia of Mongolia]*. Gen. Ed. B. Chadraa. Mongol Ulsiin Shinjlekh Ukhaanii Akadyemi [Mongolian Science Academy], 2000.

Index

About the Author

William C. Engels, Obl.S.B., was born in Seattle, Washington, and spent his childhood throughout the U.S. and in three European countries, Germany, Italy, and Greece, as the son of a career army serviceman. He received his B.A. in 1983 from the University of Arkansas and M.A. in 1992 and Ph.D. in 1998 from Saint Louis University, all in English Literature. He taught writing and literature for a total of seven years in Mongolia and South Korea and six years in Bangladesh, where he also served as an elementary school principal. Dr. Engels currently tutors part-time at the Graduate Writing Center at Washington State University in Pullman, Washington. He is an Oblate of Saint Benedict with Subiaco Abbey in Arkansas. His present hiking venture is a west-east walk, in stages, across the continental U.S.

mongolengels1@gmail.com

www.ingramcontent.com/pod-product-compliance
Lightning Source LLC
Chambersburg PA
CBHW062202270326
41930CB00009B/1618